Three *Things* *you NEED to* *Know about* ROCKETS

Three
Things
you NEED to
Know about
ROCKETS

JESSICA A FOX

First published in 2013 by
Short Books
3A Exmouth House
Pine Street
EC1R 0JH

This paperback edition published in 2013

10 9 8 7 6 5 4 3 2 1

A CIP catalogue record for this book is available
from the British Library.

ISBN 978-1-78072-171-2

Printed and bound in Great Britain by
CPI Group (UK) Ltd, Croydon, CR0 4YY

Cover design: Andy Smith

For Shaun

And for my parents and family, on both sides of the Atlantic,
without whom this adventure would have never happened.

Prologue

*T*here are three things you should know about a rocket launch. The first is that, if you sit too close, you'll be killed by the sound. Crammed into two rows of metal bleachers, we sat under the hot Florida sun miles away from the launch site, waiting in anticipation for the event. Suddenly something happened in the distance before us, across an expanse of water.

The second thing you should know is that although the launch creates sound waves, which are strong enough to kill a person, ironically the spectator's first impression is one of total silence. Silence as my fellow witnesses and I stared gaping as plumes of silver smoke, then white smoke, then fire, emerged from under the rocket. Silence as an astronaut's wife and child, who stood next to me, watched, helpless, as the countdown began. Silence as a massive wave, an actual wave, sped across the water, fish jumping all round, until it reached the shore and a wall of sound blasted our eardrums.

The third thing you should know about a rocket launch is that it is not new but old; perfectly ancient. Watching these bold pioneers defy gravity in their small vessel was something truly mythic to behold, like seeing fact and metaphor come alive at the same time; it resonated past our logic into our primal subconscious, touching on the essence of what it meant to be human, of our bold, insatiable curiosity and of leaving home for the unknown.

Joseph Campbell's Hero Journey

1) Call to Adventure
2) Refusal of the Call
3) Supernatural Aid
4) The Road of Trials
5) Apotheosis
6) The Ultimate Boon
7) Refusal of Return
8) Crossing of the Last Threshold
9) Freedom to Live

Chapter 1

"The artist's life cannot be otherwise than full of conflicts,
for two forces are at war within him; on the one hand,
the common human longing for happiness, satisfaction
and security in life and on the other, a ruthless passion for
creation which may go so far as to override every personal
desire… there are hardly any exceptions to the rule that a
person must pay dearly for the divine gift of creative fire."
— Carl Jung, THE SPIRIT OF MAN IN ART AND LITERATURE:
Psychology section, third shelf on the right in the main gallery.

A ll stories have a beginning, or so it seems. Beginnings,
middles and ends feel real, like supporting pillars that
have always been there and will always be. If they were
drawn on paper, their solid mass would look complete,
finite and separate.

On taking a closer look, however, their true nature is
revealed to be ephemeral. That solid dot that we have come
to trust as "the beginning" is in fact like a cloud, made
up of an infinite number of moments, any of which can
be broken down again into smaller and smaller moments.
This begs the question, is there really a start at all? Or do
each of us, just by existing, bend the air with narrative
threads so that every origin to any story resides not from
without but from within? The "once upon a time" that
looked like it had its origin firmly on the page is in fact

a mirror reflecting that the true source is, and always has been, you.

The honks of cars and the hum of exhaust leaking from engines reached a crescendo. I sat in the car, baking under the Hollywood sun. At 25 years old I was convinced that this is how my brief life would end. I would be found in my car, my body half hanging out the window, still stuck in traffic, having died from heat and exhaustion on an LA freeway.

My eyes squinted in the bright light, as I strained to see a line of cars ahead of me. Silver Lake Boulevard was usually free from congestion, but today the traffic wasn't moving. Hot and anxious, I looked out of the window. Next to me was the dwindling expanse of water that gave Silver Lake its name. Like most things in Los Angeles, the lake was not natural but man-made, a concrete reservoir that almost emptied, dehydrated, in summer and filled partially in winter. Looking at it made me thirsty. Seeing concrete where water should be was like seeing the feet of the wizard of Oz behind the curtain; an unattractive reminder that this was the land of make-believe, where lakes didn't exist naturally but could be conjured up by money and imagination alone.

If pressed, I couldn't articulate why I loved Los Angeles, but I did. My former Bostonian identity had disappeared as quickly as people here applied fake tans. After just a year in the sprawling suburb, I was already feeling part of the city, and the smog, the sun and the water, or lack thereof. Growing up in New England, it had felt like I had spent my whole life fighting against some invisible force that was as strong and elusive as gravity. In California, that weight had been lifted. There was nothing to fight against here – besides traffic – and even then there was little you could do but give into the slow flow of the river of cars.

My Toyota blasted cold air from its dust-covered vents. I leaned in closer, feeling the cool kiss of air against my neck. My forehead gently fell against the wheel and I hugged my arms to my chest, away from the sun. It had been a long day at work and I was tired, burnt out and I now felt my pale arms beginning to burn.

An emerging film director, I lived in a studio apartment in Silver Lake's lush, tree-covered hills, a hipster haven tucked into a small valley far away from the ocean, west of West Hollywood. It had the feeling of a real neighbourhood, not the typical billboard-and-boulevard vista that one would associate with Los Angeles. Silver Lake was ideally located between Pasadena, where my work was, and West Hollywood, where films and my social life resided.

In my street the otherwise grey sidewalks were littered with colourful petals. Bungalow houses were sweetly tucked into either side, each different in shape and size but all boasting views of snow-capped mountains and downtown Los Angeles. We were high enough to rise above the pollution – sometimes on very smoggy days, I looked down on a dark sticky cloud that hung over the city like a moth-eaten blanket.

My studio, nestled into the back of one of the bungalows, was a detached guest suite that had been converted into two studio apartments, one stacked on top of the other. I lived in the bottom studio – the bigger of the two, with private access to the garden. Out of the window of my four-walled oasis you could see, if you really craned your neck, the Hollywood sign.

My fingers gripped the steering wheel as I made a left out of the traffic and up a shady, empty side street. The backs of my hands were covered with pen-scrawled lists of to-dos, now smudged by sweat. I would joke at work that this was my version of a PalmPilot. It was engineer humour.

My full-time job was as a storyteller and media consultant for NASA, the National Aeronautics and Space Administration. I had been hired as a communication consultant to help NASA use narrative as a tool for knowledge-sharing practices. What did that mean exactly? I had been hired to help make communication between individuals, groups, departments and campuses within the whole organisation more effective. My base was at the Jet Propulsion Laboratory, a place filled with some of the most brilliant minds in the world, where people fulfilled dreams – dreams they had had from childhood – dreams of astronauts and outer space and rockets. It was an intense, inspiring campus. I walked down the same halls as Carl Sagan and Richard Feynman and future history-makers.

It was an ideal job, one that made me constantly anxious to live up to the incredible opportunities it offered. In college I had studied both mythology and astronomy, and voiced an uncompromising desire to be a film director, and many had scratched their heads as to how I would combine these interests in my future career. I was nothing if not determined. By the age of eight, on realising I could not be Hercule Poirot or Indiana Jones, I had decided the next best thing would be to become a film director. Subsequently, my whole life plan had been geared towards that vision. In the fourth grade, while other children were playing on the swings, I would make my friends stay in from recess to rehearse plays and scripts that I had borrowed from the library. Out shopping with my mother as a teenager, instead of trying on clothes to buy, I would try on long gowns and practise my Oscars award speech in the changing room while she waited patiently outside.

This determination went beyond dreaming. Every moment I had, I worked hard towards my goal; internships at public television in high school, writing and making films and, on graduating from college, spending years without a holiday. I worked on Broadway, on films and in TV. I didn't know what a life looked like without workgy. When *The Devil Wears Prada* came out, I couldn't bring myself to read it, seeing it not as an entertaining escape but as a reflection of my own existence. I realised at this point that the hard work was gaining me experience but not the freedom I craved, so I took a risk. I quit my life in New York, putting most of what I owned onto the street with a sign that read "share the love", and went to Boston to start my own production company. My first big break was filming for The Dresden Dolls, a punk cabaret band, as they went on tour throughout the US.

The call from NASA came a year later. It was from Ben Epstein at NASA headquarters in Washington, DC. He had seen my first short film and loved it. A mutual friend had told him about my background in folklore, mythology and astronomy and for 20 minutes straight we talked about storytelling, space exploration and film. I was enjoying myself so much that I forgot I was on a job interview. Ben told me of his desire to use the power of storytelling for knowledge-sharing practices at NASA. He believed everyone in the organisation had important stories to tell, but because they did not generally have a way of sharing them, their often very remarkable knowledge and experiences were lost to the community. My heart had quickened with excitement. This was something I could do, I thought. Cosmology and mythology had been my passions in life, the reason why I made films. I felt born for the position he was describing.

After several emails back and forth, I had landed an interview at HQ.

*

I rolled down the window as my small car, like The Little Train That Could, reached the peak of the hill. A fresh breeze wafted in. It was cooler up here, under the shade of the flowering trees. I felt myself relax for the first time in a week. We were working on many projects, the biggest of which was hiring an old friend and colleague, Jay O'Callahan, the world-famous storyteller, to create a story for NASA's 50th Anniversary. Nothing like this had ever been done before; we had taken a risk in hiring him, and I felt the weight of responsibility for both NASA and my dear friend firmly on my shoulders.

My car slowly circled the block again. This was a tough street to park on as few people had driveways. In my vision for the perfect Hollywood pad, I had forgotten to include a parking space.

Before coming to LA I had spent nights dreaming of my ideal place. It would be a small studio, with its own side entrance and private garden. In fact, my vision was so precise that I could see myself leaning against the sink, with a cup of steaming tea, looking out through a window at a flowering paradise. I never questioned whether it existed but rather how I would find it, and after weeks of Craigslist searchings and dead ends, I finally did. Discovering the small Silver Lake studio, hidden on the leafy hillside, had been the first good omen about my new life in California.

There had been great demand for the apartment. It was reasonably priced, in an ideal neighbourhood and very secluded. The trouble was there were a handful of equally competitive applicants who were equally convinced the place was theirs. I didn't think I was going to get it. I had given references, sent them a full resume and examples of my work and dived in determined. After a rigorous interview process, the owner left a message that his boyfriend thought I had "nice energy", so I had landed the apartment.

I popped open the trunk and removed my forlorn yoga mat, recently overlooked, and a bag of groceries, and felt glad for the walk uphill. My days had been filled with eight-hour stints staring at a computer. When I returned home, my second job would begin: running my production company. The combination left me frazzled, in that strange modern way of being constantly exhausted but under-exercised. However, my work had given me financial freedom for the first time in my young adult life. I had a car, an apartment full of IKEA furniture and, as long as I practised moderation, I could indulge in new clothes, shoes and a night out when I wished.

I looked back at my car, which was growing smaller as I climbed the street. Had I locked it? Crap. I couldn't remember. I'd been so stressed lately that whatever new information came into my mind tended to push out the small, immediate things that I should remember. My brain was leaking, and a nagging voice, like a distant bell, sounded out how desperately I was in need of a holiday.

Lazily, I decided to continue up the hill regardless of whether it was locked or not. My MIT engineer father was the one who had insisted that I avoid all cars with automatic locks and windows. His insistence stemmed from the fear that in the rare event that I drove into a massive body of water (Silver Lake's lake on a good day would barely cover my tyres), the electronic system would fail and I'd be trapped in the car and drown. Today, happily, I was safe from that eventuality – although I might have my car stolen instead.

Up ahead, the girl from the studio above me opened our gate. I felt myself quickening my pace. She was tall, blonde and an assistant to some big movie producer whom she always refused to name, which made me think he, or she, was quite a heavyweight. I took out my keys, shifting my bags to the other arm, and reached the gate, out of breath, just as she closed it and turned towards me. A smile appeared on her face as she fluttered her mascara-coated eyelashes. Before I could think of anything neighbourly to say to her, she disappeared into her car. I suddenly felt very alone. The elusive quality of LA people was deeply unsatisfying. I had friends but they were scattered throughout the city, and it took me at least a half an hour to drive to see anyone. Even then, it was rare that we'd get together in numbers of more than two. I craved a sense of cohesiveness. Other than on a film set, I had never been part of a gang or a group, and for some reason, at 25 years old, that feeling had suddenly become important. I was missing a sense of belonging.

Making my way down decking covered in potted plants and cacti, it occurred to me that I didn't even know my landlord. He lived with his boyfriend and his two tiny dogs – with whom I waged a daily battle to prevent them slipping into my apartment – in the well-groomed, stucco-style main house next door; and, from what I could tell, he seemed like a quiet, nice man. Sometimes on my way out of the gate, I would see him in his small makeshift studio in the converted garage painting these beautiful, surreal landscapes. When our eyes met he would smile and gently close the door. I got the not-so-subtle hint that he felt that, even by looking, I was intruding on his privacy.

My phone buzzed in my pocket but my arms, filled with yoga mat and groceries, stood their ground. I leaned against my door, ferreting around in my bag for my keys, when it slid open. I stumbled into my apartment. My over-worked brain had forgotten to lock my front door too. That settled it. Before I really lost my marbles – or any other possessions – I was going to take a break.

Besides a ruffled pillow and some papers knocked over by the dogs, who had clearly won today's battle and whose muddy paws had left a trail on the floor, nothing in the studio was out of order. Deliciously savouring the idea of a full night with nothing to do ahead of me, I put my groceries onto the kitchen counter. I didn't have much to unpack: canned soup, slightly melted ice cream and a chocolate bar that was now mostly liquid. I was not a chef. In fact, I despised cooking generally and had a talent for finding boyfriends who enjoyed it.

Flopping onto the couch, I took out my phone. I had a text. Probably from my friend Rose, the actress, who wanted to get together for dinner. I flipped open the phone. It was not from Rose. Instead, a horribly familiar number stared back at me and my hairs stood on end. I did not want to read it. My stomach lurched and I stood up quickly, convinced that I was going to throw up. I shut my phone and threw it onto the sofa. Suddenly, a night with only myself and the silence of my four walls seemed like a very bad idea.

*

Josh came to pick me up at 8pm. I waited outside my gate as the night grew dark. It was chillier now that the late after-noon sun had disappeared, and I rubbed my arms, my eyes scanning the street for Josh's car. I had met Josh during my first week in Los Angeles when we sat across from each other at the OM Café, a sweet coffee shop that I had claimed as my local haunt in those first few days. Josh had started up the conversation, something about where was I from and how long had I been in LA. He was a good-looking guy, tall and slim with a mop of dark hair and had a cute, slightly nerdy manner. He was a computer programmer and video game creator with many famous games to his credit. I had known only a little about that world but had known enough to be impressed. Our conversation had quickly evolved into discussing storytelling, NASA and video games. Josh had been easy to talk to and smiled at me with his handsome, dimpled cheeks. The whole package had been endearing.

Josh clearly viewed tonight as a rescue mission. He knew from the tone of my voice that I was upset and was whisking me away to his friend Tate's birthday, the biggest video game designer in LA. The party promised to be very Hollywood, very Josh. He always had interesting things going on and our adventures were never disappointing. Being a self-subscribed workaholic, I often passed on his invitations but tonight I needed to be distracted.

Headlights appeared from down the hill. With the low rumble of an engine, Josh's sports car came into sight. The car circled the narrow street and quickly pulled in front of me, and I waved.

I smiled, thinking that on our first meeting Josh had asked me if I wanted to join him in getting his nails done and drinking margaritas. "I know of a great place," he said with a smile. At first my heart had sunk, disappointed. He was gay, I thought, but quickly agreed to go, thinking at least I was making a friend. That night, when he showed up at my door with flowers, my assumptions flipped again, realising he had actually been asking me out on a date. Men in LA were just as into taking care of themselves as women were, apparently. I had entered an alternate universe – one slightly intimidating, or at least one that I didn't yet understand. That night was fun, and Josh and I had proceeded to go on three dates but it had never worked out. I wasn't ready; my heart those first months had been still entangled elsewhere. To his credit he quickly got the hint and our friendship grew. Josh had once said that I could call him day or night and he'd answer. I often put his offer to the test and he was – true to his word – consistently there for me.

As Josh unrolled the window, he smiled. "My God, you look hot," he said. "Get in before someone else tries to pick you up."

I smiled, sliding into the low black leather seat beside him. He had a talent for making me feel better.

"It's really good of you to pick me up, Josh." My voice wavered. I was still unsure if I had made the right choice to go out tonight. If I'd stayed in, I'd have spent most of the night feeling bad. This seemed like a better alternative. Every time I thought about the text, my stomach did fresh somersaults. My phone lay in my handbag like a loaded gun. The temptation to look at the text was mounting.

I turned to Josh, hesitating, "But remember if I come tonight I can't stay late, okay?"

"Uh huh. Sure."

"No, seriously, Josh." Frustrated, I shook my head. Whenever I felt myself relax, the workaholic inside me kicked in. It was always there, keeping me solidly on course.

"It's Tate's birthday – loads of producers who should meet you will be there."

Although my East Coast tradition of self-improvement had been replaced by LA's softly adapted Eastern belief in self-acceptance, my intense focus on my career had not relaxed. I had joined a meditation group, frequented by Bonnie Raitt (and her dog). I drank my weight in wheatgrass shots, had my chakras realigned and enjoyed getting free meals at all the major Hollywood spiritual institutions, from the Scientology Church to the Kabbalah Centre. Everyone and everything in LA was telling me that wisdom lay not in discipline but in letting go. Of what? Of everything, I guessed, even of that question. The hot sun had bleached out my memory of dark winter days, shopping had replaced shovelling snow and social-ising had challenged my hermit tendencies... but my work still came first.

Josh shot me his gentle smile. "You're too serious. You need to have more fun."

I looked out of the window pretending to consider what he said.

Tate lived in Los Feliz, the upscale neighbouring area to Silver Lake, with larger houses and manicured lawns. His street hugged Griffith Park, a gorgeous span of wilder-ness and according to some sources, the largest city park in the country. At the highest point in the park, connected by many walking paths, rested Griffith Observatory.

Griffith, a wealthy businessman at the turn of the 20th century, made his money in mining and then in developing Californian real estate. He had always loved astronomy and when, in the early 1900s, he had looked through the 60-inch telescope at Mt. Wilson, then the largest in the world, he had seen an image of deep space that had left him forever changed. It had transformed him into an altruist.

Griffith believed that if everyone had the opportunity

to witness such an intimate view of the cosmos, we would be able to achieve world peace. He had donated all the land in Griffith Park, along with money for the observatory, to make it possible, and free, for anyone to see deep into space. I had visited the observatory many times and was moved by his vision.

Cars spanned Tate's street and Josh pulled over.

"You should get out here so you don't have to walk." Josh glanced at my face, which wore a nervous expression. "You'll be fine, honestly, go in. Tate will remember you."

His eyes twinkled. I could tell he was feeling on top of his game, taking a young woman to a swanky Hollywood party in his sports car. He winked at me.

I stepped out of the car and laughed. "You're just like James Bond, Josh."

His grin widened. For a video game programmer, he was pretty close. Programmers and game designers were an interesting breed of Angelino. I had felt instantly comfortable in their company, perhaps because their manner and interests were akin to many of the people I met at NASA. Or perhaps they reminded me a bit of my engineer father, someone who still loved playing and inventing. Either way, they were atypical for Hollywood, like an exotic spice in the LA cupboard of ingredients. Egotists and personalities existed in the gaming community too, of course, but for the most part gamers were non-judgmental, open to new ideas and fun, if with a twinge of mild Asperger's.

I stood in front of Tate's house, uneasy about arriving alone. The great, curved wooden door facing me looked like it belonged in a castle. Large green palm leaves fanned out on either side. A lion, with a ring through its mouth, acted as the knocker in the middle. It was an entrance appropriate for a royal establishment – Tate was Hollywood elite.

The door opened to reveal Tate barefoot in khakis and an unremarkable, untucked blue button-down shirt. I felt myself slump and shift my weight. Tate was shorter than I was, up to my nose, with ice-blue eyes resting in an angular eastern European face. He stood alone in the doorway, staring at me.

"Hi Tate. I hope I'm not too early."

"You're not." He stepped aside and let me into the tiled foyer.

I held out my hand and he shook it awkwardly. Perhaps I was being too formal. "Tate. I'm Jessica, Josh's friend? We met once before."

His blank stare indicated he hadn't a clue who I was. My cheeks flushed at my bold assumption that he'd remember me. He knew so many people. I should have introduced myself at the very beginning.

"I remember." He lied politely. "Why isn't Josh with you?"

"Oh. He's parking." I shifted uncomfortably again and looked around. A large sweeping staircase curled behind him, bordered by stucco walls, with inbuilt cavern-like shelves rendered just like a period villa.

"He was supposed to come early," Tate explained, closing the door behind me. "There were people here that I wanted him to meet."

"Oh. I'm afraid he had to pick me up first." I was trying desperately to keep away the awkward silence that circles new conversations, like swatting away a hovering fly. "Well, Happy Birthday. You must be having a good time?"

"No, not really." He shrugged. While most people might have found Tate's bluntness rude, I felt myself relax. He led me into the kitchen where a large Mexican woman was leaning over a sink, washing vegetables. Steam was rising from pots on the stove and the air filled with the smell of roasted meat and sweet chilli spice. The aroma was incredible. My stomach growled.

I turned to Tate. "It's a beautiful house. When was it built?"

"Some time in the early 1920s. Typical Spanish-style villa." I followed him into a large sitting room. The floor was covered with Oriental carpets, but otherwise it was mostly empty – a piano rested in the far corner and a couple of skateboards and bean bags littered the floor around a television and video game console. The decor could have doubled as the movie set for *Big*.

"Room to play in," I said stepping into the space. I could hear my voice echo off the high ceiling.

Tate slipped behind the piano at the far end. "Exactly," he called, and began to play Bach with such precision that it caught me off guard. "Sorry I'm so rusty," he shouted over the music. Chords that a professional pianist would have been proud of effortlessly flowed from his fingertips.

My personal concert was not quite a private one though as I looked out of the sliding doors to my right. I could see guests filling the back garden, crowding on a patio and milling around a large, well-lit pool. It looked as if the party had been going for a while.

One of the windows slid open and in leaned a slim, attractive young Asian woman. She yelled over the music. "Hey, birthday boy. Time to be social."

Tate stopped playing.

The young woman was my age, mid-twenties, clad in a hot pink bikini. Tate looked distracted by her cleavage as she leaned in further. "I said, time to be social. It's your party, after all."

I suddenly felt overdressed, and a size too big, in my sundress and flats. Outside, despite the chilling night air, gorgeous women stood scantily clad in swimsuits while the men, comfortably clothed in shorts and polo shirts, looked like they just came from a round of golf. Small torches lit the way through the garden and warmed the air, as if the sun had never gone down. I dipped my hand in the pool and felt instantly sad I hadn't brought my own swimsuit. It was cosy warm, like a large bathtub.

In the far corner of the pool, a famous movie star minded his children as they splashed about the shallow end. I was about to go over and open with a "Hi, fellow Bostonian" but thought better of it. I didn't want to bother him, or sound like a nerd. There was an unspoken, "don't bother me" rule when mingling with the Hollywood elite. Saying "I'm a big fan of your work" was acceptable; acting like one was not.

There were a handful of people from TV that I recognised as well. A couple of them were mixing drinks, while two others waited in line for food. I recognised some of Josh's friends from the gaming industry too but the rest of the guests were strangers that I guessed to be film producers, their wives, girlfriends or entourage.

Josh appeared and found me in the crowd. He smiled. "Are you wearing your bathing suit?"

"No, someone forgot to tell me it was doubling up as a pool party." I watched as Josh's eyes were momentarily distracted by a stick of a woman in a red bikini with watermelon-sized breasts.

A waiter came by with a tray of pink-coloured cocktails. I took one and lowered my eyes. "This skin show is ridiculous," I said and was immediately embarrassed by my own modesty. I sounded like a disgruntled 1950s housewife.

"What do you want? They're actresses." Josh shrugged. "They see this party as one long audition."

"I guess." I suddenly wanted to go home.

"Look, there's loads of people here I want to you to meet. I've told them all about you already." Josh, in his generous way, proceeded to take me from producer to producer, as I increasingly felt like I was on some bizarre parade.

Josh consistently referred to me as the "next thing to watch" but most of the producers were more interested in why I wasn't wearing a bathing suit. "I thought it was too cold," I repeated, like a parrot. Others seemed disappointed that I wasn't an actress.

"Why an actress?" I asked Josh later, looking confused.

He whispered in my ear, "Actresses usually sleep with them."

I moaned. "Josh, I could have been on my couch in pyjamas..."

"Eating soup out of a can?" Josh laughed and shook his head. "Don't give up so easily. They'll see you're brilliant and become interested, I promise."

Josh left to network for himself. I grabbed a burger from the food table to fortify my constitution and re-entered the fray. Each conversation was more painful than the last.

One mega-producer asked what I did.

"I'm a director," I stated proudly.

He looked disappointed. "So what do you do then, chick flicks? Kid's shows?" His eyes began to wander, desperate for something more interesting to land on.

"Neither."

Suddenly he looked at me, less confused. "Oh wait, you're a lesbian."

From out of the corner of my eye, I saw a tall 30-something-year-old producer sprinting towards us. As I stepped out of the way he yelled "heads" and bashed into the man I was speaking with. Both of them went flying into the pool, fully clothed, and the loud splash sent bikini-clad actresses screaming for their lives. The two producers scrambled to give each other a head-lock, twisting in the water, while their wives looked on with faces that showed neither amusement nor interest.

I looked at them, a pair of young, idiotic walruses, who held the key to the world I so loved and wanted to enter. They splashed about in the water as if it was their own private lake, and I suddenly felt utterly depressed.

This was the land of gold dust. We were in the middle of a desert where everything was warm and bright and cities shouldn't naturally exist. Perhaps we were not in a city at all but a beautiful mirage, and I was Odysseus, journeying through Los Angeles, the city of angels: a fairy realm, a living dream, where everything was easy, comfortable and warm and where no one ever grew up.

Chapter 2

"All mass is interaction." – Richard Feynman, GENIUS: THE LIFE AND SCIENCE OF RICHARD FEYNMAN: *Biography section, across from the fireplace, under F.*

The grounds of JPL, the Jet Propulsion Laboratory, were the prettiest I'd seen at any NASA centre. Long, wide buildings, lined with large windows, were connected by shady paths and patches of green lawn with benches for repose. Trees provided shelter for tai-chi-practising astrophysicists. For the lack of a better term, it was a nerd's sanctuary, a beautiful island housing brilliant, innovative and creative minds, and I had my little patch of it – a small cubical, tucked away from the main campus, down a road, in a new building, on the first floor, all the way at the end.

I sat in my cubical, underneath the electric lighting. The walls were bare; like blank canvases, I had told my colleagues. The truth of it was I worked from home as much as I could. Even at a remarkable institution like NASA, it was hard for me to find cubical-land particularly inspiring, especially on a Friday. In 20 minutes I had a conference, so I took the rare free window of time to look through the mail on my desk. Most of it was NASA notices, and community events. JPL was a family-friendly NASA campus, unlike any other that I had visited.

Already during my time at NASA, I had visited quite a few of the campuses, which were located all over the US, mostly south of the Mason-Dixon Line. Each had its own personality, like a little microorganism that built a larger, more sophisticated, mystic-filled entity. I had been to head quarters in Washington DC, just after the cherry blossom festival, when the city exploded into all shades of pink. It had felt powerful there, tall buildings at the heart of the country's command centre. At the Glenn Research Center in Ohio, the dedication and pride of all the staff, from the janitors right up to the project managers, had been palpable. On a stone wall outside its entrance, there had been a large ticker, with bright-red numbers, showing the countdown to launch. I wondered if that accounted for the camaraderie that I felt at Glenn. Maybe it acted as a focal point around which everything else, including egos, revolved. There was a feeling there, as the great storyteller Jay O'Callahan observed, not of "I did it" but "we did it". It had been a perfect first glimpse of the magic of NASA.

At Kennedy Space Center in Florida, I had not only got to see a rocket launch, one of the most extraordinary experiences of my life, but I had walked under the new shuttle. The hairs on my arms had stood on end as I looked up at its belly, made from small foam squares, each individually crafted, each unique. What love, persistence and partnership had gone into this dream, and all for the sake of exploration. I had thought of my astronomy professor at university, Dana Backman, who stayed hours after he should have gone home, helping me through my failed physics exam. I thought of my father, how he would have loved to catch a glimpse of this, and of my great-great-grandfather – my father's great-grandfather – who had equipped ships with sails and supplies in Baltimore harbour. His ships had crossed oceans to seek new lands, while this shuttle – the ship of the future – would launch into the atmosphere to explore new worlds, riding on a vacuum of nothingness.

There were still many NASA campuses left to visit and more adventures to be had. With every visit I felt a bit of my mind expanding and my sense of what was possible growing. There was no other institution like this on the planet, perhaps the universe.

I tried to come to JPL at least twice a week to see what the knowledge management team was working on and to meet new people, hear their news. The buildings were almost vibrating with incredible, significant stories and it was my job to find a way to capture them, and the know-ledge they held, and offer them back to the NASA community. Everyone had a story to tell, many in fact, and it was overwhelming. How did you capture these stories? What kind of information did they transmit? How could you make them meaningful to others? Communication was a challenge not only across departments but across NASA campuses, located throughout the country. How could you inspire all the separate scientists and employees to listen to each other, and see the value in their stories so they could pass on knowledge, from one project to the next, one generation to the next?

You would think that at an American scientific institution, there would be a common language spoken by all, perhaps the language of astronomy or mathematics, but it wasn't so. There were many languages, which made my job more complicated. For example, engineers had a totally different vocabulary from project managers, astro-biologists may see the world differently from astro-geologists, and NASA had to bring them all together in one incredible symphony in order to complete a unified mission. The success came, I felt, despite the spectrum of specialities, languages and perspectives because in the chorus of stories I heard there was a common voice shared by all: a unified desire for knowledge and a thirst for exploration. Together they were like the fire in the belly, the jet propulsion, that motivated each individual at NASA.

When I was young I was moved by a book called *Black Elk Speaks*, a story about Black Elk, a Shaman, and the role of visions in a community. When walking through the halls of NASA, this book would often come to mind. "I think I have told you, but if I have not, you must have understood," Black Elk said, "that a man who has a vision is not able to use the power of it until after he has performed the vision on Earth for the people to see." Whether applied to creating a film, or a space mission, this continued to resonate with me.

Truly deep visions, I believe, well from our deep subconscious, holding in them a complicated mix of information, metaphor and feeling. Then, dragged up into the light of day, the vision is subjected to our many voices, each like lawyers, arguing different yet legitimate perspectives to keep us sane. Without ritual, the dream gets held up to reality, like a snowflake on the tip of your finger, ultimately to dissolve before there is time to explore its mystery. One reason I had found an instant affinity with NASA was because I knew scientists were kindred spirits when it came to mystery. An answer I heard often from my colleagues there, enunciated with a twinkle in their eye, was "I don't know" or "It leaves room for more questions". They loved the continual call of the universe for investigation; the idea that the more we know, the more mysterious things become. At NASA, visions and dreams were something that seemed to be incorporated in the totality of modern life.

Through the door of my cubical, I could see a NASA poster of the shuttle with bold lettering which read, "There are no problems, only solutions." This was their motto, along with "Failure is not an option". Both had at first sounded militaristic but, over time, had softened in my mind to seem incredibly wise: giving up is not an option, not on yourself and not on your vision.

*

My mind, like pages fluttering backwards in a book, returned to the party the previous evening. "Oh, so you're a lesbian," the producer had said before getting knocked into the pool, as if that would explain my desire to make something more substantial than the average chick flick. Many more conversations like that later, I had found myself waiting for a cab, frustrated and tearful.

The cab had appeared quickly. As I slid into its warm, comfortable seats, protected by the car's metal enclosure – my Los Angeles safety blanket – my phone beeped.

"Hello?"

Josh's voice sounded worried. "Where did you go?"

"Home. I'm sorry. I couldn't take much more." I suddenly felt guilty. Josh had only been trying to help.

"You can't take them so seriously, Jessica."

"Josh, they had zero interest in me as a director. They were more interested in why I wasn't wearing a bathing suit."

"Look," he had said, sounding exasperated. I could hear the echo of the party around him. "You're young and attractive. You've got to use it."

"I'm hanging up." The way things were hadn't been his fault and I was taking it out on him.

"Hear me out," he had persisted. "Dress sexy, charm them. Then when they find out you're smart and talented too, they'll be wowed."

"Woody Allen never had to dress sexy."

"Yeah, and look, he still struggles to get financing." Josh had a point. "Think of it like a game."

"Look, I'm sorry, I have to go." The cab had slowed and I switched off my phone.

Maybe it would be one of those memories that would improve with age? Maybe decades from now I would look back and be glad I had had that experience. For now, however, I felt disempowered, icky mortification sticking to me every time I thought back to myself standing there by the pool, the only woman fully clothed, handing out my business cards and trying desperately to be taken seriously.

Further down the hall, I could hear the voice of our project manager coming closer, pulling me out of my day dream.

"Jessica, you here for the meeting?" Nancy appeared at the doorway, smiling and leaning against the cubical wall. She gave off a glow of exuberance that only those who love their job can have.

"Yes, wouldn't miss it."

"We'll talk more about *Second Life*. There are exciting things on the horizon." She patted the top of the cubical as punctuation. "See you soon."

I gathered my things to prepare for the meeting and took out my phone. The text from the previous night was still in my inbox, waiting for me to respond. I had almost forgotten about it, distracted by the past night's events.

However, now in cubical-land, there were no distractions. No matter how many times I read the two silly sentences, a fresh flip of the stomach shocked my senses.

"I'm eating grapes right now, green ones," it read. "That's how exciting my life is now that you left."

It was Grant, trying to be funny and tempting me to respond. It was a typical Grant message, sweet and simple on the outside but completely loaded. Universes existed in between each word. This was the first I had heard from Grant in five months, since he had told me that I was keeping him from being the man he wanted to be. It had completely crushed me.

I had embraced the newness and the change that Los Angeles afforded partly because I was as far as I could possibly be from Grant and the East Coast. Ours had been a badly matched, intense and dramatic year-long affair. Grant had been one of my actors. No one else in the cast had known about our relationship, partly because we had never referred to ourselves as dating, or boyfriend and girlfriend, or in a relationship at all, but I had fallen very deeply in love with him.

Grant was charismatic and good-looking. I had loved his long dark hair, his blue eyes and broad shoulders. He was ruggedly artistic, a sensitive, motorcycle-riding actor. I was ten years younger than him, his director, and had felt incredibly powerful as a result. Most male directors had affairs with their female actresses, so here I was, turning the tides.

The belief that I was doing my share for gender equality hadn't been my only delusion about the relationship. In his company I felt giddy and uneasy, and my usual desire to be in control felt deliciously challenged. He was unpredictable and passionate, and believed in an unattached life, to anyone or anything. Our relationship was always undefined. He advocated dating many people; he was physically intimate but easily turned cold, and by the time I had fallen in love with him, I realised that this would not be the simple girl-meets-boy, girl-likes-boy, girl-dates-boy scenario.

Grant and I had agreed that when or if we wanted to see other people, we'd let each other know. We promised always to be honest, even if it hurt the other's feelings. However, I could never "let go" enough to date other people, so I was constantly worrying, wondering whether he had found someone better to move on to. I knew I was on unsteady ground, but at the same time I was determined that I could be liberal enough to love someone without wanting anything from them. That was true love after all, wasn't it?

Grant pushed my boundaries and instead of running in the opposite direction, I convinced myself that dating someone so confusing was bold and important; magic happens outside your comfort zone – well, that's what the yoga teachers say and the inspirational books tell us. This was the transcendentalist ideal, was it not? I was following Gloria Steinem's words from *Outrageous Acts and Everyday Rebellions*, "the margins are where the growth is" – by challenging myself, I believed I was expanding the person I was.

It had been after a couple of months of seeing each other that the dynamic had changed. I had woken up as usual in his bed, looking up at the flapping trash bags above me where windows should have been. Grant's house was something he was constantly working at but never quite completing – like Sisyphus attempting DIY. Outside the windowless bedroom was a funeral home. On some mornings I looked out to see a parking lot full of hearses and families dressed in black. I imagined myself among them, watching my old, confident self being carried away in the coffin. This relationship had been killing me emotionally, the lack of intimacy and affection was sticking little needles into my heart and, instead of thriving, I felt myself disappearing.

That morning I had rolled over and found Grant missing – not unusual, as he would often leave to enjoy the morning alone. Where Grant should have been I noticed he had left his journal open flat, revealing a page scrawled with writing. I sat up and glanced over my shoulder. It was too tempting not to glance; it was a rare window into the elusive mind of Grant and, as my eyes quickly flickered over it, I saw my name staring back at me in the middle of the page. I felt myself flush. Even just a glance made me feel ashamed. I was intruding. Footsteps had sounded from outside the hall and despite myself I glanced again, catching the whole sentence before the door opened.

In scratchy thoughtless letters he had written: "I'm not in love with Jessica, and that's okay."

"Ah, you're up. You want breakfast?" Grant entered the room, his towel wrapped around his perfect waist.

Something stabbed in my chest. At the time, I assumed the heartache was my own fault. What else had I expected? I had fooled myself into thinking he loved me in an alternative way, when in truth he had not loved me at all. All his rules, his lack of focus and his fiercely independent manner were not some advanced state of being, rather they were signs of a lack of emotion. I felt stupid and naive, and shook my head, politely.

Grant cocked his handsome face to the side. He could tell something was wrong. "Are you sure? Let me take you out. You're my lady, after all."

"No breakfast for me, thanks."

I did my best to distance myself from Grant. I moved back into my Boston studio apartment and tried unsuccessfully to date other people. However, six months later, when I was out with someone else, I discovered Grant did actually have feelings for me. Over the phone, on a crowded bus, he told me he loved me and promptly had a panic attack.

Two days later in Cambridge, as I sat in a production meeting at 1369 Coffee House, my "office" at the time, my phone beeped in the middle of reviewing storyboards with my production designer. I quietly slipped my phone out of my pocket, not wanting to disturb the meeting, and peeked to see it was a text from Grant. No explanation. No warning. The message was a simple, straightforward: "I can't do this any more."

My heart broke in two and spilled out onto the coffee shop floor. What I glimpsed inside that broken organ terrified me – a lonely, dark and empty centre. I quickly excused myself from the meeting and fled to the bathroom, where I cried and vomited in equal intervals. My only clear memory was the graffiti above the loo roll that read in dark ink: "Bonnie ♡ Ray 4 EVA" and "Derek is a tool".

I tried to call and text back but Grant had cut off all communication and refused to speak to me. I couldn't sleep or eat because everything about Boston and my work reminded me of him. My short film had just finished the festival circuit and at each festival I went to I had had to sit through the screening, with his face parading in front of me. Never again, I promised myself, would I date one of my actors.

When NASA offered me the chance to relocate to JPL and Los Angeles, I knew I had to take it. I would have work that I was passionate about, I thought, in a sunny land at the heart of a film centre. I could feel the power of my life's momentum pulling me far away from Boston.

I was sitting across the table from my sister in an Italian restaurant when I told her that I had got a transfer to Los Angeles.

"California! Oh Jessica, that's fantastic. You're a director. That's exactly where you should be." She was giving me all her attention and her love. "And NASA," she said, "I still can't believe you're working for NASA. That is so cool."

I raised my wine glass and clinked it to my sister's. Through its wine-soaked sides, her blurred reflection smiled back at me.

"It's your time to shine, Jessy."

With that memory frozen in my mind, my thumb hovered over Grant's message: "I'm eating grapes right now, green ones..." I pressed delete. The message was gone. I felt a sudden lightness, and made my way out of my cubicle to my meeting. As I passed the NASA "Failure is Not an Option" poster on the wall, a jolt of joy ran through my veins right to my fingertips.

*

Friday night and I was to go out on a date – my first since my manicure and margaritas evening with Josh. The previous week, I had met a talented screenwriter in Silver Lake, who had tried unsuccessfully to buy me coffee at Intelligentsia Coffeebar; on seeing I was already drinking tea, he had insisted on buying me dinner instead.

Intelligentsia was a stunning location, with brick arches and lovely tiled floors, a 1940s building beauti-fully converted for the coffee-drinking 21st century. It was the hub of hipsterville, where everyone came to faux-socialise, spending more time on their laptops than chatting to each other. A long line would always extend out the door – streaming through the outdoor seating area and acting as a slow-moving fashion show. I would get new ideas for outfits as I people-watched, waiting in line. 1980s high-waisted chino shorts, Ray-Ban-inspired sunglasses and mismatched sweater vests seemed to be the current uniform.

The screenwriter who charmed me into chatting with him had been sitting two tables over. He claimed to have written one of the *The Fast and the Furious* movies, and was now working on "something big, something indie". Staring at the people around him, he had taken a long drag of his cigarette with the jaded confidence of someone who had enjoyed early success, and exhaled slowly with the frustration of someone who hadn't had any since.

I didn't know why I said yes when he asked me to dinner. I was far more interested in his screenplays than his phone number, but after requesting the former he gave me the latter, and so I thought, why not? He said to meet him at Flore, my favourite vegan restaurant, and to bring my bicycle because he had something fun to introduce me to afterwards. It seemed mysterious and enticing enough, but the thought of going on a date made me feel agitated and I couldn't help hoping it would rain.

Of course, it didn't rain. It was, in fact, a beautiful evening like always, cool and clear. Downtown Silver Lake was buzzing with people and the excited energy of a Friday evening.

And so I found myself sitting halfway through my bean and setain burrito, enjoying the cool breeze outside the Flore café. The date was going surprising well. He had showed up on time, nicely dressed in a button-down t-shirt and khaki shorts and told me how he had been nervous to ask me out in case I turned him down. He seemed to have more depth to his personality than I first gave him credit for. Unlike most people in LA, he did not blindly follow Eckhart Tolle, he did not belong to a gym and he had never owned a pair of Ray-Ban sunglasses, nor had he wanted to. He had grown up in New York and wanted to be a journalist, when in a weird twist of fate, someone had asked him to turn one of his stories into a script. It was bought, but never made, and his future was sealed; he was hooked on the world of screenwriting.

"Journalism, goodbye, Hollywood, hello." He smiled, finishing the last of his wine. "So you work for NASA?"

"Yeah, but I'm not a scientist. I'm more on the know-ledge-sharing side of things."

The Screenwriter checked his watch, then signalled for the check. "Wait," I began to protest, "I'm only halfway through my dinner."

"You eat too slow." As the check came he grabbed it, insisting on paying. "Your job sounds cool, but you're a director. Don't you miss, you know, making films?"

"I'm still making things," I said, annoyed and still hungry. "Anyway, NASA's inspiring for any artist. I've found more creative minds there than during all of my time in TV and film put together." He didn't look convinced. "I mean it. There are more passionate, interesting people there, filled with ideas, open to innovation and new tech-nology, than any community of artists I have found." I watched while the waitress took my half-eaten meal away.

"You're going to love what I have in store for you then," he said. "Ever heard of Midnight Ridazz?"

I shook my head.

43

"Good. Come on." He grabbed my hand. We flew out of the restaurant and onto our bikes. The Screenwriter looked at my bicycle. "A vintage fixed gear – very cool."

My belly still growling, I pedalled hard to keep up with him. A couple of yards ahead, in front of Intelligentsia Coffeebar, hundreds of cyclists were grouping. There were tall bicycles, trick bicycles, on road and off road, choppers, fixed gears – I had never seen so many bicycles in one location. Many had glow-sticks decorating their frames, which, in the twilight gave our gathering the look of a junk-yard travelling circus.

A 20-something man in a racing suit, holding a megaphone, stood on one of Intelligentsia's tables. People started cheering. His words were loud and garbled. Something was about to start.

"We may lose each other," the Screenwriter shouted. "But give me a ring at the end of the night and we'll meet up again." He turned to go.

"Wait, what exactly are we doing?" I suddenly panicked. I didn't want to sound uncool but where the hell were we going? How would I get back home?

The Screenwriter disappeared into the crowd and the mass of bicycles started moving. Like a metal cloud, hundreds of noise-making, shining, fabulous bikes moved as a herd down West Sunset Boulevard – me with them.

The city looked different at night, gliding along on a bike. There were so many of us that we cycled along at a perfect cruising speed. This was an LA I never got to see because I was always in the four-walled fortress of my car. I felt as if I was on an urban safari and instead of animals there were wild houses, decaying buildings, graffiti-dressed walls, exotic-looking pedestrians, a high-rise city centre and glowing fast-food signs.

A man with a thick moustache and a speaker passed me on his bicycle, music pumping. We all cheered. Now our expedition had a soundtrack.

I hadn't enjoyed cycling so much since I was a child. Bicycles meant freedom, I had forgotten. I was getting to enjoy parts of the city I would never normally be able to explore, in the safety of a crowd and all powered by my own two feet. The soft breeze was perfect; warm enough not to chill but cool enough to wick away sweat. Night was a time when people would retreat into their caves and here we were, outside. There was a sense of magic to it all.

A girl my age, rocking knee-high socks from American Apparel and a handmade dress, cycled beside me. She was a photographer called Mini and happened to live near me in Silver Lake.

"Midnight Ridazz," she explained, "always brings out hundreds of people. Their aim is to take up a full road lane, you know, to promote cycle awareness and that kind of thing."

She asked how I had found out about them and I told her about the Screenwriter and how he had disappeared.

"Typical…" she said. We made plans to bike home together.

I met incredible people that evening, from 80-year-old cycle enthusiasts to families out for a good time. Finally, this was the community that I had been seeking in the city.

It was getting dark now, nearing midnight, and though only half of us were still cycling on, it was still quite a crowd. We turned up a steep hill and I could feel my legs were on the point of exhaustion.

The young 20-something guy with the megaphone stood in front of a tag artist's shop, shouting at everyone to come inside. Free spray paint was being given out and we all headed to the back of the shop, where four freestanding concrete walls rose into the air, covered in designs. It was a tag garden.

Mini found me and handed me a silver can. I had never done this before, and although it was obvious that the walls were built for this purpose, I had a hard time spraying over the beautiful artwork that was already there.

"This is one of the Midnight Ridazz shops," Mini coaxed. "It's okay, really." She held the gold can up and tagged her initials onto the wall. "See?"

When you're tagging, it's important to find a flow. The paint sprays out of the can in a forceful burst so you have to be ready and confident to make your mark. I decided on the "less thought, more action" approach and started spraying, watching my hand with curiosity to see what it would make. My hand swooped up and down and I drew the symbol for infinity.

I was pleased. Except, being the inexperienced tagger that I was, I had moved too slowly, so my infinity symbol dripped, streaking the wall with silver lines.

"Infinity? Typical NASA girl." I turned to see the Screenwriter behind me.

"Thanks." I gave him my spray can and walked past him. I didn't want to be rude. I owed him something, after all, for a wonderful evening, even if it wasn't spent with him.

"Where are you going?" He looked confused.

"Home," I called over my shoulder.

I met Mini outside the shop. She didn't need much convincing to go. We were both tired.

We hopped on our bikes, joined by some other people from our neighbourhood, and cruised home through the silent streets. Mini waved at me as I turned onto my road, up the hill, calling out that she'd see me at the next one.

After that night, we never would cross paths again. My velocity, my path, was about to dramatically change direction.

I crested the hill and saw my flower-covered gate only a couple of yards before me, illuminated by the streetlights. I drank in the night air, and felt a deep sense of satisfaction. With each push on the pedal, I revelled in the power of being completely self-propelled.

Chapter 3

"The great flood-gates of the wonder-world swung open."
– Herman Melville, MOBY DICK: *Fiction section, second shelf on the left in the gallery.*

Two days later, I woke up starving. My stomach rumbled and I was hungry, but craving something beyond food.

Stumbling over to the kitchen, I flicked the kettle on. My limbs ached with the sweet dull sense of having cycled days before. It was a nice reminder that the past, though past, still existed.

On Saturday I had worked all day. No fun night out, no getting dressed up. I stayed in my pyjamas ticking off a never-ending "to do" list of articles to write for NASA, website updates and correspondence catch-up. All weekend I had a lingering feeling of dissatisfaction for my cosy little work-centric life and it wasn't going away. I had tasted adventure on my bicycle and it had awakened a thirst in me for more.

I flopped into my desk chair, opening up my notebook. It was my morning ritual to meditate by the window with the sun pouring in. I had always felt that filmmakers, just like other artists, needed a time in the day in which to experiment and play. Joseph Campbell wrote in his journal that it was a necessity for every body to have a place or time each day "where you don't know what was in the newspapers that morning, you don't know who your friends are, you don't know what you owe anybody, you don't know what anybody owes to you. This is a place where you can simply experience and bring forth what you are and what you might be. This is the place of creative incubation."

This was my time to dream, to write, to doodle and to listen to music, all the while conjuring up images that felt as real to me as the view outside my window. Anything that came to mind I treated as sacred and I would write it down in my book.

Some sculptors feel that rather than carving their vision into something, they are instead uncovering a form that had always existed there. I felt that way about screenwriting. My job was not to carve an image out of words, but rather to act like a scribe as images mysteriously unfolded before me. This type of writing, the mysticism and mystery of it all, kept me interested in the process. Some images wouldn't lead anywhere, and others held worlds that would open up to me the more I explored them.

When I got stuck I often found myself turning to Herman Melville. *Moby Dick* was one of my favourite books and I often pictured Melville, clad in his period garb, sitting on my IKEA sofa, a little bewildered as he suspiciously eyed the green tea I had given him, and wondered how on earth he had got there. He would then passionately yell at me to dig deeper into the bowels of my soul and not rest until I had satisfied my own sense of the beautiful and the mysterious. Melville, to me, represented someone who had had the freedom to let his creative imagination lead him wherever he wanted to go. His writing still held a fresh, exciting tension because he had been brave, inventing sentences, images and story tangents with an intelligent confidence. Whenever I felt lost in my writing, Melville was like a lighthouse, steering me around the rocks of my subconscious self-doubt.

I poured myself some tea and returned to my note book. My current vision, half finished, stared back at me and I closed my eyes: a girl, wrapped in a wooly jumper sat behind a long wooden desk in a secondhand-book shop somewhere by the sea in Scotland. She leaned back in her chair, her feet up on the desk, watching the world go by outside her window.

I could see the Bookshop clearly before me: tall wooden shelves filled with a mismatch of beautiful old books. I could smell the shop's damp, musty perfume. The girl behind the counter huddled deeper into her jumper – it must have been on the cusp of autumn and winter because the steam from her tea swirled in the air in front of her. She was lost in her thoughts, calm and at peace, when a brass bell, which hung above the door, rang clear and interrupted her dreaming.

I opened my eyes, surprised to see my sun-drenched LA studio still there. The feeling of calm drained quickly away. This same image had been coming back to me off and on for about a year, which was unusual, and more unusual still, the girl in the vision looked unsettlingly like me. I constantly thought about other worlds or characters, but had never had a vision with me in it.

I sketched a bit more in my notebook. As I drew, a thought flickered briefly in my mind. Perhaps this was not a vision for a screenplay at all. The hairs on my arms stood on end. Perhaps this was a vision about my life. Suddenly, it was as if doors flew open and images started flooding into my mind. I closed my eyes.

I was on a red bicycle with a basket in front, filled with my lunch.

I was cycling along a single-track road surrounded by rolling green hills and the sea crashing far below me.

I was eating my lunch, my own private picnic, with the wind whipping my hair. My eyes looked out over the endless ocean while I pondered the universe.

I was in a pub. It was night and I was warm, surrounded by fresh faces and the smell of beer. I had to excuse myself, saying it was time for me to write. A chorus of friendly voices called me back but I walked outside, apologising for leaving early.

Then… then… nothing. Blank screen. As if the reel in my mind had run out of film, the images suddenly came to an end. I opened my eyes and stared at my notebook, surprised. I quickly started scribbling away.

My phone, like a Mexican jumping bean, buzzed impatiently on the counter. The sound in turn made me jump. With one hand, I flipped it open. It was a text from Rose: "Where the hell are you?"

I looked at the time. I hadn't realised it was already so late.

*

Rose was a good friend from college – a gorgeous, talented actress who, after a couple of years in LA, had started making small waves for herself. In addition to a string of admirers, and a sweet dog, she had a lovely apartment in the centre of a palm tree-lined street in West Hollywood.

I had crashed on Rose's couch for my first two months in LA. It was because of her generosity that I had had such an easy time settling in. She had showed me the city and I had had the time and freedom to acclimatise, with a home and kindred company to come back to.

Every Sunday Rose and I went to Greenblats for our weekend brunch ritual. Greenblats was one of LA's finest Jewish delis. We had our usual booth, up the stairs from the main restaurant, huddled into a corner at the far end. The food was better than your grandma could make it; the bagels and lox, divine. The essential part of our weekly ritual, however, was that while stuffing ourselves, Rose and I would dish over our weekend's adventures. Hers, full of star-filled parties and bizarre dating stories, were far more Hollywoodtastic (as she would say) than my NASA trips or Saturdays filled with paperwork. We entertained each other with glimpses into these different worlds.

Today, we had started with matzo ball soup, over which I had heard all about Rose's "quiet night", a roof party with B-list celebrities where she had landed an invite to the Playboy mansion. By the time we were devouring our usual lox spread, I had told her about my evening at Tate's birthday, after which she held up her hand, giggling, claiming if I told her any more she'd throw up her food.

On the bench opposite, Rose tucked her long legs up next to her, sighing and placing a hand on her flat belly.

"I have a food baby," she said.

Bits of lettuce were all that remained on the platter in front of us.

I looked over our carnage, and still craved something more. Perhaps that deep-felt longing, which had been there since I had woken up that morning, had actually just been for Greenblats' chocolate cake. While we waited for it to come, I told her about the screenwriter.

"What a waste of time. You should be happy to be rid of him." She said, sipping on her diet Coke.

"Maybe. I think he was playing some kind of hard-to-get game."

"Probably." Rose stretched. "Sounds like a drama queen. Think about it this way, do you really want to spend your pretty on that?"

I smiled. Rose, in addition to making me feel welcome when I first arrived in Los Angeles, had helped me work through my broken heart. On days when I had felt like never getting out of bed and staying in my pyjamas, she wouldn't let me. Instead, she took me shopping, to the movies, anywhere to distract me from thoughts of Grant. She, in the kindest way, had whipped me into feeling fabulous again.

"Always feel fabulous, Jessica," were Rose's words. But in her philosophy lay a deep wisdom that went beyond the superficial. When a relationship has lacked the basic capacity to make you feel cared for, cracks appear in your spirit, like fault lines, undermining your foundations and draining joy and energy, leaving you empty. Rose's solution, showing me that the powers of feeling fabulous lay in my own hands, may sound small, but in truth was profound. It filled me up again.

"What's bothering you?" Rose asked, as a massive piece of chocolate cake, smothered in icing, was placed before me. Rose practised what she preached. She always looked radiant, even at Greenblats in just a simple white T-shirt and jeans.

"Nothing really. I'm just a bit burnt out. I think I'm craving a bit of adventure."

Rose nodded. "I know, LA can do that to you. Channel that energy into your screenplays, though. It's good."

"I don't know. I'm starting to feel that there is something more out there than just film."

She looked worried. "Like what?"

"Well…" I couldn't believe I was about to say it out loud. "I was thinking, I've always wanted to work in a secondhand-book shop by the sea in Scotland."

Rose was silent for a moment, then she suddenly broke out in a smile. "You know, I've always wanted to work in a flower shop in Amsterdam."

"I'm serious, Rose."

"I know, so am I." I thought I knew Rose well but it was the first time she had ever mentioned this to me. She waved her hand in the air as if to dispel the idea. "But that's just LA burn-out talking. Honestly, you're building momentum here. You don't want to lose that by going away. Just look at you."

I shrugged.

"You're working for NASA," Rose continued. "You have one film in the festivals, another one getting made, you've just finished your website…"

"I know, I know. Perhaps you're right."

"I am. Anyway," she continued, "it sounds like you're already having loads of adventures. Just look at your weekend."

It wasn't the same. I wanted to tell Rose that maybe too often we keep our visions for the page and not as direction for our own lives. I wanted to tell her that if she truly yearned to work in a flower shop in Amsterdam, if she could smell what it would be like to be inside it, if she could see the colour of the tulips in the window, or feel the apron around her waist as she tied the strings at the back, if she could feel the scissors in her hand as she cut the stems of fresh roses, then she should do it. With all her heart she should make her life as rich as her imaging of it.

Rose flipped open her phone. "Oh my God. It's already 3pm." She started putting her credit card out on the table. "How did that happen?"

"Rose. You got it last time. This one is on me."

"You sure?"

I nodded.

"All right, lover." She packed up her purse and slid her sunglasses on. "Don't go skipping out of LA on me."

*

The conversation with Rose was still playing in my head, round and round in circles like an aeroplane in a holding pattern, when I pulled out onto Sunset Boulevard. She was right, of course. I had worked hard to establish myself in Los Angeles, and it would be an insane career choice to leave just as things were becoming exciting. She was the voice of reason, reflecting the would-be reaction of my family and friends – all of whom, I knew, had my best intentions at heart. A career move wasn't the point, however. It was a holiday, a chance to get away from work. A month perhaps? Two, tops?

Traffic stretched on before me and I looked down at my phone, thinking of who I hadn't spoken to in a while.

I called my mom.

"Jessica, it's so good to hear from you, sweetie," Mom said in her happy, lyrical way.

I sighed. "Thanks, Mom, it's good to hear your voice."

"What's wrong?"

"Nothing."

"Jessica."

"Nothing. Really. Just. Mom, how would you feel if I went to Scotland to work in a secondhand-book shop?"

There was a long silence.

"I'm just saying if."

"Fine, as long as you didn't fall in love with anyone there."

"Mom…"

"I'm serious."

I rolled my eyes. "Okay, fine, sure. But otherwise…"

"Otherwise." She sighed. She was used to my daydreams, "In the world of the hypothetical, it sounds like fun."

Suddenly I was aware that traffic was moving fast and I was back near Silver Lake. Einstein's theory of relativity could easily be proved when thinking of troubling issues while driving.

Minutes later, I was back in my studio. On one side of my laptop rested a pile of paperwork I still had to get through before the next morning's meeting. Although it was now late afternoon, the LA sun poured in with such intense heat that my thighs were stuck with commitment to my leather desk chair.

My computer screen showed Google. "Used book shop Scotland" waited patiently in the search box. I closed my eyes. I could see it as clearly as if I were there already. It would be a cold, wet day and I would be sitting with my feet resting against a long wooden counter. I would be worlds away from LA, in a small Scottish town right by the sea, enjoying a solitary afternoon in a bookshop. Wrapped in a large sweater, in my hands would be a torn copy of *Pride and Prejudice*, a dusty tome I had pulled out from the many shelves that surrounded me. The bookshop would be quiet and empty and my eyes would drift dreamily out of the window, taking in the green hills and the sea beyond.

"This is insane." A little voice crept into my vision, its doubting tone breaking apart my dream, particle by particle, until it evaporated and my eyes fluttered open. My heart was beating so loud that I couldn't tell if I was excited or terrified.

Then a big voice thundered in... I could actually do this. Not just dream it. I could make this happen, I could for once listen to that instinct that Jay O'Callahan had articulated about NASA, not "why" but "why not?"

Maybe the dream, or the process of dreaming, was the point, not executing it, I thought, but then what would happen if I did? What if I took all the imagination and creativity that I poured into my screenplays and invested it in my own life? I saw Melville before me, sitting on my sofa, drinking tea.

"Why let your characters have all the fun?" he said and immediately spat the hot drink back into the cup. "You call this tea? It's green."

I looked around my apartment. The four white walls I was so proud of, piled with books and scripts and stacks of work, now felt like the four walls of a big cubical. My life had become so myopic, so focused on my career, that I was living in a self-imposed box. When was the last time I had done something without calculating how it benefited my ambition? The lack of an answer made me sad. There was nothing wrong with being ambitious or having large aspirations. That had been a part of me ever since I was born, and I felt at home in that space, but I also felt I was missing out on something else, something I was hungry for and which I couldn't put into words.

It brought to mind the months I had spent as a student in Prague. There, sitting in my usual little nook by the window of Beas, the best Indian restaurant in Europe, I had read Joseph Campbell's book, *Hero with a Thousand Faces* – a seminal work of comparative mythology in which he outlined the German ethnologist Leo Frobenius' idea of "the night sea journey of the solar hero" and Toynbee's "Palingenesia", a continual reoccurrence of birth within the soul. Campbell explains the ideal hero journey as one of continual growth, and not just growth in one direction – even in an environment of constant challenges or constant change, we acclimatise, and our growth plateaus.

I rummaged around in my desk and found my journal from Prague. I leafed through a couple of pages until I found my notes on "Palingenesia". In familiar hand-writing, on a page partly stained with curry, I saw my younger self trying to figure out what constituted the perfect journey, what would allow someone to continually grow. On the bottom of the page I had concluded that our journey through life must be self-directed, for as we allowed ourselves to change, the shape of our journey would change, too.

I shut the journal, my mind buzzing with a sense of purpose. My birthday was coming up in a couple of months, and it suddenly occurred to me that the timing couldn't be better. I would gift myself a holiday. A leap into the unknown wherever that took me, following my instincts – this would be my 26th birthday present to myself.

My hand hit the enter key on "Used book shop Scotland". Immediately the results page appeared, and "Wigtown, Scotland's National Book Town" stood clear and bold at the top of the list.

"Wigtown, Scotland's National Book Town," I said out loud. I clicked on the link and my heart jumped into my throat. The website was modest and had a list of book-shops to choose from. I couldn't believe it. Wigtown was a town of 1,000 people and sixteen bookshops, right by the sea in Scotland. That small voice thundered in my chest, "See, you can make things happen."

Chapter 4

"When you choose one way out of many, all the ways you
don't take are snuffed out like candles, as if they'd never
existed. At that moment all Will's choices existed at once.
But to keep them all in existence meant doing nothing. He
had to choose, after all." – Philip Pullman, THE AMBER
SPYGLASS: *Children's section, across from stairwell, right shelf.*

My finger quivered as it rested on my laptop. I
scanned the names of the different bookshops and
was attracted to the third on the list: "The Bookshop,
Scotland's largest used-book shop". I tried to justify why
I felt compelled by this one – it was the largest, it had a
straightforward title – and then I decided it didn't matter.
This trip was about instinct.

The Bookshop's website was simple and unremarkable,
with a little video on one page offering a music-accom-
panied tour through its many rooms. The video was a bit
blurry but funny, with "it's massive" appearing in bold
text at the end. There was also a page linking to a holiday
home, which the owner evidently let out in the town.
"Promising!" I said to myself. Especially if I wanted to do
some kind of live/work exchange. It looked like a lovely
two-bedroom cottage, perfect for a month's stay. That
would certainly cut down on the costs of the trip. My heart
started to pound. It was too exciting. It actually all existed,

the bookshops, the town – now I just had to get work in one of them.

I saw a contact page on The Bookshop's website and clicked on the email address. What would I write? Sound enthusiastic but not crazy, Jessica, I thought. Keep your vision to yourself. Sound normal. Whatever you do, sound totally not-crazy and nice. I took a deep breath and began.

To whom it may concern,

I hope this email finds you well. I am a 25-year-old film director and writer from the States, looking to spend a couple of months in my favourite country, Scotland, starting this fall.

I've read the wonderful reviews of your bookshop and I was hoping, with any luck, you would be open to live/work volunteer opportunities that allow young writers to volunteer and help at the shop in exchange for living accommodation. I hold a BA in Folklore and Mythology and currently work for NASA as a storytelling consultant and media director. Information about my education and work history is available upon request. Taking a month to visit and write in Scotland has always been a dream of mine, and as I have a deep affinity for used-book shops, I cannot think of any better way to spend my time there.

Thank you so much for your time and I look forward to hearing from you.

Much warmth,
Jessica

I pressed "send" and exhaled. It was good to get it off quickly, like sending off a flare. The message was out there now, travelling through the ether.

Suddenly I didn't know what to do with myself. I couldn't sit still. I made more tea, I flipped through books without actually reading anything. I called Josh back, thanking him for including me at the party. He sounded cheery, completely unfazed by my earlier rudeness. The party had been a great success for him. The people Tate wanted him to meet were impressed by Josh's ideas. He had made important contacts.

Half an hour later when I sat back down at my desk and opened my computer, I was stunned. I had a new email.

Dear Jessica thank you for your letter could you please tell me more about yourself Euan

The message, though short, felt promising. It wasn't a "no", rather, it was a question, an opening for possibility. I had sent an email out into the unknown and heard the echo of someone receiving it half a world away. That in itself was exciting.

However, the lack of punctuation and capitalisation in the one-line response was confusing: it made me feel I had discovered someone not well used to digital technology – some 80-something proprietor of a dusty old bookshop, staring in awe and bemusement at an ancient computer. I pictured this man, surrounded by his grandchildren as they helped him figure out this "newfangled thing called email", while he painstakingly typed out his response, one arthritic finger at a time.

Excited, I wrote straight back. As requested, I told him more about myself, in clear language that an 80-year-old could understand, as well as giving him a very profession-al-sounding list of my abilities, plus my CV. For good measure, I also attached a picture of myself waving, with "hi" written on my hand.

The next day Euan wrote back stating my CV looked impressive. This email was lengthier, casual and humorous. I wondered if I had misjudged my 80-year-old bookseller.

The Bookshop already has plenty of help, however I live in a big, old house above the shop and often host artists and writers.

As I kept on reading, it all felt more and more surreal.

Wigtown is a beautiful place to visit, but remote. We could find you transportation if you felt like exploring the area while you are here. It is cold too, so best to come in the spring.

I looked at the computer screen, amazed. Euan was an incredibly generous person, clearly. He had responded to the extension of my hand into the unknown not with suspicion but with a friendly handshake. I couldn't believe everything was flowing so easily.

Immediately I received another email from Euan.

In fact, he said, perhaps on second thoughts I should come in September – only weeks away and much earlier than I had planned – for the Wigtown Book Festival. He wrote that his house was the centre of activity during that time and would be full of authors, speakers and interesting people. The town, he explained, would be buzzing with activity. He still had one spare room left where I could stay and write and enjoy the town at its best.

I hope we'll be able to keep you amused while you're here. You may find you get quite good at lighting wood-burning stoves.

Without another thought, I booked my ticket.

Chapter 5

"Careful the tale you tell, that is the spell." – Stephen
Sondheim and James Lapine, INTO THE WOODS:
Music section, front room, middle shelf on the left.

A t passport control at Heathrow Airport, the security
official asked why I was visiting the country. I stumbled, struggling to find a simple answer.

"To visit a friend," I said.

Had I ever met the person I was staying with?

"Honestly, no."

How had we met?

"Online."

My face flushed. Aloud, it sounded so mail-order-bride.

If the universe is truly infinite then theoretically there
are an endless number of Jessicas who, at airport security
check points like these, might have decided to answer differently. Perhaps one of those Jessicas would have told the
officer the insane truth, that she was following her golden
guide because of a vision she had had of a bookshop. This
Jessica, however, decided that would be worse.

Undaunted, the security official let me through. That in
itself was disturbing. How often must he get people travelling across the world because of someone they had met
online? Often enough to be unruffled by it, apparently.

I headed to the boarding gate for my connecting flight to Scotland. In an hour or so I would be in Glasgow, where Euan said he'd pick me up. Wigtown was that remote. The journey, he had written, would be mostly on single-track roads and would take about two hours each way.

I could see down the departures hall that a queue had already started forming in front of the boarding gate. I hurried to get in line as a well of uneasiness sprang up inside. What, in God's name, was I doing? By asking simple questions, the security official had stripped away the romantic narrative in my mind, and for a brief moment I had seen my journey as he had: I was going to a tiny town in a country I knew nothing about, to live with a complete stranger.

A crowd of people piled in behind me, all holding boarding cards. The line moved forward and I felt stuck – hemmed in by people on all sides, trapped in the current of the extraordinary events that I had started.

I boarded my plane to Glasgow, found my seat, and freaked out.

Chapter 6

"'The inhabitant or soul of the universe,' Najagneg said, 'is never seen; its voice alone is heard. All we know is that it has a gentle voice, like a woman, a voice so fine and gentle that even children cannot be afraid. And what it says is: Sila ersinar sinivdluge, 'Be not afraid of the universe'." – Joseph Campbell, MYTHS TO LIVE BY: *Mythology section, front room, second shelf from the bottom.*

In the long mirror, under the electric lighting, I looked at my reflection. Staring back at me was a pale, dishevelled, sleep-deprived, mid-twenty-year-old with dark circles hanging under her eyes – I hardly recognised myself. It was not the look I was going for to start my new adventure, and the ambience of the airport's public bathroom wasn't doing me any favours either. I tried to put on a brave smile. I was one floor above the arrivals hall, where Euan would be waiting for me. Despite appearances, I felt awake, alive and extremely nervous.

"I'm not going to hold up a sign like an idiot," he had written. "I don't need one. You'll recognise me. I'm tall with a mass of curly ginger hair. I stand out in a crowd." I detected a note of pride in his words.

It was my first clue as to what Euan was really like. He was wittily self-conscious and a bit of a contradiction. I had once taken a workshop with the great performer and clown, Bill Irwin, who had asserted that character equalled contrast. While Euan didn't want to stand out in a crowd by holding a sign, he was happy to let his appearance set him apart.

I brushed my teeth and felt instantly refreshed. Dabbing concealer to hide my dark circles, I went through my make-up ritual: light eyeshadow over my lid, a darker shade in a thin line around the eye and a dusting of gold in the corners. In less than a minute, I felt like myself again.

Two other women entered the bathroom and brushed past me. Through the swinging door I caught a glimpse of the escalator leading to the arrivals hall, and felt aware that imminently I would be leaving the safety of the bathroom. I took a step back to inspect myself. In jeans, an "I ♡ LA" tank top and with my long dark hair and fringe, I looked very Californian. Perhaps I should have tried to blend in more and not look so American. I sighed. I wouldn't be able to change now; there wasn't enough time. I grabbed my small suitcase and pocketbook, and ventured out.

The escalator was empty. I stepped onto its moving teeth, feeling the velocity pulling me down. There was no turning back. In the waiting room below were a handful of families, looking expectantly up at me. When I fully materialised and they realised I was not the person they were hoping for, they looked disappointed. I smiled, apologetically.

In the far corner of the room, sitting on a bench, there was a man who I thought had to be Euan. A large newspaper was opened before him and covered most of his body, so all I could see were his arms, in a brown jacket, and a mop of ginger-blond hair sticking up over the top.

I put on my best, friendly, I'm-very-normal smile and walked boldly over to him.

"Are you Euan?" I said in my thick American accent. Euan would later tease me that I had pronounced his name with a nasal "Eu-aaan".

He looked up from his reading, as if startled. "Jessica." His voice was deep and sounded perfectly round, like a classic BBC broadcaster's.

He stood up and we looked at each other with a faint sense of recognition. He was far from the 80-year old that I had imagined. For a moment we each smiled with surprised pleasure. Perhaps it was what Anne of Green Gables would have explained as the thrill of instantly spotting a kindred spirit. Or perhaps it was the relief that neither of us looked outwardly insane.

As Euan grabbed my bags and paid for parking, I took a moment to study him. He was tall, 30-something and slim, with wire-framed glasses on a round, good-looking face, big hands. On glancing down, I was delighted to see brown, suede shoes. Everything about him was neat and tidy, except for his hair, which rested like a nest of chaos on his head.

Despite my being instantly comfortable in his company, there was also something that felt very distant and unreal. Perhaps the distance was because I had dreamed this world up, and was now suspicious about its reality.

It was a sunny and unseasonably warm afternoon, and Euan led me through the busy Glasgow parking lot to where he had parked his bright-red van. The five-year-old in me did a somersault. The van had no other markings; it was just cherry-red and big, and looked far more fun than a regular car. This was a good sign of things to come.

But then, as we approached, I saw on the dashboard a sticker reading, "I ♡ Tongue". Interesting and, I thought to myself, surprisingly raunchy. Euan slipped my bag into the back. "Is this all you brought?" His voice was rich, almost heavy, an intriguing contrast to his light, easy demeanour.

"I don't like packing much."

"Neither do I." He smiled and walked around to the front. I started to follow him but quickly remembered that passengers went on the left. Other side of the car, shaking my head, I sighed: we're not in Kansas now, Dorothy.

"It's really good of you to have me," I breathed as I pulled myself up into the van and slid into my seat. "I can't believe I'm here."

"Why?"

"Well..." There was an electric buzz in the air. I couldn't tell if he felt it too, or if my excitement at realising my dream was overflowing. "I'm a complete stranger. I can't believe you said yes, actually."

"Well, it's really great of you to want to come," Euan said as he drove out of the parking lot. "When I got your email I thought, this girl must be really brave to write out of the blue and travel to a strange town across the ocean alone. It was very cool of you. I decided that anything I could do to help, I would."

I was touched by the way he viewed my seemingly random impulse to work at a bookshop by the sea as brave.

He smiled, continuing, "Anyway, it's not every day we get someone so determined to come to Wigtown."

We pulled out into the highway. Although we were still in the city, the relatively empty, four-lane motorway seemed small and quaint compared to the eight-lane, congested traffic madness that greeted me each morning in LA.

Everything out of the window looked green and alive; the browns of winter had yet to arrive. The open landscape was filled with petrol stations (or, as I noted then, "gas stations"), unexcitingly familiar fast-food joints and pebble-dashed houses. Euan would later tell me, to my surprise, that the houses were low-income council houses. To my untrained American eyes, they looked like expensive, country holiday cottages. I realised then that I had entered a truly different world, one not just with different social cues, but with different visual cues, and I would be completely hopeless at reading both.

Euan started chuckling, as he glanced across at my glowing face and Cheshire-cat smile.

"It's so beautiful here," I said, half delirious from jet-lag and half believing this was a lucid dream.

"Just you wait. We're barely out of Glasgow yet." Euan's phone buzzed; as he checked it, his face clouded over.

I suddenly wondered if my presence there was an imposition. "Everything okay?" I hadn't thought of it before, but Euan had driven two hours to pick me up, on a work day.

He shook his head, like an etch-a-sketch, as if he wanted to erase whatever thought had just come to mind. "It's fine. Not a problem." He slid his phone into his pocket and adjusted his glasses.

The facts of my current situation might, on paper, have looked worrisome: I was alone, without any kind of (what my father would call) "communication device", in another country, unaware of where I was going, alone with a stranger in his van. However, I felt completely safe. It wasn't that I had a naive or happy-go-lucky personality. The opposite, in fact, was true.

At eight years old, I had been obsessed with a missing girl my age, named Molly, who had been picked up by strangers on a country road in New Hampshire. Missing posters of her were plastered around my town and littered the memory of my childhood. Daily walks to the elementary school then became a personal battle. My mind filled with abducting scenarios and I used to run the entire way there, my heavy backpack thudding up and down on my small shoulders, in an effort to make myself impossible to kidnap. Later, as a teenager, that fear still there, I would walk to school in my steel-toed Doc Martens, confident for the first time since I hit puberty that I could look after myself.

And yet here I was, in a seemingly vulnerable situation, completely at ease. If I had thought about it more at the time, I would have realised it was either a miracle or a testament to the flow of fate. Or more likely my serenity was because of Euan. It was as easy to see that he was a gentle, generous soul as it was to see his bright blue eyes through his clear glasses.

As if Euan could read my thoughts, he mused, "So was I your first choice of bookshop?"

"First… and only," I said. "I didn't contact anyone else."

"Really? You have no idea how lucky you are."

I raised an eyebrow.

"Not to say I'm great or anything," he continued, "but, you'll see."

"See what?"

"Someone else may have made you work." He was teasing, but I detected some truth in his "you have no idea how lucky you are" and it made me curious. I knew Euan had grown up in the area, and he was young and that he was a key figure in the literary life of Wigtown. Though I hadn't been able to learn much about the town or the other bookshops online, I could guess at what Euan meant. In terms of timing, my age and interests, I might well have hit the jackpot.

"Well, I have to admit I was agreeing with you, until thoughts that I might have been entrapped by a sexual deviant crossed my mind." I pointed to his "I ♡ Tongue" sticker on the window.

Euan laughed and blushed. "Tongue is a place I visited. An old lady was selling those – she had no idea why they were funny, which made it all the better."

"But this is your work car. Clients see that when you do book deals?"

"Yes," he said proudly. It was another interesting contrast to his personality; sincerity coated with a thin veneer of punk rock.

He slipped his phone out of his pocket, typed in a number and handed it to me. It was already ringing. "Tell the shop we'll be a bit late. There's something I want to show you on the way home. That is, if you're not too tired?"

I wasn't. I was more awake, more alive, than I had been in years.

Chapter 7

"Far away in the heavenly abode of the great god Indra, there is a wonderful net which has been hung by some cunning artificer in such a manner that it stretches out indefinitely in all directions. In accordance with the extravagant tastes of the deities, the artificer has hung a single glittering jewel at the net's every node, and since the net itself is infinite in dimension, the jewels are infinite in number. There hang the jewels, glittering like stars of the first magnitude, a wonderful sight to behold. If we now arbitrarily select one of these jewels for inspection and look closely at it, we will discover that in its polished surface there are reflected all the other jewels in the net, infinite in number. Not only that, but each of the jewels reflected in this one jewel is also reflecting all the other jewels, so that the process of reflection is infinite." – The Avatamska Sutra described by Francis H. Cook, HUA-YEN BUDDHISM: THE JEWEL NET OF INDRA: *Philosophy section, last bookshelf by the back door on the left.*

The way to Wigtown was long. Out of the window, the suburbs gradually gave way to green fields, interrupted only by cows and ancient stone cottages. It was like an idyllic Scottish postcard had come to life. The farther south we went, the more dramatic the topography became, as if the rolling fields were reflected in a fairground mirror, with vast expanses of dipping canyons and dramatic hills. Waterfalls and meandering rivers cut into the landscape, trees disappeared and were replaced, now and then, by wind farms. Herds of rugged sheep ambled down from the hillsides onto the road. We slowed to let them cross, their deep baas echoing in the van as we inched along the winding road. The further we went, the smaller the road and the more exotic the world became.

Conversation flowed easily between us. Euan asked me what I thought of the upcoming American presidential election, and of the democratic candidates, Hillary Clinton and Barack Obama. I was surprised by how informed he was on American politics and history. He had studied it at school. Nervous that I would get into a political disagreement this early into my trip, I tried to stay neutral, but Euan seemed to agree with every point I made.

"You're not just being polite?" I asked.

"No, honestly. I would have said the same things myself." He looked a bit bewildered. It was as if he had found an alien from another planet, only to find it spoke the same language.

The large red van made its way over ever-narrower, precarious one-track roads. Euan, with the grace of someone well practised, manoeuvred the hair-raising turns with ease. I looked out of the opposite window, down at the sheer cliff to my right, and wondered how long the narrow road would go on for.

Euan, it transpired, had wanted to be a filmmaker before owning The Bookshop. It was at this moment that I started to wonder if someone would shake me awake. He told me he had worked on the sound for some BBC documentaries, and although it was hard to break into the industry, he had never lost the bug for creating films. We tripped over each other, listing films that had inspired us.

Once high into the hills, the landscape changed again and became intimidatingly remote. The stone cottages disappeared revealing on either side a wilderness of long brown grass, rust-coloured bracken and wandering sheep. The horizon was gone too; the once open views were now blocked out by a sea of dark-green pines.

"It's an ugly tree," Euan sighed, looking out the window, "and not native to Scotland. They planted it because they needed fast-growing lumber after cutting down most of the trees for the First World War."

"It certainly feels a bit desolate here." I hoped I sounded sympathetic rather than critical.

"It is. You have to be especially careful in the winter," Euan said. "A long time back, a postman and his truck got stuck up here in a snowdrift for days. No one came by and the poor man died."

If the landscape hadn't done it, Euan's story painted a lasting picture in my mind. We were not just rambling along some country lane; we were now far away, utterly disconnected from the modern world, in some liminal realm between farmland and whatever lay beyond. I could feel myself nodding off, soothed by the gentle bends in the road and the warmth of the car.

*

"Sleeping Fox, wake up," Euan gently shook my shoulder.

I jolted awake. The sun was now shining in the car with an increased intensity. I could hear the murmur of people, a sound that meant we were back in society, down from the hills.

Blinking the fog of jet-lag away, my voice sounded sleepy and quiet. "Where are we?"

"I thought I'd show you Culzean Castle. It has lovely grounds, right on the cliffs." Euan hopped out of the van, and I followed, the promise of my first castle rousing me instantly.

My childhood dream, besides being an Agatha Christie detective, had been to live in a castle, though I had never seen a real one. Perhaps this vision was not a unique one for a little girl, but mine did not involve me being a princess in fancy dress. Rather, I wanted to run around with a sword and dig in the back garden for treasure. Now, walking over an impressive stone bridge, watching as the grand Culzean Castle rose before us, I realised that the dream still held appeal.

The gardens were surprisingly tropical-looking, with long stretches of manicured lawns and palm trees. The castle itself did not have the sense of dilapidated mystery that I was expecting. It was disappointingly well maintained, as if it had been built yesterday, though Euan explained that was far from the case.

"Eisenhower stayed here but the original tower is from the fifteenth century," he explained.

"Wow," I tried to sound impressed, though I would have liked it more if he had told me the place was haunted.

As we approached the castle's wind-whipped front courtyard and looked down over the white foamy waves smashing against the cliffs below us, my desire for a sense of majesty was finally met. In front of us the blue horizon, as far as I could see, was sky meeting water.

Euan smiled, watching my thoughts written clear across my face. "It's an amazing spot, isn't it?" he yelled over the wind.

I nodded. "It's really kind of you to have brought me here. I realise it's a work day for you." I moved the windblown wisps of hair from my face and found Euan staring at me. He quickly looked away.

"It's a pleasure." He shoved his hands in his pockets and the first awkward moment passed between us. He immediately turned on his heels and disappeared down the path into the castle.

After the windswept walk and then a tour of the castle's elaborate interior, I was wide awake. Euan, however, had grown quiet, and even as we emerged back into the gardens, he said nothing. We walked in silence under a grey stormy sky, and I hoped I hadn't offended him somehow. He smiled when I re-thanked him for taking me there, but I felt something had shifted. I was growing concerned that because of the ease of our conversation in the van, I had assumed a level of immediate intimacy that didn't actually exist.

I wrapped my jacket tighter around me. The sky was becoming dark and the air had a slicing chill. It was a damp cold that seemed to seep into every pore. I shivered as we reached the red van, a beacon of cheerfulness in an otherwise grey car park.

"Here," Euan suddenly said, his voice formal and distant. "You can help me load."

He walked to the small gift shop on the other side of the car park and emerged with a large box of books. "There's more in there." He gestured behind him with a nod.

Just as he passed me, he reached into his coat pocket. "Oh. I got you this."

I took the package from his hands and opened it. It was a book, *Folktales of Scotland*. "I thought you'd like it." Euan shifted nervously.

"Thank you." He had remembered that I had studied stories. I looked at him curiously, unable to read his mood changes. "That's so thoughtful. I am sure I will love it."

Euan shrugged and walked towards the van. I said nothing else and headed into the gift shop. Box after box, I helped load the van till my skin, chilled from the sea air became flushed with heat and a sticky sweat clung to my neck. This, and not the castle, I realised, was my true baptism by fire. I was actually working for a bookshop by the sea in Scotland.

Chapter 8

"Imagination is a monastery and I am its monk." – John
Keats, from a letter to Percy Bysshe Shelley, August 1820,
LETTERS OF JOHN KEATS: *Letters and Diaries section, after
staircase in gallery on left.*

The sound of a cow mooing roused me from a deep
slumber. My body felt heavy, drugged by jet-lag. My
legs shifted beneath stiff, white sheets, and my nose tickled
with the scent of lavender – alerting my consciousness
to the alien air, sounds and smells that surrounded me.
I was not in LA, I thought. I was actually here. I was in
Wigtown.

The room was still dark. It must be about 6 or 7am,
I guessed, but it was hard to tell as my blurry, tired eyes
began to adjust and take everything in. Willing myself
to sit upright, I looked past the foot of the bed at a large
window covered by a long, heavy curtain that cloaked the
morning sun. A sliver of bright light came in though the
cracks, illuminating the white wall behind me.

I was in the largest of Euan's three guest rooms. He
had kept it empty of authors this past week, leading up to
the festival, especially for my arrival. The other two rooms
were empty for now but one was reserved for a visiting
author and the other for the imminent arrival of his cousin
and best friend.

"But don't worry. You'll be staying in the big guest room for the whole time you're here," Euan had casually mentioned. He made it seem like no big deal, but I knew he had probably said no to many people in order to let me stay.

I was warm enough under the covers, but the cold, early-autumn air greeted me outside the duvet. I quickly tucked my arms back underneath, happy to stay in bed a while longer and look around the bedroom. There were a couple of nice bits of antique furniture; carefully hung oil paintings decorated the walls, and a small fireplace with a wood-burning stove, with a vase full of dried lavender on the mantel, dominated the far end. I felt like one of Jane Austen's heroines – either Marianne or Elizabeth – as they woke in their quaint country homes.

My eyes closed. The journey to the castle had been beautiful enough, but the last leg – as we continued on through Galloway to Wigtown itself – had been spectacular. Galloway afforded the most pristine view of Scotland's best-kept secret: the Machars, a peninsula with its series of small parishes between Wigtown Bay and Luce Bay, boasting soft rolling hills, majestic and gentle, against an ever-changing backdrop of dramatic snow-capped mountains, indigenous forests and the sea.

"My grandmother would say it's like mini-Scotland," Euan had said suddenly. He had been answering the expression of bewilderment on my face, and broke the long stretch of silence in the car. "It's like all the most wonderful parts of Scotland rolled into one. You have everything here, sea, mountains, forest, highlands."

"It's the most beautiful place I have ever seen," I said and I wasn't exaggerating. Euan laughed. "I'm serious. Why isn't this place more loaded with visitors? Doesn't everyone come here?"

I had felt as if I'd discovered the holy grail of beauty. Expanses of green, rugged open coastline would pass without any house to interrupt the view, except for the odd stone cottage or mysterious ruin. Empty beaches flashed by, with caves and coves to explore. The landscape was pure, remote and breathtaking. This was a Scotland that I hadn't believed still existed. There was no sign of tourist buses, or billboards, or commercialism of any kind. It was timeless, untouched.

Euan had shrugged. "Probably because it's hard to get to, but the fact that it's still undiscovered is one of its charms." Euan had then pointed to a large brown sign that read in clear white letters: "Scotland's National Book Town, Next Left". "We're almost there."

We'd arrived at The Bookshop as it was getting dark – following the main road into Wigtown until it came to an end in a large town square. This was unlike any town square that my New England eyes were used to, where there would have been wooden colonial houses, large side yards and perhaps a church, sitting highest in its centre, like the crown jewel. Instead, lining Wigtown's square and glowing in the setting sun, there were ancient stone cottages painted in pastel colours: mint, peach and white. On one side of the square rested a Victorian red-brick town hall while, opposite, a road wound its way up a hill and disappeared at its crest.

Bookshops were everywhere, or so it had seemed through the delirium of my exhaustion and the dwindling light. I passed signs above doors that read "The Book Corner", "Reading Lasses", and the "Old Bank Bookshop" and more, out of eyesight, extended down the street.

Euan pulled the red van up in front of a large Georgian town house with a shop below. Peering through the windscreen at the sign above, I made out the words "The Bookshop" in green paint and gold letters. Two book spirals, DNA helixes of literature, rose on either side of the door like columns.

A thrill shot through me. Here I was, about to step into a town that I had conjured up in my imagination when I sat in my hot studio apartment in LA. I felt as if I was Neil Armstrong, about to take my momentous first step onto the moon. I was nervous, perhaps like Armstrong, wondering if the ground below was not solid but dust. Was all this really happening or was it only in the ephemeral ether of my imagination?

Euan opened up the side door of the van and stood aside for me to grab my things. I struggled with all my bags, and followed him past the two columns of spiralling books into the dark interior of The Bookshop. A sweet, clear clang rang out as we passed through, and I looked up to see a golden bell. I held my breath. It had been just like the one in my dream and was hanging delicately above the door, as real as the pavement beneath my feet just a moment before.

Set aglow by the setting sun, the magic of The Bookshop was on display. Dark wooden shelves stuffed with books surrounded me as the room opened into a large gallery. My nostrils were filled with the musky aroma of old pages and dust. There were original fireplaces set into the walls, hardwood floors that seemed to stretch on and on, chandeliers overhead, and, in the shadows of the evening, I could see that there were little treasures and trinkets everywhere to reward the observer, creating an atmosphere that was both intimate and grand. Oil paintings rested against walls while random antiques – a bowler hat here or a stuffed pheasant there – were artfully and often humorously set on display. Through another doorway, past the Children's section and into a long hall, Euan pointed above me and I looked up to see a skeleton hanging from the ceiling, playing the violin.

"This is amazing; it can't be real," I had repeated like an incantation. Euan laughed at my American enthusiasm.

"I'm glad you like it." His eyes twinkled and I could tell he was pleased.

"How big is it? It goes on for ever," I said as Euan led the way.

As we continued further in, rooms opened on to each other, each with its own character. "The Transportation Room" was a small stone room off the main hall filled with books on transportation of all kinds. Under the room's wooden floor Euan opened a trap door to reveal a working model train, which rode through a replica of Wigtown's square – it was so secret and hidden that no one would have known it was there. Further down was the large "Scottish Room", with shelves that rose to the ceiling filled with books on all things Scotland, including a whole section dedicated to Sir Walter Scott. The hall then led to a door into the garden, where there was a small stone building aptly named "The Garden Room", stuffed full of more books and antiques.

Back in the main bookshop, as we walked through the winding hall towards the staircase, there were even more fireplaces and interesting nooks and crannies to get lost in. The setting was like something out of *Harry Potter*. It was, indeed, the ideal bookshop.

Sweeping up a gracious, bookshelf-lined flight of stairs, we stopped at the first landing, which opened onto a hallway, connecting different rooms. A large stag's head looked down on me disapprovingly as I stood taking it all in. The hall, too, felt grandly eccentric, decorated with oil paintings of dark and mysterious landscapes in gilt frames. I craned my neck, looking up through the stairwell to see two more flights topped by an arched ceiling that seemed to go to true cathedral height, lined with ornate cornicing.

"This is incredible," I said, immediately feeling like a broken record. "Sorry I keep on repeating myself, but your house is making me speechless."

Euan laughed again. I blushed but secretly felt jubilant. I had no idea I was so amusing.

"I promise to give you a proper tour tomorrow, when it's light," he said, opening the door to his right. "For now you must be hungry."

I smiled politely but had absolutely no desire to eat. All I really wanted to do was explore the stacks of books downstairs. The impulse that had brought me here, my dream, had suddenly taken on a life of its own, showing me things that were beyond and better than anything I could have imagined. Having followed the white rabbit, I was now tumbling down the rabbit hole and I wanted to see everything it had to offer.

Euan opened the door to our right and the soft murmur of chatter escaped into the hall. Other guests? Faced with such unexpected socialising, my excitement drained away and I felt all of a sudden incredibly tired. Euan beckoned me to follow. Obediently, I slipped through the doorway and found myself in a large, charming, dimly lit kitchen with cream-coloured walls and mint-green cabinets. On one side of the room laundry hung from an old-fashioned wooden rack, attached to the ceiling on a pulley. A large schoolhouse clock hung over a flower-filled mantelpiece and a cast-iron stove glowed in the fireplace. Candles flickered on the table, among a mass of empty bottles and glasses.

Around the large wooden table were seated four guests, two women and two men, and they all looked up expectantly. The men quickly stood when they saw me. I couldn't have imagined the same kind of gentlemanly courtesy in America, let alone at an LA dinner party.

In a tangled chorus of friendly hellos, the guests viewed me with curiosity. One of them, a young woman with long blonde hair and blue eyes, pushed out a chair.

"Don't be rude, Euan," she said with a secret delight all of her own and watched as Euan made his way to the table. Her voice was musical, with a rounded Wigtownshire accent. "Be a good host and get the American a drink. We've been waiting for you. Come sit by me. I'm Hannah. Have some pie."

As commanded, I found a chair near Hannah and she slid over a plate of bramble tart. Her beautiful, open face was as disarming as her manner. My fork dipped into the pie but I was exhausted. Jet-lag had now firmly taken hold.

"That's Hannah," Euan said and stressed the next words. "My employee."

"Favourite employee," she interrupted.

Euan shook his head. "Troubled employee."

I laughed and Hannah pretended to look offended while Euan shot me a playful glance. On the other side of Hannah, sat a woman in a thick fuchsia jumper that clung to her curvy figure. She had long dark hair and looked young, though I guessed she was in her late thirties, like Euan.

A man in his forties with pretty, almost feminine features, extended his hand awkwardly. "Hi, I'm Eliot."

To my inexperienced American ears, Eliot didn't sound Scottish but had an accent like Bingley in *Pride and Prejudice*: posh and from London.

"Eliot," the woman in the fuchsia jumper had piped up, "is the festival dictator."

"Director," Eliot corrected quickly.

"And I'm Laura, Euan's friend," she said, then added, "Euan's only friend."

"What about me?" Hannah smacked her in the arm.

"You're more like my enemy," Euan said.

Hannah smiled, satisfied.

If I had thought NASA was full of different languages, this room proved to be even more complicated. No one spoke with the same accent and my ears kept on retuning, adjusting to the ever-changing inflections.

"Hello, happy to meet you." The last guest chimed in with a thick Northern Irish accent. "I'm Callum." He was tall and broad and peered at me through his wire-framed glasses. Callum extended his hand and I shook it, with a firm, friendly confidence.

"Shall I relight the fire?" Euan asked, handing me a glass of wine. No one answered. All eyes and ears were upon me.

"So where do you come from?" Callum asked.

"America, duh." Hannah rolled her eyes and tried to kick Euan, who was opening the old iron stove, filling it with kindling and newspaper.

"Well, recently?" I tried to speak through a mouthful of bramble tart. "I'm from LA."

"We couldn't tell." Laura had been staring at my "I heart LA" tank top. My face flushed and I suddenly wished I hadn't worn it. If my accent and manners hadn't been screaming American, my apparel was.

"Well, anyway, happy to see that you're real," Callum smiled, toasting me with his beer. "We thought you may be a figment of Euan's imagination."

Hannah shot across the table, trying to smack him on the arm. She seemed to like hitting people. "Ignore him, do continue."

"I am a film director. Well, I actually work for NASA." It never got easier trying to explain what I did.

"So you came to Wigtown?" Eliot's eyebrows furrowed.

"I wanted a holiday where I could stay in a usedbook-shop in Scotland."

"And you got stuck with us lot, the poor dear," Laura teased. Though sharp, there was a warmth to her wit. I liked her immediately. "Euan's lured you..."

"I haven't lured anyone," Euan yelled in protest from the fireplace.

"...into the middle of nowhere in this freezing house," Laura ignored him. "That's okay. You have your American optimism to keep you warm."

"I'm trying to light the fire as fast as I can," Euan's muffled voice shouted.

"Why did you choose Wigtown?" Eliot looked horrified.

"You know why," Hannah said. "We all read the emails."

I suddenly felt embarrassed. There didn't seem to be much privacy in Wigtown.

"What were you doing for NASA?" Callum sat back and took out a small tin from his pocket. He opened it, revealing tobacco and smoking papers inside.

"Euan, you seem to have a talent for convincing attractive young women to come to Wigtown." Eliot poured himself more wine. "Any chance your dream included working at a festival?"

Laura smiled and winked at me. I had never been good with teasing but this was different. Perhaps it was the large dose of British comedy that I had watched while growing up, but I got the rhythm and sense of humour immediately. Though I couldn't dish it, I could take it, and that seemed to be enough to get me accepted. I looked around the room, my mouth full of pie, and smiled.

In high school, people had written in my yearbook that I was "nice" – no other adjectives, nouns or verbs. Perhaps they did not know me well enough to be more explicit. I hadn't been weird enough for the drama crowd, or mainstream enough for the cool kids or even academic enough for the nerds. I slipped into the cracks between groups, blending into the background of the suburban high school landscape, and because I was neither this nor that, I never felt part of anything. I would smile my "nice" smile, butterflying my way through the school cafeteria in social purgatory, never sitting with anyone in particular.

I thought this would change in college. Anne of Green Gables, on growing past her teenage years, had said that kindred spirits weren't as rare as she used to think. After a month at the liberal arts college of Franklin and Marshall, I saw Anne was right, but not in the way I had anticipated. I had desired a community, my very own gang, but instead found kindred spirits randomly, and often in the most unlikely of places. There was the one boy from class, another girl down the hall, a handful of my professors. I found kindred spirits in the voices of some of the authors I was reading, and even in some of the fictional characters that they wrote about.

But for all my adventures since college, I still craved that sense of belonging. Though I was lucky enough to have close friends scattered all over the world, it just wasn't the same as having a group, a gang, a clan. Now, as I sat among Wigtown Book Festival's witty, self-effacing elite, in a stranger's house above a bookshop, halfway across the world, in a remote part of Scotland, I marvelled that I might finally have found a taste of that long-desired sense of community.

What was certain was that, if this was my personal Algonquin round table, I was currently its soberest member. After another half-hour of their acrid irony and drunken teasing, I pleaded exhaustion and climbed the stairs to my room, where, lulled by the laughter and chatter below the floorboards, I fell quickly into a deep, contented sleep.

*

In the dim light of the morning, as the memory of the previous night echoed in my mind, I became aware of the silence within the house, and the growing sound of a morning chorus outside.

Raised in the suburbs of Boston, the sounds that had greeted me in the mornings were usually human – the soft drone of someone pushing a lawnmower, an angry beep from a frustrated driver, my sister's muffled radio, my father singing in the shower or my mother's light steps on the stairs. Living in LA, I had grown used to silent mornings. I had been so high in the hills, in a new, sound-proofed, earthquake-friendly construction, that nothing, not even the sound of traffic from nearby Sunset Boulevard, seeped through.

I had assumed that in the Scottish countryside I would wake to equally silent mornings, but I had assumed wrong.

I listened with keen interest to the orchestra outside my window. It was magical to hear so many different birdcalls, mixed in, of course, with the occasional baritone moo.

I slipped out of bed, braving the cold, and opened the curtains. It was a brilliant, bright day outside and an assortment of Wigtown rooftops greeted me. It was the most unexpected and enchanting sight – slated rooftops of different shapes and sizes stretched before me; the stones grey green and blue, each unique, filled with personality age and a weather-beaten history. Crooked little chimneys climbed on for ever, covered with stubborn flowers and wisps of grass, a reminder of Galloway's wet, temperate climate.

To the right, I could peek into neighbouring gardens, as cobbled and quaint as the rooftops. Each one seemed to reflect the inner life of the owners who lived there: some were low maintenance, mostly paved and decorated with potted plants, others were overgrown and forgotten, and many were lush and manicured, with laundry hanging to dry and little spots for repose. Stone walls and fences separated the gardens, some new, some Victorian, time-battered and ivy-covered. Beyond the gardens, a vibrant green hill arched into the sky. Atop sat a tall stone monument. Cows and sheep were grazing on the hill, standing in stark contrast to the blue sky beyond. I was in sensory heaven. Everything was so beautiful, so clean, green and fresh.

I looked down to see light-green lichen on the stone window sill. Its rough silvery fronds crawled along the outside of the window. They were a sign of good air, a friend had once told me. "You're not in Kansas any more, Dorothy," I said to myself again, thinking of the familiar thick cloud of smog that hung over Los Angeles.

I slid open the window and took a nice deep breath. My starved lungs sang and my head buzzed. I turned to my left, and outside on the buttress, near the gutter, I discovered a small stone-carved face. It must have been very old. The carving was weatherworn, tinted green and smiling with eyes shut, reflecting perfectly if not my expression, then my mood.

When was the last time, I asked myself, that I had rested my ears? They drank in the silence and birdsong as greedily as my lungs did the air. My thoughts were free to ramble, uninterrupted. I was completely disconnected and off the grid here without a list of to-dos, without a car, without even a cell phone. A growing, mysterious sensation warmed my body despite the cold air, though it quickly disappeared the moment I thought about how many emails would be piling up in my inbox.

Chapter 9

"Bypasses are devices that allow some people to dash from point A to point B very fast while other people dash from point B to point A very fast. People living at point C, being a point directly in between, are often given to wonder what's so great about point A that so many people from point B are so keen to get there and what's so great about point B that so many people from point A are so keen to get there. They often wish that people would just once and for all work out where the hell they wanted to be." – Douglas Adams, THE HITCHHIKER'S GUIDE TO THE GALAXY: *Fiction section, front room, under A in hardbacks.*

During my first few days in Wigtown, I would wake early and go running. It was the same every morning. Greeted by the cool crisp early-autumnal air outside The Bookshop, I would survey the landscape – my eyes slowly taking in the empty street, sun pouring over the silent, colourful stone walls of the houses and the flowers, dew-covered in their small hanging baskets. You could see the whole of Wigtown, from one end to the other, if you stepped out into the middle of the main road. This did not make me feel claustrophobic, in fact, quite the opposite. I found the small village liberating. Instead of being stuck in wall-to-wall traffic, here I had open space.

I would slip on my earphones and take time selecting the perfect track on my iPod. I'd turn left, jogging lightly in my American Apparel short shorts, down Wigtown's only road.

Today the large, empty town square was covered by a massive white tent. A wind had blown in, and the empty tent flapped in the breeze, anxiously waiting for the festival to begin. There was only a week to go until the ten-day literary event that took place every year in Wigtown from the last weekend in September to the first weekend in October. It was supposed to transform this sleepy town into a bustling, event-filled sanctuary for the UK's literary elite, and I could already see evidence of the metamorphosis everywhere.

The Bookshop, as if foreshadowing the changes to come, had morphed from a quiet refuge into a hive of activity, filled with Hannah's and Laura's energetic chatter. Catering equipment arrived and folding chairs seemed to be on constant parade, going up and down the stairs. The shop was increasingly packed with tourists and festival volunteers. Time suddenly felt like it was speeding up in some strange quantum anomaly, and I had to remind myself that after the festival, I would have just one further week to enjoy Wigtown, before heading back to hot Los Angeles.

A creature of habit and ritual, I found morning runs were the key to helping me adjust to my reality. The Bookshop had appeared so like my vision of it – even, to my shock, having a long wooden counter that you could sit behind, like the one I had seen in my daydream in LA, and a window that looked out onto the street. The crossover between dream and reality could easily have given me a god-like complex, but Wigtown exceeded my expectations and repeatedly surprised me, reminding me that I was just an explorer along this journey, not its sole creator. The place had a spirit, energy and mystery all of its own.

On one of my runs, a few days previously, the rare sound of tyres on gravel had interrupted my rambling thoughts. I had just sprinted over a bridge, under which flowed a small brook that went through marshlands out to sea, and there wasn't much room to manoeuvre. I moved onto the grass embankment to let the car pass.

Instead of passing, the car slowed and stopped. Great, I thought, I'm going to get harassed. Even in Wigtown a woman couldn't go running without some jerk thinking its an open invitation to yell lewd obscenities. I turned towards the car, defensive.

Facing me, to my surprise, was an elderly couple in their Subaru Forester. Two yelping dogs were panting excitedly in the back. The old man rolled down the window.

"My dear," he said, blinking into the sunshine, "are you all right?"

This confused me. I stopped jogging to catch my breath. "Yes, I'm fine, thank you."

"But," the old lady leaned over so she could see me, "what are you running from?"

It suddenly dawned on me that they thought I was in trouble. "Oh no, no. I'm perfectly fine. Just out for some exercise."

The old man smiled and held up his hand as he rolled up the window. I watched in amazement as the car drove off and disappeared down the road.

The cast of characters I met along my morning runs was quickly becoming as familiar to me as the brush strokes of a favourite painting. There was the group of tracksuit-wearing children who yelled "running lady" – perhaps not the most inventive insult – at me on their way to school. The friendlier town residents would wave as they watered their plants in the morning. There was the woman who drove a hearse with red velvet seats, who would smile at me in her goth clothing as she took her child and dog into town. There was the elderly gentleman, always immaculate in a refined tweed suit, neatly pinned at the shoulder where one arm was missing. He took a while to charm but eventually greeted me as warmly as he did the rest of the neighbourhood. Then there was the postman, a truly jolly postman, who knew my name within a day of me being there.

The one person I struggled to connect with, however, was Euan, who remained quiet and elusive. One day, when the shop was still quiet, he had taken me to see Wigtown's old stone church, which had an extensive ancient graveyard. It had been foggy, but the church was down the road, an easy walk from The Bookshop. We walked in silence, and I stared at Euan curiously, feeling the soft mist on my cheeks. We had spent hardly any time together since our initial drive from the airport. He had his hands full preparing for the festival and running the shop, but I couldn't tell if he was actually that busy or purposefully being hard to pin down.

"I love days like this," I said, my arms restraining the urge to swim through the air.

"It's the har, rolling in from the sea," Euan responded in his usual deep tone.

To my right, down the sloping hill, rested the silvery marshland, and beyond it the mist had grown thick, resting above a hidden sea. "This is the most beautiful place in the world," I gasped.

"You're so dramatic, Jessica." He laughed. His arm had grazed my side but he quickly moved away.

I still didn't know much about Euan. He was as mysterious – I dreamily noted – as *Jane Eyre*'s Mr. Rochester. He would be quite friendly one minute and look distant the next. Sometimes he disappeared for hours at a time, and when he returned he'd walk past me as if I were invisible, looking stressed. There always seemed to be shadows of women surrounding him, like crows flying high around a scarecrow. I was aware of detached voices on the phone or fleeting guests showing up at The Bookshop, but nothing tangible enough to know whether he was dating any of them.

We had entered the churchyard to our left, past an iron gate, and the scene before us suddenly came into focus. Stone graves rose in all directions out of the ground, reminding me of old, crooked teeth pushing out of the wet, mossy earth. There were patches of brambles growing, intertwined with the graves, and Euan picked me a blackberry. I had taken it and nibbled at it, chillily, thinking of the soil out of which it came.

The gloomy scene of that churchyard visit felt worlds away as I stepped out into the morning sunshine for my run. The day promised to be clear and bright – no sign of clouds or fog – so I decided to run a bit farther than usual. Normally I turned downhill, in the direction of the sea, past rolling marshland and gently grazing cows. Today I needed time to think so I would make a right where I usually made a left, and head towards the expanse of blue sky, over the hill and away from Wigtown.

Though I didn't yet have the red bicycle from my dream, I had been writing, every day, and making slow but sure headway. I was supposed to be working on my new screenplay. An investor in Boston had asked to see it when

Jessica A. Fox

I returned and I was feeling the pressure. Deadlines were good for writing; the pressure of expectations was not.

I tried to increase the pace, willing my legs to move faster. My heart beat steadily in my chest to a stubborn rhythm, only quickening when I thought of Euan. Even when I tried to think of other things, my thoughts would wrap around back to him.

I had found an article in the shop, which described Euan as "Wigtown's heart-throb". He had grown red as I teased him about it.

"It's biased. The man who wrote it was hitting on me," he had protested. Clearly I hadn't been the only person who found the contrast between his shy, quiet demeanour and his tall, shaggy-haired, boyish good looks attractive.

"I prefer what the poet Rab Wilson called me," he said.

"Oh, what's that?"

"A cultured minotour," Euan answered, looking pleased.

As I ran, my feet hitting upon the soft grass, I felt them throb and ache. I was sore.

Euan had taken me night mountain-biking with Callum the night before. We had worn headlamps and crashed up and down hills through the dark woods. I hadn't done anything so physically fear-inducing in years. I had done well though, keeping free of crashes, and had met Euan and Callum back at the van only minutes after they had finished the course. A good thing, as they hadn't once slowed to help me through the course, or even checked in with me to see if I was okay. Euan's disregard had been so blatant that I worried I had started to become a burden to him – one more person to chauffeur around and be nice to, while he ran the shop, attended to visitors and prepared for the festival.

I turned past a bend in the road and open farmland appeared. Above me was as dramatic as the landscape, with large clouds now hanging low in the sky. I stopped to catch my breath. Why couldn't I stop thinking of him? He was intriguing, kind and mysterious, but I wasn't getting any signals that my interest was being returned.

A lone cow approached the fence where I was standing, looking mournfully sympathetic.

"I didn't come all this way to open up my heart again," I found myself saying aloud. "This is supposed to be Me Time. Like a Buddhist monk I am here in remote, beautiful Wigtown for writing and inward reflection only."

The cow, maintaining a diplomatic silence, began to eat grass. I stretched my legs before me and started to run again. Yes, I had learned from the past, I thought to myself, this time with a twinge of pride. Grant had satisfied my thirst for unrequited love enough to last a lifetime, and any sniff of indifference now would send me running for the hills. Literally. I hopped over a fence into a rising field and headed up a steep green slope.

That morning I had received an email about NASA. It was the first unwanted intrusion into my adventure, and had woken me from what had become my fully immersive, intoxicating Scottish dream. Quantum physicists don't need mathematics or hypothetical worlds to believe in parallel universes; Wigtown was enough of an example that I was living in one. Checking my packed inbox, filled with pages of unopened messages, had reminded me that in another reality my old life still existed, and would be waiting for me when this adventure was done.

The NASA email was marked as urgent, so reluctantly I had opened it. My project was going well, it said, but my department was experiencing budget cuts. The last two words made my stomach flip. Budget cuts were never a good sign and the tone of the email was one of apology. Pounding up the side of the hill, I told myself to use this solitary time to think about where I was heading. Not just on my run, but in my career, in my life.

I crested the hill, out of breath. The moment I had been hired, I had known my job at NASA wouldn't last for ever. I was a film director after all, and my trajectory, with or without budget cuts, would have led me in a different direction eventually. Perhaps it was time to jump into the unknown again and make a feature? I waited for that pang of intense "YES" to fill my heart, but it didn't come. I felt nothing. No excitement filled my fingertips in the usual way. The only thing I felt strongly pulled to at the moment was this eccentric seaside town.

Keeping an eye out for bulls, I continued on my way. Yesterday, Euan had explained to me the "Right to Roam", a brilliant Scottish concept of walkers being free to walk anywhere.

"Just be careful," he had warned; "you don't want to end up in a field with a bull."

"What happens if I do?" I had asked, never having seen a bull before in my life.

Euan had turned serious. "Run. Fast. And get over any wall or fence you can."

So it was with great caution that I began descending the other side of the hill into a neighbouring field, one part of my mind looking out for a large cow without an udder, the rest lost in thought.

This particular hill was empty, and for a moment I felt like Maria from *The Sound of Music*. I held out my arms, just like Julie Andrews, and started twirling, singing, out of breath, "The hills are alive..."

I laughed as I twirled, feeling dizzy and disoriented. As I dropped to my knees to catch my breath and looked at the new scenery, I suddenly realised how far I had strayed from my known route. Carefully scanning the horizon to take in my surroundings, all I saw were green hills – no sign of the sea, no houses, no sign of Wigtown's monument or large town hall steeple.

The euphoria wore off, and panic quickly set in. I was far from Wigtown. Without a phone, and no sense of direction, I had, in fact, no idea where I was or how I could get back. I was lost.

Chapter 10

"C'est la personnalité qui conte." – Antoine Bourdelle quoted in Joseph Campbell: A Fire in the Mind by Stephen and Robin Larsen: *Biography section, under C.*

The sea of green hills stretching before me was as disorienting as a wall of mirrors. I staggered downhill, in no direction in particular, having answered the question of "where am I headed" in a very literal way: I had absolutely no idea. However, stumbling somewhere along the path less travelled seemed better than nowhere. Robert Frost would be proud, I thought, as my steps started to gain confidence again.

My arms into my chest and I was suddenly hungry. I scanned myself for provisions, but had no pockets to carry snacks or water. I did have a now sweaty five-pound note stuck in my shoe; brilliant forethought, I congratulated myself, until I realised there would be nowhere to spend it. As I descended the muddy hillside, the world before me was empty farmland as far as the eye could see.

Almost as soon as I got to the road, a red van appeared in the distance. My heart quickened. I tried to keep calm; it could be either Euan's van, or the Royal Mail's for they looked quite similar. As the van drew near, I discerned the familiar ginger curls of a cultured minotaur in the driver's seat.

I didn't know what to do. If I just waved he might think I was saying hello and not stop. It was a bit dramatic to stand in the middle of the road, or wave my arms, so I opted for the cool, thumbs-up hitch-hiking stance.

Euan's van slowed when he saw me, and he rolled down the window. "You need a lift?"

"That would be great, thanks."

As I climbed in, I could see Euan looking bewildered. "What are you doing all the way out here?"

"I got a bit lost."

"I can see that." Euan tightened his jaw, trying not to laugh. "There are just so many roads out here, I can see how it would be confusing for an American."

I smacked him on the arm. "I took short cuts, over the hills. I think I paid more attention to whether there were bulls than the direction I was going in."

"Clearly." Euan was smiling.

"You know, if you hadn't come along, I would have found my way back." I folded my arms, annoyed by how much he was enjoying this.

"Uh huh." Euan's smile widened.

The van sped down a one-track road and over a small hill, finally turning where the road widened into a larger road that I recognised. The familiar snow-peaked mountains and marshland came into view.

"It's Big Bang Day today," I said, trying to make conversation, instantly wishing I had picked a cooler topic. But Euan's amusement seemed to be growing.

"Really?"

"The Large Hadron Collider is supposed to smash its first atoms together." I couldn't help myself.

"I heard that on the radio," Euan said. "Apparently it could create a massive black hole. I'd better get my errands done before that happens. You don't mind, do you?"

"Not at all." Errands in a new land were an adventure. I was relaxing, enjoying his company. Euan turned up the volume on the radio. "What are we listening to now?"

"Radio 4," Euan said, handing me an open pack of Maltesers, which I had miss-called Maltese Balls, much to everyone's amusement. I relished the milky chocolate as it melted in my mouth. "There's BBC Radio 1, 2, 3, 4," Euan said, in response to my questioning expression.

"There are only four radio stations? I don't understand."

"What's so hard to understand?" Euan was looking amused again.

"It just feels so... so... socialist."

"What?" Euan looked surprised. "That's ridiculous. BBC Radio is highly regarded worldwide for being the most unbiased media." He seemed personally insulted. "I can't believe you think it's socialist."

Coming from a world where the American dream was synonymous with choice, and support for public broadcasting was ever being cut, I couldn't imagine people embracing four government-funded channels for their radio.

"I didn't mean the content," I said quietly.

His expression lightened and he shot me a playful glance. "It's not like the American drivel you're used to, I suppose."

We rode in silence, up the highway, the sparkling sea beside us extending into Wigtown Bay. I could see Wigtown on the other side of the water, resting like an ideal city upon the hill.

*

The week before the festival passed in a blur of unrelenting rain. The postman stopped and slid a couple of envelopes marked for Euan into my hands.

"It's dreech out there," he said. "Dreech," he repeated, as he searched my puzzled face. "It's Scottish for…"

"Dreary?" I offered.

"No, not really, it's not depressing enough. It's Scottish for… for… this." He pointed out of the window. Having said his piece, he left.

Wigtown was shrouded in a silvery haze and each day was like the next, damp and dreech, but I didn't mind. I was in love with the place. Like a golden child, everything it did in my eyes was perfect. The weather, trees, hills, town and people all added to my rose-tinted bliss. My heart, which had always been missing something, slightly askew with a constant, mysterious pang of homesickness – for what, I could never put my finger on – for the first time in my life, felt whole and content.

Tennyson's Ulysses explained his constant thirst for something intangible as "all experience is an arch where-thro'/Gleams that untravelled world whose margin fades/For ever and ever when I move". However, among the green hills and open spaces of Galloway, my unrest was gone. There was no *shpilkus*. It was as if all along my true home had been out there, in that "untravelled world" and it was just a matter of finding it…

NASA had continued to send me emails, each more worrying than the last and rousing fresh concern – like a car kicking up dust, my thoughts dashed about in different directions with the velocity of Brownian Motion. The investor wanted to see a screenplay soon too, and Josh had been trying to contact me. The other world, my life in America, was no longer politely ringing the doorbell but banging on the door, and I avoided answering these unwanted intrusions by volunteering in the shop. My help was needed as the lead-up to the festival began in earnest and there were chairs to be moved, tables to be brought out of storage and people to meet and greet. I felt distracted – far away from LA – but couldn't hide from the anxiety of what I would do next, which hung like an impending question mark before me.

"I haven't seen him, Eliot, sorry," I said, moving a stack of books that had fallen over. Eliot had popped in, panicked, looking for Euan. He needed Euan, or more precisely Euan's van, to shuttle cases of wine for the festival's opening party. Though it seemed like a small task, it was an important one, almost more crucial to the festival's success than the books.

"I thought you two were tied at the hip," Eliot said, pacing back and forth. He was leafing through pieces of paper that he found crumpled in his pocket. "Right, fine. Next task. I need to know where we put the gift bags for the authors."

I shrugged. Eliot was panicking because the festival was starting the next day and his panic was contagious. My stomach churned in sympathy and I began to feel as agitated as he looked.

"Great. Fine. Right. That's okay." Eliot waved his hands in the air. Quickly realising I was completely useless, he turned on his heels and left. I found myself alone in the shop, heart racing.

I used the nervous energy to tidy shelves, explore the nooks and crannies of the Scottish Room, warm up by the roaring fire next to the Poetry section – Euan was seriously lacking in E.E. Cummings, I noted, disappointed – and finally, realise my dream of sitting back behind the long wooden counter. Just as if my dream had been real, I sat snug in Euan's woolly jumper, contemplating the universe as I looked out of the window, my vision of my journey complete.

Outside, the large white tent for the festival was getting pounded with wind and rain. A car pulled up into the empty street, and I was delighted to see an elegantly dressed woman emerge, shield herself from the weather and head bravely towards the shop. The little bell rang loud and clear.

Soaked but glamorous in a raincoat, tasteful pearls setting off a round pretty face with a hint of lipstick, my customer lifted a bag onto the counter in front of me. It fell open to reveal a bevy of warm jumpers and socks.

"You must be the poor American," she said with a warm smile. "I'm Deirdre, Euan's mum." Her eyes were just like Euan's, radiating warmth. I watched as she pulled off her rain-soaked hood. "Now I brought you some cosy things. God knows how you're surviving in this weather, all the way from California."

"I'm Jessica." I walked past her outstretched hand and gave her a hug. She seemed surprised but pleased. I liked Deirdre immediately and was certain I could detect a kindred spirit in her. "Thank you for the clothes. Can I get you tea to warm you up?"

"No, no, I mustn't. Very kind of you." Deirdre had a wonderfully melodic Irish accent, and her voice an expressive, sing-song quality. As she insisted about needing to go, she settled down beside me, pulling jumpers out of her bag. "If something doesn't fit, no matter, I can always take it back."

"Deirdre, this is too kind," I began to protest.

"Well, someone needs to look after you while you're here. Your poor mother, watching you go off to live in

God knows where, with God knows who..." She smiled. "I'll say you've come at the exact right time. It's all a-go now for the festival."

"I'm looking forward to it. I hear Princess Anne is coming."

"Oh yes," Deirdre said with equal delight. "We must arrange for you to meet her. And Euan's cousin Eve will be arriving soon. You two will get on like a house on fire. She always livens the place up." I couldn't get enough of Deirdre's energy. I wanted to tell her that she too livened the place up.

"I love it here," I said, suddenly but sincerely.

Deirdre looked touched. "I know you do. Euan says he couldn't believe how well you fit in here."

The comment took me by surprise.

"It takes a special person, you know," she continued and glanced at the clock behind me. "Oh my dear, the time. I could chat to you all afternoon but I really must run." She moved towards the door, searching for her keys. "I hope the jumpers fit. I'll see you soon." The bell above the door chimed and she disappeared back into the rain.

*

Euan appeared right before closing time and asked if I'd like to come with him to meet Callum and Eliot in the pub. I had never been to a pub before and after a day of solitude, looked forward to the outing.

"Jessica, you're kidding. Don't they have pubs in America?" Euan asked as we stepped outside and the damp air met us. It had finally stopped raining.

"Of course, but they're more bars than what I'd imagine a pub to be." Overhead the moon was full and bright. The once overcast sky was now a clear, inky dome of twinkling stars.

Euan was smiling again. "Well, don't get your hopes up. I'm starting to learn about the heights of your imagination."

He had no idea about the real, Everest-like heights of my mind, I thought. If he had, I'm sure he'd have had me committed. I decided it would be better not to tell him about my vision of the shop.

"Eliot came looking for you today," I said as we walked slowly across the road.

"Uh huh." Euan pushed his hands into his pockets. I wondered if he would say anything else, perhaps about where he had been. Instead he went quiet.

The walk to the pub, silent beneath those stars, ruined all subsequent night walks for me for ever. It was the most glorious way to get to a pub, so glorious, in fact, that I couldn't imagine the pub living up to the journey there.

The pub was small inside, dark and, in my memory, smoke-filled, but that would have been impossible because of the indoor smoking ban. The people were as thick as fog, however, and the warm, steamy air made for a hazy atmosphere. Everyone knew Euan. He was like the unofficial mayor, shaking hands and joking with the local farmers. No matter their age or background, everyone met him with the same friendly affection, except for Hannah. She was behind the bar, carefully filling a glass with honey-coloured beer and, on seeing Euan, she quickly shoved two fingers in the shape of a "v" into the air. To my American eyes, it looked like a peace sign but, from Euan's expression, I assumed it meant otherwise. Euan yelled something offensive back and Hannah grinned.

No one eyed me with the least amount of interest or suspicion as I walked behind Euan. Either they were used to him bringing different women into the pub, or they were displaying Wigtown's famous nonchalant attitude that I had grown to love so much already. This was not a small town that had any of the judgement or Puritan scrutiny that I was used to. My New England home town, with its population of 31,000, felt claustrophobic by comparison with Wigtown and its 1,000 residents. Growing up in a wealthy suburb of Boston, there had been an ever-present pressure to try and meet an unspoken intellectual and socioeconomic ideal. The pressure was subtle but real, an invisible pink elephant standing on everyone's manicured lawns.

In the few weeks I had lived there, I had found Galloway's mind-your-own-business, look-the-other-way acceptance incredibly liberating. Wigtown in particular, isolated and idiosyncratic, seemed to welcome the same qualities in its residents. It was an attitude I embraced with increasing enthusiasm. One sunny afternoon, after a full day of writing, I had walked into the town's small grocery store, in my tiny retro running shorts and slippers, Euan's jumper and massive Lolita heart sunglasses. Euan had described my outfit as looking like a blind woman who had stumbled into a charity shop. No one in the grocery store batted an eyelid, however. The only person who paid me any attention was an elderly lady who had asked, in an admiring way, where I had bought my "footwear".

The experience of shopping in Wigtown's Co-op was a lesson in eccentricity itself. I learned never to go with a list of what I wanted, because it was just a recipe for disappointment. Depending on which day you went in, the

Co-op could be a fu lly stocked wonderland of food, filled with surprises and yummy treats. On the wrong day it could look like a ration depot from the second World War, having run out of even the essentials. No one seemed to be able to figure out when was the best time to go; the good days changed weekly, keeping the residents on their toes. I was hooked with a gambler's enthusiasm on its unpredictability, as exciting as playing the lottery.

As we moved further into the pub, Euan spotted Callum waving at us from a small table in the corner and grabbed my hand, pushing through the crowd. His hand was large and warm, and like magic, the Red Sea of people parted long enough for me to squeeze through.

Euan went off to the bar for drinks and I slipped into the booth next to a smiling Callum. "Just in time to hear me sing," he said, his Northern Irish accent well oiled from beer.

"So what song?"

"Not sure yet. You play?"

I shook my head. "I dabble with the banjo, though."

"Dabble?" A guitar rested in Callum's lap, over which his fingers were diligently rolling a cigarette. The same small tin was open by his side, filled with tobacco and papers. My eyes caught sight of something moving and I looked up to see Eliot shifting in the corner. I hadn't noticed he was there and he waved at me without making eye contact. He sat curled around his cell phone, struggling to hear.

"You coming to the festival?" I asked Callum while Euan dropped a pint of beer in front of me.

Callum shrugged with indifference. "It's tomorrow?"

"Tomorrow night," Eliot corrected, looking stressed, and quickly returned to his phone call.

Before he could sit down, Euan's phone rang and he excused himself from the table.

"Everyone's on their cell phones; I could be back in LA." I sipped my beer and watched disappointed as Euan disappeared into the sea of locals.

"Spoiled for choice." Callum shot me a knowing glance. Though we were all speaking English, I felt like Callum understood me better than the others. My face had been rosy already from the heat of the pub, and I was glad Callum couldn't see me blush.

"Let's go outside for some air," I suggested.

"Good. I want to smoke this anyway." He finished rolling his cigarette and licked it closed.

Outside in the cool dark evening, musicians sat, smoking and playing folk music. Callum lit his cigarette and put the guitar on a bench nearby, content to listen to the music around him.

"You settling in here okay?" he asked.

"I do love it here." I shrugged. "I just hope I'm not a burden to Euan."

Callum raised a questioning eyebrow.

"It's hard for me to tell. He's always so nice."

"That's a boarding school thing. We've been drilled to be nice and polite." Callum stretched his legs out before him. "But don't worry about it. He likes having you here."

"How can you tell?"

"I can tell," Callum said in his straightforward way.

Euan reappeared looking drawn and sat on the bench next to Callum, smiling apologetically. "So, what have you fools been doing?"

"Talking about you," Callum teased with an air of satisfaction and drew on his cigarette. It was Euan's turn to blush.

I turned my attention from them to the music echoing through the dark beer garden. The voices were strong and clear, hitting every bittersweet note with skilled passion. The folk songs felt as much a part of the Galloway landscape as the moon above us, or the trees or the hills beyond. My time here was moving too quickly. The festival would soon be upon us and then in a couple of weeks I would be leaving again. In the heat of a Los Angeles afternoon, I hated to think this mysterious, mossy, majestic Wigtown would feel more like a dream than it ever had.

I suddenly felt swept away in a mood of sadness. My father had been a folk singer, and sometimes before I went to bed when I was young, he would sing me traditional folk songs that came from Appalachia but whose origins were in Ireland, Scotland and England. They were full of jilted or star-crossed lovers, tragic deaths and mystical happenings. There was a sense of otherworldliness and longing in the beauty and simplicity of the melodies that had transported me as a child. Now, all grown up, I was hearing the music at its source and felt so close to it that beneath the singing and guitar strings, I could almost hear a heartbeat.

Chapter 11

"O would some power the giftie gie us to see ourselves as others see us." Robert Burns, POEM "TO A LOUSE" : *Scottish Room, Burns section, second shelf from the bottom.*

O f the first night of the festival, two moments remain vivid in my memory. The first: a sudden announcement that Richard Heckler, the famous footballer, would not be able to appear that evening for the festival's headlining event. Second, was the look on Eliot's face when he told us the news.

Eliot had pulled off a real coup in getting Heckler on the programme. Wigtown Festival, though small, had a growing reputation for being both an intimate literary event and attracting speakers of a high calibre. Eliot had turned programming into a work of art, and included an eclectic group of literary elite and popular speakers. Ticket sales had been up this year, and the anticipation of Heckler's presence had brought fresh faces to the festival, mixing sports enthusiasts with book fans.

It was exciting. Wigtown was buzzing with false sightings. "I think I saw him," I heard a woman say. "Don't be ridiculous," shouted another. "It's too early."

People had come in droves, pouring in from every part of the country, specifically to see the inaugural event of the festival. This was important.

I was hiding upstairs in Euan's large sitting room, completely unaware of the impending crisis when it happened, engrossed in a conversation with Euan's cousin Eve. She had just arrived from Ireland for her yearly trip to The Bookshop to visit Euan and, of course, attend the festival.

She had bounded into the sitting room with a magnetic energy, smiling broadly after a hellish drive, declaring, "Where's my loathsome cousin? I can smell his putrid scent so he can't be far." Euan had appeared behind her.

"Ah, evil." Euan had struggled to hide his pleasure.

I introduced myself immediately, thinking: be cool, be cool.

"Hi, I'm Jessica, the American."

Eve had raised her eyebrows. "I couldn't tell." Eve, like Deirdre, spoke with a lyrical, rounded accent, but Eve's had a hint of self-enjoyment at your expense. I adored it.

"Ha, yeah, well…"

"I won't hold it against you."

It did not take long before we were drinking and gabbing away. Euan's sitting room, converted for the festival, was empty except for catering equipment and a long banquet table, covered in a white cloth and flowers. We sat at the table like lone royalty, a fire blazing in the large fireplace, bottles of Prosecco opened and most of our conversation geared to insulting Euan. I laughed until my sides hurt. Between gasps for air, I realised I hadn't had this much fun in ages. Eve's warmth, determined enjoyment of whatever came her way and her piercing wit left me feeling that my own personality could use a few improvements.

"You're not drinking enough, dear, have some more," Eve said, filling my glass.

As I watched the golden liquid pour into my glass, I felt giddy with happiness. If only Josh could see me now. He wouldn't have recognised the former workaholic, now grinning from ear to ear, completely content with Euan and Eve, half listening to their laughter and insults and half looking out of the large windows at the crowds of people gathered around the main marquee.

The festival's opening event was just an hour away from starting, and everything was feeling fresh and filled with possibility.

"So what's happening this evening?" Eve took another sip of her drink, while staring at the programme. "Oooh, a Burns supper."

I tried to offer something. "After that there's a ceilidh... What's a ceilidh?"

Euan leaned back. "A dance. It's fun."

Suddenly, the door flew open and Eliot tornadoed into the room, looking frantic. I could almost see invisible papers flying in his wake. "This is not happening," he muttered to himself over and over, as he paced through the room.

"Hi, Eliot," Eve chirped. He didn't seem to notice.

I stood and walked towards him. "What's wrong?"

Eliot waved his hands in the air, trying to dismiss whatever cloud of chaos hung around him. "Heckler missed his flight. We don't know where he is."

Eliot ran over to the window and watched the crowds gathering outside the marquee. "This is not happening. Fuck fuck fuck. Fuck." Taking out an inhaler from his pocket, Eliot held it up to his mouth and a soft hissing sound was heard. He inhaled deeply.

Eliot's phone rang. He let out his breath and answered. "Hello. (Pause). Yeah, I know, so where is he? (Pause). What? WHAT!"

Euan shot me a look. This wasn't good. The mood, which moments before had been exuberant, suddenly shifted.

"Oh my God!" Eliot began to pace again. "When? (Pause). We're just going to have to tell them. Refunds, tickets for next week, whatever. We'll fix it. (Pause). Thanks – I suppose."

Eliot shoved his phone back into his pocket, slowly raising his eyes. His expression was that of someone who had completely accepted the imminent arrival of the apoca-lypse. He leaned against a chair, and drew a breath in. "Heckler isn't coming."

"What?" Euan yelled, and Eve and I joined in.

"He'll come next month."

I resisted the urge to hug Eliot. I didn't think it would make him feel any better. In fact, I'd been in Wigtown long enough now to know that it would most definitely add to his discomfort.

"Right." He sighed. "It will be fine. It will have to be fine. We'll just apologise, offer free tickets and that's that."

He didn't say goodbye, just disappeared through the door as quickly as he came. I stood there amazed, and impressed. Although it may not have felt like it at the time, it was a heroic moment for him. He had handled a near catastrophe with perfect grace.

Euan's gaze returned to me and seemed to read my thoughts. He quickly filled the silence with "Heckler is a wanker".

Eve nodded, then proceeded to pour everyone more Prosecco.

We watched from the windows for a while. The fall out of the Heckler debacle was chaotic. As quickly as the guests had disappeared into the white marquee, they poured out again in hordes, like the carnival trick of clowns emerging from a clown car. Eliot commanded his post heroically, herding angry festival patrons to and fro, calming the masses and reinstating order.

With near disaster evaded, we thought we'd get Eve settled in before guests filtered back to the sitting room for the Burns supper.

Eve had arrived not only bearing gifts of chocolate – enormous Toblerones – but also groceries, booze and a shocking amount of personal luggage. We stood in the hall surveying her substantial entourage.

"How long are you staying for exactly?" I smiled, suddenly feeling that I had approached travelling all wrong. I always tried to pack as little as possible, but Eve had not stinted on one creature comfort and I had become an immediate convert to her pack-all, want-not philosophy.

Euan tried to pick one case up. "Jesus," he exclaimed. I quickly tried to grab the other end and grunted, feeling a deep twang in my lower back.

"Shut it, all of you." Eve proceeded to bound up the stairs with her other trunk, putting Euan and me to shame.

Euan grabbed the suitcase from me. "I got this, Fox." His tone carried the same ease that I was used to hearing from Rose or Josh. In a week and a half, despite mysterious moods and my assumptions to the contrary, we had become friends. Euan quickly disappeared up the stairs and I felt supremely happy.

An echo from a book I once read, by the German philosopher Novalis, came back to me: "The seat of the soul is there, where the inner and outer worlds meet." Perhaps I had stumbled upon my seat here, standing alone in a dark hallway, halfway across the world. For weeks it had felt as if I had been living in a liminal realm between the imagination and reality. It was weird, fantastic and empowering. What if, I mused, Wigtown only existed because I dreamed it? Quickly I shook the self-deluding notion away. Better to think that, in all likelihood, Wigtown was dreaming me.

Suddenly I felt that I was not alone. I had assumed it was just me, my thoughts and the darkness of the hall, but I got the prickly sensation of another presence. Eve and Euan were still upstairs. I could hear their footsteps and the occasional cackle of laughter drift down. I had been so engrossed in my daydreams that I hadn't noticed that someone had brushed by me in the hall. From behind, the whirring of a toilet flush sounded. The "other presence" emerged from the bathroom and I turned, expecting to see Laura.

But instead out walked a giant bear. I took a couple of steps back, stunned. In the dim hall light he emerged from the shadow and I saw that he was more half-man, half-bear. Massively tall and broad, his thick, jet-black beard cascaded upwards into a forest of hair. He coughed.

"Excuse me." His voice was deep and grizzly, with a hint of eastern Europe. When he breathed, the buttons strained on his jacket and I imagined that his suit was too tight, not because of his belly, but because of the massive amounts of fur that lay underneath.

"Can I help you?" I took a step back as he walked towards me. He held out his arm and I fully expected to see a paw, but instead his hand looked convincingly human. It was large and covered with dark, rough skin.

"I'm Miroslav," he growled.

"Oh, hi." My hand disappeared in his and his eyes bored into me as if looking for something in particular. I imagined that I would fall in his estimation if he didn't find it.

"Why do you look so scared?" He stood back, surveying me closely.

"I thought you were a bear." It fell out of my mouth before I could stop it.

Miroslav threw his head back and rumbled with laughter. His eyes returned to me looking bright and delighted. "You're far more entertaining than Richard Heckler."

My face flushed.

Eve vaulted down the stairs behind me. With one hand she shook Miroslav's while she wrapped her other arm around my waist affectionately. "Hello there, I'm Eve."

The Grizzly Bear smiled. "Miroslav."

"I remember you from last year." She tugged on my side knowingly. "Can I get you a drink?"

How did Eve do it? It seemed she always knew what to say. The Grizzly Bear looked relieved and replied in low Slavic tones, "Those Scots are complete Scrooges with their whisky. Show me the way, fairy lady. I want to have at least a glass to myself before the vultures come."

It wasn't long before the authors descended into the sitting room, setting it alight with their rosy, inebriated glow. I stood among the crowds, and noticed how suddenly the energy in the room had changed from a peaceful quiet into a chattering buzz. I looked up at the gorgeous Georgian ceiling, ornate with inlay and intricate carvings, and listened to   and whispers about the Burns supper – mostly descriptions of the infamous Burns impersonator.

The reason why Miroslav was thirsty for his whisky was that the Burns impersonator had found, and drained, most of the bottles before the dinner had even begun. By the time Robert Burns was supposed to give his recitation, his voice was so slurred that the audience had had to finish the poems for him. Burns had only been able to do a couple of lines before wandering off somewhere, shouting into the ether. Everyone had enjoyed it immensely.

One of the guests suggested that Burns was a method actor, and that his drunken manner and complete disregard for authority was a genius attempt at an accurate historical portrayal.

"He's here." Eve suddenly appeared and shot through the doorway. As if on cue, Robert Burns stumbled into the room.

"Where is that beautiful woman?" Burns demanded, searching the room for Eve but she was carefully hidden behind Euan. Giving up his search with an ease not befitting a romantic poet, he locked me with his unsteady gaze and made a beeline. I held out my wine glass.

"There you are," I said, hoping the ruby-red wine would distract him. It worked. He took it from me and sat in the closest chair. It was already occupied by a famous local poet but Burns didn't seem to mind the extra cushioning.

*

Bang. Thwap. Crackle. In the night sky above Wigtown's square a dizzying spectacle of fireworks exploded. Laura and Eve stood on either side of me, and we leaned in together, trying to keep warm. A crowd had gathered in their winter hats and jackets, looking up at the smoky sky. In bursts of blues, pinks and whites, the festival had officially begun.

Eve handed me her phone, smiling. I pressed it to my ear, trying to make out the voice in between the bursts of fireworks.

"Hi, it's Robert Burns." The voice message began. His voice seemed sober and tired. "I seem to have lost my sideburns. If you find them, please would you mind posting them to the following address…"

Chapter 12

"Let Ahab beware of Ahab." – Herman Melville, MOBY
DICK: *Fiction section, second shelf on the left in the gallery.*

On the second day of the festival, Stanley appeared. He stepped off the bus, landing firmly in Wigtown Square among the hustle and bustle of the festival tents. With a VHS tape of his documentary film under his arm, he had made the journey all the way from Zimbabwe, and now happily travelled the extra two blocks to the festival offices on foot.

I was hiding in the kitchen when he arrived. Two days into the festival and I had already become wary of the sitting room, with its endless stream of authors, dishes to clear and kettles to refill. On the whole the authors were incredibly kind, pitching in and helping to keep the sitting room tidy. There were always those, however, admittedly few and far between, who treated us like indentured servants, and me with something bordering disdain (was it my accent?) until they heard I worked for NASA. Then I became worthy of eye contact when spoken to. It was such a strange phenomenon that I liked keeping the fact I worked there in my back pocket, like a wild card, pulling it out if I felt that an author was judging a book by its cover.

Stanley wandered into the kitchen, looking lost in his oversized leather jacket. "Excuse me," he asked in a warm,

African accent. "Is this the authors' room?"

"No, you're not far off though." I wiped my hands dry and led him into the sitting room. He flashed a smile, looking up at the large ceiling, then taking in the long dining table surrounded by authors feasting on lobster.

"You've come on the right day," I continued. "On the weekends authors are treated to lobster."

"I impregnated a woman who looked like you," said Stanley, catching me off guard, while Eve who overheard, snickered into her wine. From that moment on, everything suddenly became very bizarre.

Stanley, it soon transpired, with his sincere, smiling face, and his home-made documentary, was a rampant Mugabe supporter, and a possible sociopath. He changed careers as often as he changed seats, first saying he was a supermarket owner, then a music producer and finally a bookshop owner, all the while professing his undying loyalty to his holy Mugabe, and ingratiating himself with people with rape jokes. Within five minutes in the authors' room, he had succeeded in offending everyone sitting near him.

Eliot appeared, sheet white, as people evacuated the room. "What the hell is happening?"

Stanley attempted to snap a lobster claw off and it went airborne, hitting Eliot squarely in the forehead. Eliot dropped his folder and looked frightened, as if his fears of festival mutiny were being realised.

"How the hell did he get here?" I whispered, searching Eliot's confused face. "Was he invited?"

"No, he just showed up. I have put him on the African panel this afternoon." Eliot, bewildered, looked from Stanley to the now empty table littered with half eaten lobsters.

At the African panel, Eve and I sat in the back row. The moment Stanley saw us in the crowd, he waved happily, like a child who had glimpsed his parents in the audience of a school play. He proceeded to upstage each speaker during the debate by pointing to his own self-published book.

"When did you lose your virginity?" he asked one stunned writer, who had opened the floor to questions about his book recounting years spent as a hostage in Lebanon. Promptly asked to leave, Stanley wandered into another tent, trying to open-trade for books in exchange for his "many trinkets".

In the middle of the chaos, between keeping tabs on Stanley and taking care of the authors in the sitting room, I hardly noticed the reporters wandering through to the back of the shop.

"Do you mind if we take your picture for a small article?" they asked as I brought more teacups into the sitting room.

"Sure," I said, on "perfect host" automatic pilot, and followed them downstairs, where they asked me to hold a book, and flashed their camera. A day later a festival patron came up to me, pointing. So you're the girl, they said, holding up a copy of *The Big Issue*. My face was enlarged over an entire page.

By the second day, we were taking shifts buying Stanley rounds at the Wigtown Ploughman, keeping him far from anyone he could offend. Eventually Eliot person-ally escorted him to the bus station, waving him off and watching with relief as his bus disappeared over the hill. And thus, Stanley vanished as quickly as he had arrived.

Chapter 13

"An event is something that happens at a particular point in space and at a particular time." – Stephen Hawking, A Brief History of Time: *Science section, Transportation Room, left of spiral staircase.*

Royal can be an adjective and a noun, which is appropriate, because royalty in Scotland, to my fresh American eyes, seemed like two things at once or, for lack of a better word, a contradiction. Scotland was a free, separate state of mind to that of England and an undercurrent of rebellion towards its parent country or anything English still ran strong in its proud veins. However, when it was announced that Her Royal Highness, the Princess Royal, was to appear at the festival, the entire town gathered in excited reverence to see her.

I was also desperate to see Princess Anne. Americans are perhaps more obsessed with the idea of royalty than our long-lost British brothers; our taste for anything royal, never satiated in a true democracy, manifests itself in the canonising of celebrities and their families and mass idealisation of political dynasties like the Kennedys. I'd say our fascination with royalty is a perversion from the Revolutionary War, a desperate longing, perhaps, to reconnect with our parent country. But my family tree on both sides is Jewish from eastern Europe. My father's family extends back a couple of generations in America and my mother, born in Germany, is the child of two Holocaust survivors. As things stand, I have no colonial ties. Yet, faced there in Wigtown with the imminent arrival of Princess Anne, I was still royally inspired. As I leaned against the window, neglecting my cleaning duties in the sitting room, I watched as my breath created a fog against the glass, hoping I would catch a glimpse of her.

I heard she was only staying a couple of hours, having arrived earlier that afternoon by helicopter. She would wave and plant a tree, but no speeches. That was in her contract.

"Where is she? She's missing all the excitement. Jessica? Yoohoo!" I heard a familiar voice echo from the hall. Deirdre bounded into the sitting room full of her usual, infectious enthusiasm. My day suddenly brightened.

"What are you doing up here, silly girl? All the excitement is happening downstairs."

"I know," I said, feeling a bit like Cinderella missing the ball. "I'm supposed to be manning the authors' room this afternoon."

"Oh stuff and nonsense!" Deirdre grabbed my hand and gave it an affectionate squeeze. "I'm taking you to see her. This is an opportunity you cannot miss."

The large cream tent was filled with the smell of plastic. It was the first time I had been inside and I was impressed with its scale. I had no idea there was so much room on Wigtown green.

We walked past the entrance, full of tables with pamphlets, raffles and books for sale.

Deirde pushed me ahead into the next room which opened up into a grand space with plastic windows and a draped ceiling. The sound of chatter bounced off the walls and a sea of chairs, filled with expectant festival-goers, stretched out before us.

"Deirdre, I don't think there's anywhere to sit," I whispered.

Patting me on the hand, Deirdre led me to two open seats at the far end of the back row. On the stage, at the podium, Eliot cleared his throat. He saw us and smiled, and I shifted to the edge of my seat. The room suddenly became quiet – the anticipation was palpable. Deirdre searched my face for signs of approval and I glanced at her, smiling broadly. I was about to see my first princess.

*

Was it already over? That was it? We walked into the reception area after our brief public audience with Her Royal Highness, the Princess Royal. Clad in a tartan skirt suit, with a string of pearls, gloved hands and impeccably done hair, she had been on stage all of ten minutes. She had waved, her secretary had read a letter and then she had accepted a book from a small child (quite sweet). Then she had left to tour the garden. I had been all set to meet her, and had been practising my "Ma'am as in ham not Mum as in hum". There was something so impressive about her, her etiquette, posture, poise. To me, she felt royal... if such a thing existed.

I excused myself from Deirdre, anxious to get back to my abandoned post in the authors' room. I was also anxious to break free from the smell of plastic. As I stepped into the fresh morning air outside the tent, I took a deep breath. Smell has always been a very vivid sense for me, ever since I was little. Right now I could smell the whiff of powdery perfume from a lady who had brushed up next to me as I had slid through the door. I could smell the chalky dust of the gravel beneath my feet, mixed with the grease from a distant chip van, flowers in bloom and the fresh salt sea air.

Crossing the street, I stood watching Princess Anne surrounded by an adoring crowd. She held a shovel in her gloved hand, and she smiled as her picture was taken next to a newly planted tree. She looked up and saw me standing away from the crowds, lingering outside The Bookshop. Our eyes met and I'm still not quite certain if this next part was in my imagination, but she lifted her hand and waved. I waved back, filled with a sense of destiny. Wigtown was magic, everything about this moment was magic. As soon as our eyes met, Her Royal Highness, the Princess Royal shifted her gaze.

Chapter 14

"Some beautiful morning she will just wake up and find it is Tomorrow. Not Today but Tomorrow. And things will happen... wonderful things." — L.M. Montgomery, ANNE OF THE ISLAND: *Children's section, top shelf on the right.*

The rain beat down in steady, rhythmic torrents onto the roof of the red van. I felt as if I was inside a large kettle drum. We had abandoned the festival for an afternoon and were making our way slowly along the western side of the peninsula from Wigtown, the Monreith coast.

"It's around here somewhere," Euan said, bending over the steering wheel. Eve and I leaned forward, too. Sandwiched in the front of the van, we struggled to see out beyond the foggy windshield. Stone houses appeared every now and then in the rain-soaked fields, breaking up the rolling pastureland. The van slowed as we approached two horses — one brown, one white — that stood in a fenced-in pasture near the road, heads down, braving the elements.

"That must be them," Eve said, delighted, reaching her arm across me and pointing out the window. I snuggled back into the warm seat. The thought of emerging from the van's cocoon-like warmth into this damp weather made me shiver. Euan's neighbour owned these horses and had made kind and generous offer that we could ride them any time we wanted. Neither Euan nor I had any experience of riding but Eve had a passion for horses, and on hearing that there were some nearby, had been determined to make the most of it.

As the rain continued to pelt down, Euan and I stood, soaked, and watched Eve walk alone across the wet field. She was fearless, as her tiny frame approached the massive and slightly jumpy white horse. In the distance, it looked as if she was bewitching the wild creature, throwing a bridle over its head and instantly coaxing it to walk with her. I looked on, fascinated, as she returned to us, beaming through the rain.

"Well now," she said, patting the horse behind her as if they were old friends. "Who's going to have the first go? Jessica?"

"No, thanks. I'm here to watch, not ride."

I stepped back, intimidated by the horse, which reared its head at me. The only time I had ever ridden was during a family vacation to Arizona. My father had been in his element, trying out the whoops and whistles he had heard as a child on *The Lone Ranger*. I had not been so at ease, however. The pony I was placed on had a rash on its belly. As I tried to follow my parents and sister as we trekked through wild backcountry trails, the pony would compulsively walk into shrubs and trees in the hope of alleviating its belly itch, scratching me in the process.

"Come on, where's that American confidence?" Euan looked at me.

"I'm wearing a dress."

"And fishnets." Eve looked at my soaked fishnet stockings, undeterred. "Step on here," she said as she pointed to a broken part of the fence, "and I'll help you get on."

"But there's no saddle." I argued, firmly placing my hands on my hips. "I can't ride bareback."

Eve cocked her head and it seemed the horse did the same. The horse glowed white in the misty green that surrounded us. I could hear the ocean roaring not far off. It was an intoxicating atmosphere, pregnant with challenge, and I felt my resistance waning.

"You do yoga - it's the same muscles." Eve held out her hand and I reluctantly took it. "Trust me."

*

I stood, dripping wet, in the hall at the top of the stairs, triumphant. I had done it. Today I had been on a great adventure and satisfied a lifelong romantic ambition – riding through the mist-covered hills bareback on a white horse with the ocean roaring close by. Only in those dreams I had been wearing a cape, not fishnets and a mini-dress.

Eve had been an excellent teacher, walking the horse slowly as I felt its muscular body beneath me. Rain poured down, making it hard to see and I had struggled to gain balance at first, tipping from one side to the other. As Eve began to pick up the pace, I had clung to the horse terrified, but slowly began to feel a rhythm. My own muscles quickly synced with the slightest shifts in the horse and, between gulps of fear, I began to feel almost powerful. It was, again, the magic of the festival. Between dishes and authors and chaos, incredible moments bloomed. They had become more plentiful thanks to Eve's fearlessness and sense of fun.

"See you later, losers." Eve bounded up the stairs for a bath. Standing alone in the hall, I could hear the water start to rush through the pipes, before the sound of approaching footsteps made me turn.

A man with dark hair, bearing a suitcase and a bewildered expression, appeared at the top of the stairs. He cleared his throat awkwardly.

"Oh, are you just arriving?" I said, aware that my dripping appearance was more appropriate for a rain-soaked lady of the night than the host of a literary festival.

"Yes, hi." He spoke with a soft English accent, but there was a twinge of American about him. "I'm Thomas, Eve's friend. Well, not friend exactly."

"Enemy?"

Thomas blinked at me. I was in complete festival mode and forgot that to someone who had just arrived, we all probably seemed raving mad. "She's just in the bath, but come in," I said, finding my manners, and led Thomas into the sitting room. It was empty. All the authors were either hosting events or at them. Thomas's eyes grew wide, looking from the marble fireplace to the high ornate ceiling, then finally resting on the piano.

"Do you play?" I asked hopefully.

"A little." Thomas smiled and dropped his bags. He sat on the piano stool. "You said Eve was in the bath?"

"I think so."

At this, Thomas's fingers hit the keys with confident determination and he started playing "Rule Britannia". The cheery sound echoed through the house and up the stairs.

"Thomas! You foul wretch!" Eve's voice exploded from the upstairs bathroom and Thomas's smile widened as we heard her splashing in protest.

Chapter 15

"It is quite a three pipe problem." – Arthur Conan Doyle,
THE RED-HEADED LEAGUE: *Mystery section, across from
the spiral staircase.*

When the clock struck midnight there was a lull in
conversation. Around the long table, its cloth
stained with food and wine, a handful of authors sat,
smoking and sipping the last of the wine in a rare silence.
The light was low and moody as the candles, now down to
their last inches, were dwindling. Everyone was drooping,
leaning at augmented angles, fighting off the growing urge
to go to sleep.

I looked around the room in a drowsy haze. We were
having a pipe party. It began when Euan saw a Sherlock
Holmes pipe sticking out of my pocket – I had forgotten
to leave it on my desk. I would often pretend to puff it
while writing – a sensible trick to put me in a thoughtful
mood, but more to keep me from eating copious amounts
as I worked through my screenplays. Euan proceeded to
take out two pipes of his own. Thomas brought a pipe
and the room suddenly overflowed with pipes and pipe
appreciation.

I had never actually smoked mine, its sole use being as
an adult pacifier. But now burnt-vanilla tobacco filled the
bowl, and, having puffed away half the night, my throat

felt like a charred house. My mind buzzed and was as light as a hot-air balloon.

At the far end of the table sat Eve, pipe in hand, puffing away with grim determination, eyes slanted, looking questioningly at Peter, the author across from her. Peter, a tall, thin, kind man, in his early forties, wrote for one of the major Scottish papers and had recently had a work of short fiction published. He had been one of the few healthy specimens during the festival, abstaining from drink, but now, under Eve's glare, he obediently picked up a rouge pipe and took a great puff.

Next to Peter sat a couple, her tall, him short, both in black. They were engrossed in a deep, drunken conversation. I peered at the open programme in front of me. Two small square photos of them stared back with a heading below that read "The History of Keys". Laura, to my left, leaned over to me, bumping heads.

"Ow." I tried to move away but she grabbed my arm, pulling me close.

"I heard she's a man."

I rubbed my head. "Who? Her?"

I looked back to the woman in black. Laura nodded.

Next to Laura sat two other authors, both men in their mid-fifties. They had been arguing about the state of the Middle East and their conversation, heated (especially for this hour of the night) had risen and fallen in volume; they now sat, slumped, in silence. I leafed through the programme to find out who exactly they were. My American ignorance of the UK's literary elite embarrassed me, but during the festival my cluelessness had been mistaken for confidence. I hadn't been intimidated by, nor had I pandered to the intellectual giants and I had treated everyone equally, not out of some enlightened state of being – I'd be the first to get tongue-tied – but simply because I had no idea who they were. Euan had suggested I study the programme before the festival began, but I was enjoying my unexpected autonomy.

As my eyes scanned the smoke-filled room, I noticed Euan was missing. He was the only one of our gang who was unaccounted for besides Thomas, who had gone up to sleep.

I quietly slipped out of the sitting room into the dark hall. Fresh air. My eyes slowly adjusted and I took a deep breath. It was significantly cooler out here and I stretched my bare arms out, welcoming the chill. In the soft silence, I could hear Euan's voice echoing from the kitchen. I couldn't remember when I had seen him last, and I approached the door, listening to see if I could hear who he was talking to.

"He's always been like that."

I turned to see Laura sitting behind me on the steps leading upstairs. In her hands was a full bottle of wine, and as I stared at it, she followed my gaze.

"If I don't guard it," she smiled, "those bastards will drink it all."

Euan's voice grew louder. Laura looked up, as if her ears too were perked.

"For as long as I've known Euan, women have adored him," she said, as she took a sip from the bottle, before offering it to me. I shook my head, and she continued, "I'll never forget one year, on Valentine's Day, when we were at Tesco and he had to buy four different Valentine's Day cards."

I didn't want to hear this.

"One for this girl he was sort of seeing," she went on, "one for his ex, well, sort of ex, one for this French girl.

It was hilarious." Laura took another swig from her bottle and searched my expression. "Don't get me wrong, he's the best man I know. You see, he's too nice. He didn't want to hurt their feelings."

Laura's voice faded out and my ears pulsed. All the humiliation I had suffered while with Grant flooded back: the feelings of being worthless and shrinking inside started tumbling through my nervous system again. My heart suddenly went out to those women whom Euan had juggled on Valentine's Day. I had no right to be angry and I was. I was furious. I needed to calm down. It was none of my business what Euan did or didn't do. I was just a guest here, nothing more. I needed to breathe, to come back into this moment, to find a distraction.

"Laura, we're going to do a talent show." I brightened as if charm alone could sell the idea.

She didn't look enthused.

"It will be fun, I promise."

"You're so American," she said as she followed me back into the siitting room, clutching the wine bottle under her arm.

Eve stared at the piece of paper before her. There was a line down the centre and one side read "Name" and the other "Talent". She blew smoke on it from her pipe, which was, I was impressed to see, still lit.

"I'm not having any part of this. I don't perform."

"Why?"

"I'm happy to say, I'm not talented."

I wasn't swayed. "The 'key' couple are listing obscure trivia, Laura is singing" — Eve shot Laura a "you must be kidding" glance which I pretended not to see — "and Peter is tap-dancing while hammering a nail up his nose."

This impressed Eve. "What about those guys?"

"Those guys" — I pointed to the Middle East lecturers — "are telling jokes. It would be weird if you didn't do something."

Eve thought for a second. "I'll host."

The night went off with a bang. What had begun as a desperate attempt to distract myself grew into the festival's first fringe event. By 1am a large crowd had gathered upstairs and the sitting room was suddenly alive again. Thanks to Eve's hosting skills, everyone was enjoying themselves. Peter, true to his word, hammered a nail up his nose while tap-dancing and unanimously won the heart of the audience. The judges, three intoxicated festival patrons who were scooped off the street on their way home from the pub, to everyone's surprise, picked the Middle East lecturers as the winners, perhaps impressed after a day of arguing that they possessed a sense of humour at all. The prize given at the end was Ferrero Rocher chocolates that Eve had super-glued into a massive golden pyramid. In what turned out to be an ironic gesture of good will, the winners passed the pyramid around to be shared, not knowing that it was glued together, and watched in horror as everyone clawed unsuccessfully to get their piece of it.

*

"Let's leave it for tomorrow. I'll clean up in the morning." I slouched even deeper into my chair, debating whether climbing the stairs to bed was too much of an effort at this point. It was 2am. Eve, Laura and I sat relaxing in the now empty sitting room. Somewhere between a second wind and pure exhaustion, I scanned the post-talent-show carnage: cups, wrappers, plates, jackets.

Euan, to my surprise, emerged holding juggling clubs and lighter fluid. "I missed it, didn't I?"

I raised an eyebrow. "Never too late."

Laura started to applaud. Eve leaned forward and tried to prise some chocolate from the pyramid, which had been abandoned in the middle of the table.

Euan walked over to me, his face wearing signs of emotional exhaustion. "I didn't want to do this while everyone was here." I looked away, feeling for the first time the need to guard myself around him.

He stepped back and lit the clubs. They burst into bright flames, and Euan juggled three, easily and rhythmically. I blinked slowly as if my eyelids were shutters, trying to take a snapshot of this moment for my memory. I was in a beautiful Georgian sitting room in a remote part of Scotland, having just hosted some of the brightest minds in the UK, with a fire-juggler in front of me, who I couldn't take my eyes off.

Chapter 16

"Now behind the eyes and secrets of the dreamers in the
streets rocked to sleep by the sea, see the titbits and topsy-
turvies, bobs and buttontops, bags and bones, ash and rind
and dandruff and nailparings, saliva and snowflakes and
moulted feathers of dreams, the wrecks and sprats and
shells and fishbones, whale-juice and moonshine and small
salt fry dished up by the hidden sea." – Dylan Thomas,
UNDER MILK WOOD: *Poetry section, right of the fireplace,
under T.*

Finally I found the Folklore/Mythology section. It was
high up on a shelf, tucked away across from Travel
and next to Foreign Language. Typically in bookshops, if
the section was hidden away in the little corners of bookshelf obscurity, there was a reason.

I peered up to see a nearly empty shelf, with a volume
of Greek mythology, Joseph Campbell's series, The
Masks of God, and golden flecks of dust swirling in the
space between. My nerdy need to surround myself with a
familiar fortress of tomes on "the call to adventure" and
"symbolism of the sun gods" would not be satiated by this
shelf. Bookless, I felt oddly exposed and vulnerable.

To my surprise, I glanced down to see the Grizzly Bear
standing in front of me, stroking his full black beard. He
eyed me with intense curiosity, looking amused.

I flushed, annoyed. My rare solitary afternoon had been full of intrusions like this one. There was nowhere to hide during the festival. Every nook and cranny of the house and shop was a hub of activity. Silence was an even rarer commodity than space. The house was constantly humming, a beehive whose buzz of chatter droned on till the wee hours of the morning. I had been in Wigtown now for over two weeks with hardly a moment alone. It had been a welcome change from my tower of isolation in LA, but still, it was a change, and in that moment I just wanted to be by myself.

"Have you found some treasure?" his deep voice rumbled.

"Not yet."

He remained silent. I hated it when people did that. His lack of a silver tongue was not the soft quiet between two friends, but the mute expectation of an audience member, waiting to see what his entertainment would do or say. I could have ignored him, but the awkwardness compelled me to babble uncontrollably.

"It's the anticipation of finding treasure, not the having it, which is the thrill for me," I said pretentiously. My mouth kept on moving, despite being horrified that I had said something so trite aloud. "Dusty books waiting to be discovered, you know, and that kind of thing." Still, the Grizzly just stared, so I continued. "I had always thought that was what the Holy Grail was all about."

The Grizzly shifted. He seemed interested. "The Holy Grail?"

I could tell his big brain, filled with knowledge and books and things not yet written, had finally found something with which to entertain itself. He waited, wanting me to say more, but I had always felt self-conscious talking about mythology. I was not Joseph Campbell, nor Sir Frazier, and my arms were empty, with no books to use as shields.

"It occurred to me," I continued tentatively, "that the Holy Grail is not the treasure but the dream, like the carrot before the horse. It's the impulse that gets you off the couch and propels your journey. The problem arises when you don't allow your dream to change. In that case, if you seek it, hopefully you won't find it."

"Why?"

"Well, that would be a mid-life crisis, wouldn't it? You finally get what you want, but didn't realise that the journey to getting it has informed who you are, so the grail you once dreamed about, that was supposed to bring perfect happiness – whether a car, house with a white picket fence or dream job – is, most likely, not going to make the current you feel fulfilled."

The Grizzly Bear's mouth twitched. It could have been a smile but it extinguished quickly. "I should be leaving."

Leaving? I looked at him like a leaf falling in August, an unwanted harbinger that autumn was on its way and things were ebbing and fading away. All of a sudden I didn't want this conversation to end. I didn't want any of it to end. Although craving some solitude, tired and over-worked, I wanted to drag my feet in the sand, to slow time down, to make it last longer.

The Grizzly Bear stretched past me, his powerful arms easily reaching the first Joseph Campbell book high on the shelf.

"So this is your Mr. Campbell?" His bushy eyebrows were raised, as he held *The Masks of God: Occidental Mythology* in his paws.

I could feel my heart growing for the Grizzly Bear. "It's very good."

His thick fingers took out a slip from the front cover. The series was a first edition, £235 for each book.

"On your recommendation, I'll take it. " He looked at me, closing the book. "It had better be good."

I lingered at the bottom of the stairs, looking through the doorway as the Grizzly Bear made his way to the front of the shop. I could hear the distant murmur of the "key" lecture, given by the couple from the pipe party, echo from the main tent and I watched the shuffle of more customers, aglow with the late-afternoon light, pouring in.

Euan looked up from the counter, sipping on a glass of champagne. The Grizzly Bear dropped his luggage down with a large thud and slid the Campbell volumes onto the counter. "I'm getting these because of the American."

Euan smiled. "She's bossy, isn't she?"

The Grizzly Bear shook his furry head. "She's rare."

Euan, with his angelic halo of ginger curls, glanced over at me.

*

The sitting room was a chorus of conversation. This Saturday was the pinnacle of the festival, the last full day and traditionally the most decadent, a literary mardi gras. Happy writers, agents and speakers occupied every chair and leaned against the walls, their clinking glasses echoing off the large windows and high ceilings. I should have been attending to the litter of empty teacups and plates, but instead I sat down in the closest empty chair and grabbed a half-full glass of wine. Glimpsing the end of my adventure had drained me of the will to be helpful.

Suddenly a hand landed on my shoulder and a bathing suit fell into my lap. Eve stood next to me. "Stop feeling sorry for yourself. We're going swimming."

In my mind, everyone has their own personal super-hero's ability, and this was Eve's. She knew exactly when and what to say to motivate people and get them out of the labyrinth of their own thoughts.

In the hall, Laura emerged from the kitchen, holding a refreshed glass of wine. "Swimming?" she said, eyeing the bathing suit in my arms, "Excellent."

"Swimming?" Euan clambered up the lower stairs, two at a time, with the familiarity of someone who had done this too many times to count. Euan's house these past ten days, from his kitchen to his sitting room, had been completely taken over for the festival. I searched his face for strain but saw none. He, in his typical generous way, looked quite at ease sharing so much without ever asking anything in return. "Let's go." He reached the top landing just in time to miss a playful swipe from Eve.

Outside, we made our way across the street to the red van. Our gang had snowballed into a motley crew of five – Euan, Eve, Laura, Thomas and me.

"You're very quiet," Euan said as we headed to the car.

Though I didn't feel like it, I smiled. "Really? I'm fine."

Before sliding into the driver's seat, Euan looked at me. "Don't worry." He squeezed my hand. Again it felt strong and warm. "There's loads of time before you leave."

My heart fluttered. My thoughts about him were like a tennis ball, flipping back and forth between two sides. I couldn't deny that I was growing fond of him. He was playful, generous, incredibly kind, and increasingly there was a connection between us. I could feel it. Then again, sometimes there wasn't. Sometimes he felt distant, and from what I observed I thought perhaps he was in romantic overload, the women in his life creating a prism for his affections and emotions. It would be too complicated to add myself to the mix.

I buckled myself into the van, sandwiched between Eve and Laura, with both my legs over Thomas. What a place to have an emotional epiphany — but it struck me that I didn't have to decide what my feelings were because there was one point on which I would not compromise: though relationships are never clear, the next man I would be with had to be clear, above all else, in his desire to be with me.

It was a grey, windy day in Monreith. One of the prettiest spots in Galloway, Monreith's sandy beach stretched in both directions, with steep cliffs of rocks and coves behind.

I was the first to head for the water. I wanted to look fearless, to impress my new friends, and ran overly zealously at the towering waves. Now only a couple of inches in, I regretted every hubristic second. The waves today were dramatic, frothing with peaks and foam. The water pulled forcefully under my feet and swelled around my ankles. It was so cold it burned.

After a couple of seconds, goosebumps stood ridged like armour all over my skin and I couldn't feel the wind any more. I was numb and shaking all over. My brain wouldn't stop thinking about leaving, like a jukebox running compulsively over and over the same song. Heart pounding, I closed my eyes and took a step deeper into the ocean. A blast of cold shot up my legs. I wanted to scream. My body was as rigid as a board. "Enjoy this moment, Jessica," I whispered. "You are in Scotland, in the most beautiful place on Earth, with your Bookshop owner and kindred spirits. I'm lucky, I'm so lucky." I turned to see Laura, Thomas and Euan running towards me.

Eve was missing. I scanned the shoreline to find her sitting wrapped in everyone's jackets, waving. Was this not the woman who had got us all out here? God, she's good. And what was I doing out here? I wasn't even in a bathing suit, but my underwear. I hated the cold. I tried to wave back but my hands were stubbornly tucked under my arms.

Euan, as smooth as a sea lion, dived into an oncoming wave. I was in awe. He resurfaced, his head bobbing up and down, wearing a big grin. Thomas, with the same determination, ran past me, diving into the foamy water. Laura slowly walked by me, yelling over the wind, "Come on," and disappeared deeper into the sea.

I was frozen, watching all of them in amazement. This was a challenge I just didn't think I could meet. Jumping onto a plane, travelling across the world to live in the middle of nowhere with strangers, no problem. Here, thigh-deep in icy water, I had found my limit. Thomas cocked his head, shouting, "Come on NASA girl, live a little!"

I was uncomfortable and started to turn around. How many times did we really go to where was uncomfortable? I had with Grant, and look how that had turned out. But – actually – how had that turned out? At the time it was horrific, but now I was living my dream. This was a paradox. I turned to face the crashing waves.

"Let's go, Jessica!" Euan yelled. I told myself this would be a Palingenesia baptism.

I took a deep breath. Stretching my arms towards the grey, swelling sea, without another thought, I plunged into the ice-cold water.

Chapter 17

"We are all filled with a longing for the wild... No matter where we are, the shadow that trots behind us is definitely four-footed." – Clarissa Pinkola Estes, WOMEN WHO RUN WITH WOLVES: *Psychology section, third shelf from the bottom all the way to the right.*

The festival ended not with a bang but with a whimper. Everyone disappeared one by one, like Agatha Christie's Ten Little Indians, until there were none. There were many heartfelt goodbyes: Eve made me promise to visit her in Ireland, Thomas pressed a leather journal into my hands and insisted that I keep up with my writing and Laura whispered in my ear that they would all be devastated when I left. She had looked at me without a trace of her signature sarcasm when she added, "Especially Euan."

By Sunday evening, all was calm and Wigtown had begun to return to its normal state, though Euan's house still looked like a scene from the aftermath of a revolution. There were more cups to clean, more tables to clear and we, including Hannah and Eliot who stayed on to help, were still all running on no sleep. Euan and I hardly said a word to each other. In fact, the whole house was silent. There was a shared solemnity to the end of the festival, and the atmosphere in the sitting room, which had recently been sparkling and vibrant with the guests' energy, now hung heavy and empty.

On Euan's insistence, I spent the next couple of days in Edinburgh with his sister and her boyfriend. I was reluctant to leave Wigtown – and Euan – in my last week, but he had encouraged me to see more of Scotland before I left.

"It is time," he said, "to see something outside Wigtown." He was right.

Euan's sister and her boyfriend welcomed me into their home with the same generosity that seemed to permeate through the whole family. In addition to sleeping (I hadn't realised how exhausted I was from the festival madness), I explored the wonderful city.

Walking around Edinburgh was like entering a classical painting, especially in Old Town. I couldn't get enough of the stone passageways, crumbling buildings, green cliffs and bicycles. To me, bicycles were a yard-stick of happiness for a city and in Edinburgh bicycles were everywhere. My heart leapt when I saw a young woman, her long brown coat billowing in the wind, cycling past old buildings and along a path of trees, whose leaves were raining down in a shower of oranges and browns. Autumn. I suddenly ached to be living in a place with seasons, and among old buildings, a place with deep roots and history.

After living like a settled resident in Wigtown, here I suddenly became a tourist. I went to the castle and museums and bought a warm blueberry scone from a market, letting the delicious buttery cake melt in my mouth as I wandered through the city's gardens. I climbed up to the park with its half-colosseum and breathtaking views, and stared at Arthur's Seat, a steep, dramatic cliff, jutting out completely naked into the sky. Looking at it, I felt a familiar childhood longing: a deeply intimate craving for something wild.

On the train back from Edinburgh, I stared out of the window, lost in thought, as the familiar green fields and stone cottages greeted me, and a glimmer of a new idea began to ignite. Perhaps the thrill of the unexpected was more intense and satisfying than the thrill of planning and executing something new. Stephen Hawking writes in *A Brief History of Time* that "it seems the uncertainty principle is a fundamental feature of the universe we live in". Perhaps this was my way of adding an uncertainty principal to my grand unifying theory. All the best parts of this adventure, after all – Euan, Eve, Deirdre, Edinburgh and all that I adored about Wigtown – had been outside the possibilities of my imagination.

I got off the train at Glasgow where Euan had promised to be waiting. My eyes darted over the handful of people on the platform. He was there in his brown jacket, tall and slim, his familiar curls bobbing above the crowds. I noticed he had dressed in his casual best to pick me up. I smiled and without thinking, I ran up to him and gave him a hug. At first he seemed surprised but slowly he returned the gesture. His familiar cologne surrounded me and I felt instantly at home again. I pulled away, trying to act relaxed.

"So, did you miss me?" I asked as he took my bags, realising how much I had missed him.

"Not at all," Euan said. I smacked him and he moved away laughing. "Stop dawdling, Fox, I have something to show you."

As we drove along in the red van in contented silence, Euan pointed out of the window at the most extraordinary cows. They were like Oreo cookies, black in front, black at the back, with one white stripe in the middle.

"Belted Galloways," Euan said, scanning my delighted expression.

They were all over the landscape, even sweet-looking Beltie calfs. I couldn't believe I hadn't noticed them before. A horrible pang pierced my heart. There was still so much to discover. I couldn't leave yet.

"Where are we going?" I asked Euan, trying to distract myself.

"My old school."

"Is it a castle?"

"No," Euan laughed, "but it's a beautiful building. I thought you'd like to see it, and it's on the way home."

We pulled up a long drive, overgrown with rhododendron bushes. I had no idea they could grow so big, almost into trees. Euan had taught me you could tell how well established an estate was by the size of the rhododendrons because they took so long to grow. In the house I grew up in in Lexington, we had rhododendron bushes outside but they were barely as tall as I was.

As we approached a large, dreary-looking Victorian building, Euan stopped the car. "It looks abandoned now," he said, "but it used to be quite a nice building."

A lone, and slightly deranged, orange cat sat on the front courtyard, now covered with grass and weeds. Despite the cat's unfriendly hiss, I walked a bit closer and stared up at the building's high stone walls and dark windows.

"You went to school here?" The place felt cold and sad, more like an institution than the colourful, sticker-filled elementary school I was used to.

Euan nodded. "I started boarding here when I was seven."

In the silence that followed, Euan quickly turned on his heels. As he headed back to the van, I felt like I was seeing a lost little boy. I ran after him.

"Seven? Weren't you lonely?"

"You're so American, Fox." Euan handed me a now half-empty bag of "maltese balls". "Always wanting to talk about feelings."

We headed back down the drive in silence, leaving the orange cat blinking back at us.

Chapter 18

"All things are one thing and that one thing is all things –
plankton, a shimmering phosphorescence on the sea and
the spinning of the planets and an expanding universe,
all bound together by the elastic string of time." – John
Steinbeck & Edward F. Ricketts, SEA OF CORTEZ: A
LEISURELY JOURNAL OF TRAVEL AND RESEARCH: *Biography
section, across from the fireplace, under S.*

When we pulled into Wigtown, the buildings were
dipping into shadow as the sun disappeared behind
the hills. Euan got out of the van and went inside, but I
lingered outside, struck by an exquisite sense of pre-emptive homesickness.

In the few days that I had been gone, I had longed for
the town's soft beauty, the quirky square filled with stone
houses, the vast expanse of fields and sky that encircled
it, the marsh and the sea. It inspired not a restless sense
of adventure in me, like Edinburgh had, but a deep sense
of rightness and calm. It reminded me of the story of the
Buddha, who found his immovable spot underneath the
Bodhi tree and once settled there, didn't want to leave.

I had only spent a month here out of my 25 years
but already, mysteriously, it had come to feel like home.
My analytical brain whirred with "how is this possible?"
but the truth of the answer was, it just was. Perhaps my

atoms had once resided in the sea salt of Wigtown Bay. Or perhaps hundreds of years ago the elements that now made up my arms and legs had once formed a bee, buzzing and collecting pollen from the bluebells in the Galloway forests. Or perhaps it was not a literal connection at all but, as Freud would suggest, the landscape of my interior world matched the landscape of Wigtown.

Herman Melville tapped on the glass behind me and I whirled around, surprised to see him sitting comfortably in the van. He rolled down the window, sticking his head out and pressing his hat firmly to his head.

"It's none of those things," he declared. "This place called to you and you to it for reasons neither of you completely understood." Satisfied, he rolled the window back up and leaned into the van's seat, settling in for a nap.

*

My feet pounded hard against the paved main road. I was running – fast – down the hill, past the church and graveyard. I shot past Devorguilla's old stone house and glanced quickly over the wall to see my favourite view of the marshlands. My legs wouldn't slow down. My breath was erratic, gasping for oxygen while by body was alight with adrenaline. I found myself rounding the corner onto the path for the Martyr's Stake.

This was my favourite spot in Galloway. A small track, surrounded by grasslands and dappled with pools of water, led you out into open marshland with views extending in all directions. Beside me in the distance, Wigtown's soft green-brown coastline fell gently into the blue bay, which sparkled with flashes of brilliant, bright light. A wetlands bird sanctuary also resided there and the cacophony of chirps travelled across the open space through the crystal-clean air. Far in front of me, there was a range of mountains. The largest and closest was Cairnsmore, which I was told shone like a green emerald in summer but browned in winter, and was often topped white with snow.

I followed the track to the middle of the marsh where a small stone monument stood, sinking into the earth below. Carved into the stone were the words: "This is the site of the Martyr's stake." It, and I, would often share the solitary spot in the enormousness of the landscape. The only other visitors there, on most days, were the cows, which grazed on the salt marsh's rich sea minerals.

In the dusk light, a couple of stars twinkled above and I could still see shadows of birds descending into the tall grasses. There was space here, and softness. Beyond the stone statue, purple hills bled into the sky and my ears filled with the wind, with distant birdcalls and the low rumble of cows. I had to fight the urge to cry. The light was growing dim and I knew it was time to go back. Euan, if he had noticed I was gone by now, would be wondering where I was. I closed my eyes, not to say, but to feel a goodbye, then picked my way back along the track towards Wigtown.

When I entered the kitchen, Euan was busily making dinner. The smell of cooking sausages and warm bread was intoxicating. He bent over the oven and pulled out a tray.

"Have you ever had toad-in-the-hole?" he asked without turning around. He didn't ask where I had been or why I had disappeared.

"No." I said. "It smells good though."

Euan had already eaten, but he told me to sit at the table and placed a plate before me. toad-in-the-hole looked like a doughy popover with a plump sausage in the middle, covered in gravy.

"It's pretty disgusting. You don't have to eat it."

I took a bite. The flavours were salty and rich and the texture was addictive – the juicy sausage burst in my mouth as the batter melted away.

"Oh my God, this is delicious."

Euan smiled and started cleaning the dishes while I ate. I wished he would sit down and keep me company, but an awkward silence had descended between us again. I wasn't sure what the dinner meant, whether he was sad I was leaving, or thanking me for helping in the festival, but it was certainly a gesture. toad-in-the-hole had been an undertaking, and I could see evidence of his effort – mixing bowls and pans stacked in the sink.

I was feeling so sad: sad that this was to be my last dinner in the big country kitchen, and sad that Euan seemed so distant. The moment I cleared my plate, Euan said that he wanted to show me something.

We walked in silence out into the dark. Euan brought a flash light, and we made our way behind the stone houses, along Wigtown's empty streets and up a path. A breeze lightly touched my face. I looked up to see bats overhead. They were like elegant dive-bombers, and some got so close that I could feel the air from their wings brush past. Every time that happened I would jump and I could hear Euan's muffled laugh.

"They have very good sonar," he said. "Don't worry, they'll get close but they won't touch you."

We reached the crest of the hill and surveyed the view beyond – of Wigtown, its houses and streetlights twinkling in the dark. Behind the town was the sea, lit only by the half-moon, which hung bright in the sky.

"I love Wigtown," I said softly. I felt a lump in my throat. "I really love it here. I think it's the most beautiful place in the world."

Euan was quiet for a moment. "I'm glad you think so." He said it in a tone that was deeply sincere.

Another silence descended, and after lingering for a moment, we turned back towards home. My head was now swimming in confusion. Was that as romantic as it felt? It could have easily been Euan just being nice on my last night. He was so kind, to everyone, it was difficult to tell whether he would have treated another person who had come to stay any differently. When we returned, Euan made some excuse that he was going out to the garden, and I didn't see him for the rest of the evening.

I stayed up much of the night writing thank-you letters. I had bought cards for Eve, Laura, Euan and his parents and found myself facing blank pages, unsure of what to write. I could embrace my inner American and as Euan teased, "talk about my feelings all the time", or I could write a short, heartfelt thank-you. I decided on something in between, and by 3am, I had finished them all. I still wasn't tired so I sat looking around the bedroom, blinking slowly, trying to capture an exact mental picture for my memory. I never wanted to forget a single inch of The Bookshop.

The next morning, at the airport, I thought my heart would split in two. I felt physically ill as Euan helped me with my luggage to the boarding gate. The long car ride had been in complete silence, as had our seemingly longer ascent to the top of the airport escalator, beyond which visitors were not allowed. He handed me my bags and shoved his hands in his pockets.

"Thank you for everything, Euan. This has been…" I trailed off as he interrupted me.

"No, thank you for coming." Euan stood in the airport's electric light, looking as tall and alone as the Martyr's Stake. His curls, brown jacket and sloping shoulders felt as familiar to me now as my own reflection.

Without thinking, I gave him a hug. Moving through the embarrassment, I leaned in. I could smell his cologne, and for a moment I felt him return the embrace, before his arms, as quickly as they had wrapped around me, retracted and dropped back at his sides.

Without looking up, I grabbed my things and turned, heading down the terminal. I did not allow myself to glance back to see if he was still there, watching me go.

Chapter 19

"The beauty of things was born before eyes and sufficient to itself; the heartbreaking beauty will remain when there is no heart to break for it." – Robinson Jeffers, CREDO: *Poetry section, gallery, right of the fireplace.*

A plane, once airborne, flies at an average speed of 480 kilometres per hour. I could feel myself being hurled through space, every atom silently protesting at the growing separation between myself and Wigtown. No matter how much my will tried to turn the plane around, I was caught in my own velocity, heading towards California, trading the Galloway hills back for the Hollywood hills. The farther we flew over the ocean, the more vivid the image of Euan standing alone at the airport became, while Wigtown and moments from the festival flashed through my mind, and broke my heart.

Chapter 20

"Coming back to where you started is not the same as never leaving." – Terry Pratchett, A Hat Full of Sky: *Fiction section, hardbacks, under P.*

It was hot in Los Angeles. The studio hadn't been aired in a month, and the stale smell of dust and heat was dizzying. I dropped my bags and flung myself on my bed. Little tan hairs clung to the brown duvet cover. The dogs had obviously been in here, enjoying my studio as their vacation pad while I was away.

Otherwise, everything was as I had left it. The shades were still drawn, my closet, half opened, spilled out with a pile of clothes that I had decided not to take on my journey. My desk, sofa and television were in the exact position I had left them a month earlier. Everything sat in an eerie stillness. I wanted to feel a sense of calm and belonging on returning home, but I did not.

I checked my phone messages, expecting after a month to find it full. To my surprise, there were only four voicemails. One was from Rose, insisting that I call her when I returned. One was from Josh to say he missed me, and another from my parents, wishing me a safe return. The last was from my boss.

"Hi there Jessica" he said, in a friendly but concerned tone, "I know you're on holiday, hope you're having fun.

Please call as soon as you return. I need to talk with you."
My heart flipped. His voice sounded urgent. "All sorts of
shifting going on here. Not sure how things will pan out
but please know I'm doing everything I can."

That was it? His message was vague and I wasn't sure if
I wanted to hear how "things panned out" but with shaky
hands I quickly sat up and called him. Part of me hoped he
wouldn't pick up the phone.

He was usually away at meetings and I prepared myself
to leave a voicemail. Unfortunately, on this rare occasion,
I had "good timing" and he answered.

"Hi, Jessica," he said. "Welcome back."

"Thanks. It's good to be home. I literally just walked
through the door." My heart was pounding so loud I
wondered if he could hear it through the phone. "I have to
say, your message left me a little concerned."

He took a deep breath in, slow and deliberate. "Yes,
there have been some changes while you were away.
Budget cuts, unfortunately."

"It sounded like that from your message." We weren't
getting anywhere. "So what does this mean?"

"Well, there are many changes. Right now I'm trying
to get you on as a contractor," he said, hiding a bad kind of
change in a nicely structured sentence.

"Oh." My head fell into my heads. "What exactly does
that mean?"

"We'll try to hire you back directly," he said, "not
through a consulting company. It's the best we can do,
I'm afraid. It was impossible to keep you on in the same
capacity. Many of your colleagues are gone."

"Gone?" The realisation that I was being laid off
sidelined my sensations. I couldn't feel my legs and my
mouth went dry. I had never been fired before. "What

about all my projects? And Jay? We're halfway through producing his story." It felt like someone was breaking up with me.

"So we'll be in touch soon," he continued. "View it as a transition. NASA is doing everything it can to bring you on board directly."

"Oh." I wanted to believe him. "Thanks. When should I expect to hear from you?"

"Jessica, I'm late for a meeting. I'll be in touch soon." He was getting impatient. "We're trying our best for you. Okay?"

"Great. Sure, okay."

He hung up the phone.

I curled up on my side, thinking. Was this a dream? Perhaps I'd wake up to find myself still in Euan's guest room, with the cows and the dawn chorus gently rousing me awake.

I walked over to the window and lifted up the shades. The blinding Los Angeles sun poured in, a glaring reminder of how far, in truth, I was from Wigtown. I noticed that in the bleached light the tropical garden outside looked frozen in time. Leafy, plastic-looking plants curled up trellises and big colourful flowers grew in wild abundance. It was just like when I had left it, as if Wigtown had never happened. I craned my neck, and past the tree-covered Silver Lake hills, I could see the Hollywood sign. This image, which had once filled me with a sense of purpose and destiny now made me shrink back into the shadow of my studio.

I had just been laid off. That had really happened. NASA had just fired me. I felt sick. I had loved my job. I comforted myself by replaying the part of the conversation where he said I'd be rehired. He wanted me there.

It wasn't me; it was the budget cuts. I walked around my silent studio apartment feeling restless and dissatisfied.

In the pauses between my thoughts, Euan came to mind. It was evening in Wigtown and he would be closing the shop. After walking up the steps to the kitchen, he'd cook dinner while listing to Radio 4. As things simmered, he would step out into the garden, enjoying the cool evening sea breeze. I smiled. For an instant I felt transported.

Chapter 21

"But in her web she still delights
To weave the mirror's magic sights,
For often thro' the silent nights
A funeral, with plumes and lights,
And music, went to Camelot:
Or when the moon was overhead,
Came two young lovers lately wed;
'I'm half-sick of shadows' said,
The Lady of Shalott."
– Alfred Lord Tennyson, THE LADY OF SHALOTT:
Poetry section, right of the fireplace.

Euan called me the next morning. His voice sounded distorted over the phone, and I sat up in bed, straining to hear through the bad connection. My heart wanted to burst when I heard him say his familiar "Good morning, Fox." Part of me had expected never to hear from him again, and now, here I was, being woken up by his deep voice.

"How are you doing?" he asked. I shrugged, as if he could see me.

"I miss Wigtown." Instead of feeling the cool air of his guest bedroom, I was now sitting bleary-eyed in my hot studio apartment.

"Just Wigtown?"

"And you, of course."

"Me too, Fox." It didn't matter how delayed the connection was, those three words thrilled me to my fingertips.

"Really?"

"Yeah, after you left I sat in the van in a numb daze. I just couldn't believe you were gone."

It was my turn to say, "Me too." I leaned back into my pillows, my heart quickening. This way of speaking to each other was new – it was like the distance made it okay for Blake's "doors of perception" to open.

The opportunity for us to linger in the wonderfully open doorway lasted only a moment or two, however. It was treading too close to the dangerously American realm of feelings, and Euan quickly turned the conversation over to other things, like work and Wigtown.

"There were loud, annoying American customers in the shop today," he lamented. "Uncivilised lot, you are, wasting perfectly good tea by dumping it into the harbour."

I got out of bed and began to dress, holding the phone awkwardly as I slipped a T-shirt over my head. I looked at my reflection, horrified to see dark jet-lag circles under my eyes. I had a production meeting in an hour with the producer for my company's new short in West Hollywood. It was at a café that had outdoor seating and if I was lucky, we'd sit in the sun so I could hide my exhausted face behind my sunglasses the whole time.

Euan's deep voice continued in the background as I got ready. I hurried around the studio, trying to collect my things and brush my teeth without interrupting the conversation. I didn't want this phone call to end, but I was going to be late, so when the easy banter began to run dry, I offered a segway.

"Well, this is probably a costly phone call," I apologised.

"Yeah, my phone card is almost gone," he said. There was an awkward pause before a quick goodbye. My heart sank as he hung up the phone. I had to get it through my stubborn head that Euan was just being nice because that's who he is. He might miss me today, but it wouldn't last.

Down the hill from my studio, I pulled out onto thick traffic on West Sunset Boulevard. My car baked as I inched forward. I hadn't missed this part of Los Angeles. The sun poured in, burning my pale, exposed arms. There was no shade, nowhere to hide.

Finally, the traffic loosened and I moved ahead in the queue. I looked out of the window, and instead of Belted Galloways, there were belted Hipsters mingling on the sidewalks. Wigtown's charming stone cottages had been replaced by funky wooden houses, stucco apartment buildings and parking lots, and where there had been an expanse of marshland and sea, there now was a sea of cars and endless highways.

My producer sat across from me, looking disappointed. He wasn't happy and drummed his finger on the table in staccatos of disapproval. A short film I had been making, and he had invested in, was behind schedule in Boston. We were experimenting with a new way of doing animation, somewhere between stop motion and modern animation, and it was exciting, but the learning curve was an unpredictably painstakingly slow process. My collaborators had had to take other jobs in the meantime as we raised more funds.

The producer and I sat under a large red umbrella, our lunch of Caesar salads half finished. I had reluctantly taken off my sunglasses and felt self-conscious, worried that I looked as much of a mess as I felt. He wasn't angry, which made it worse. He kept on repeating that he was concerned. For my sake, he said, he thought we should finish it soon.

"Your career has a momentum," he waved for the check. "Don't kill it. You're too talented to pull some bookshop stunt and run away to Scotland."

"I wasn't running away, it was a vacation."

"Whatever. This is the time to push yourself." He paid for the lunch, ignoring my protests. "I believe in you, you're a brilliant director. The problem is *you* don't believe in you."

I started to get angry, perhaps because he was right. "I'm trying as hard as I can to move things forward."

He waved his hand in the air, as if banishing my excuses. "Look, you're the director. Ultimately the responsibility rests on you. If you can't finish it, let me know."

The producer's cell phone rang. When he took the call, I knew it was a cue for me to leave. I stood, slowly, feeling both embarrassed and unsettled. My *shpilkus* had returned.

Every year or two, since graduating from college, I had moved to a different city. Before LA I had lived in Boston, New York, Hawai'i, Pennsylvania and Prague and each move was motivated by a sense of growing dissatisfaction. My grandmother would call it *shpilkus*, a Yiddish word for restlessness. The word has an onomatopoeic quality to it, literally meaning "sitting on pins", and includes the idea of restlessness in both a physical and emotional sense. As strange as it sounds, Wigtown, the town of 1,000 people and sixteen bookshops, in rural Galloway, was one of the first places in which my *shpilkus* had disappeared. In fact, it had become such a part of me that it wasn't until now, on feeling my *shpilkus* return, that I was aware that it had been gone at all.

It was dusk as I turned onto my flower-covered street. The sky was full of silvery pinks and purples, another of the gorgeous Los Angeles sunsets that ironically came from the polluted clouds of smog that hung over the city. My head filled with my producer's words, "This is the time to push yourself… the problem is *you* don't believe in you."

He was right but the more I tried to immerse myself in the film, the more I could not. I had thought it was because of my break-up with Grant that I had been distracted. Now, however, I was still having a hard time and I was distracted for another reason. Somewhere, in the deep, mysterious caverns of my heart, where I would once have felt fulfilment, I felt nothing and it made me panic. For my whole life I had wanted to be a director and make films, but now, instead of grabbing this opportunity, all I saw before me was a lonely road and I wanted to run far from it.

I parked my car, and walked up the hill towards my studio. Where had the pieces of me gone that were once so integral to my personality? My thirst for ambition, my compulsive drive had lost their motor and I felt adrift. Life in the fairy realm of Los Angeles may have been the same, but I was not.

Chapter 22

"You are that vast thing that you see far, far off with great telescopes." – Alan Watts, TAO OF PHILOSOPHY: *Philosophy section, last bookshelf in the Scottish Room.*

"Hello, Jessica?" My boss at NASA's voice sounded distant on the phone. "Did I wake you?"

"No, not at all," I said and quickly shot up in bed. He had. It was eight in the morning. My alarm clock was switched off.

Ever since I had returned from Wigtown, my life had become an unstructured mess. All the puzzle pieces, which had fitted so neatly before and that I had worked so hard to achieve, were scattered or lost. I had no job, no sense of purpose and was getting up later and later. I enjoyed my empty afternoons, filling my time with lunch dates and friends. For someone who had never taken a holiday before Wigtown, I was moving quite effortlessly into a life that resembled early retirement. In my more productive hours, I played my banjo and forced myself to work on the short film, but a nagging feeling lingered in the background – a growing discomfort with my directionless spirit. If I were to have given it a voice, it would have croaked, "You are lost."

I had tried to put some order back in the chaos. First, I thought I needed to get back my body, which had grown

plump and unfit after a gluttonous yet informative exploration of Scotland's confectionery offerings. So every
morning when I woke up, the sun already hot and bright
in the hazy Los Angeles sky, I stepped out into my private
garden, the two dogs waiting patiently by my door, and
practiced yoga while they ran around my heels. Then I
made green tea and showered, taking time to do my hair
and make-up. But the routine did little to settle my sense
of impending entropy.

Euan had not only called the first morning I had
returned, but the morning after that, and the morning
after that, until we were talking every day, at the same
time, over our computers. It had become a daily ritual.
After meeting Rose at Greenblats, or Josh for tea, I'd rush
home in time to see Euan waiting for me on my computer.
All my friends were curious about him, and my sense of
curiosity was growing, too. Rose declared I was going to
abandon her and go to Scotland "to have loads of babies
with a Sean Connery lookalike". Josh was more silent on
the issue, changing the subject any time my conversation
came round to Euan or Wigtown.

There had been nothing inherently romantic about
my conversations with Euan at first. We'd discuss music,
movies, the Wigtown gossip and stories from our day –
even things as benign as the weather. But however casual,
each call had ended with "I miss you", which had grown
more intense with every conversation. "I really miss you"
had turned into "I really really miss you". I was becoming
attached. And it worried me. Our Skype sessions provided
the only structure to my day and although I looked forward
to chatting with him, I always felt more alone afterwards.

"I can call back at another time," my boss suggested,
interrupting the pause on the phone. I became concerned

that he could hear sleep in my voice. I would have to speak loudly and clearly to compensate.

"No, please. Right now is perfectly fine." I looked around for a pen. I don't know why, but it made me feel more prepared. Who knows, I might have to take notes. "Do you have any news for me?"

On my bedside table rested my favourite pen and a card with the name "Mark" and a number. My heart sank. I forgot I had made plans to go out tonight – part of a bid to bring a bit of romance into my life as a solution to my waning inspiration. In theory this had seemed promising, but in reality it was a disaster. I always came home feeling more alone than when I had left, Euan somehow at the forefront of my mind.

I had also tried filling my days with all the things I had once loved to do in Los Angeles. It was as if I thought that the beauty of the Getty Museum or the stillness of Griffith Park could erase my longing for Galloway, but not even a visit to the drive-through deliciousness of In and Out Burger could replace the taste I had developed for Wigtown.

Tonight, I decided, I would have to cancel with Mark because I needed to be home for Euan's Skype call. I could see in myself that I was starting to arrange my life around Euan but I didn't care. I moved Mark's card away and reached for the pen. I had my pen. I felt prepared.

"Things are so tight here, you know." I heard my boss echoing. "So we've moved you on as a contractor."

"Oh, that's good news," I said, writing down contractor.

My boss coughed. I could tell he was nervous. "Look, we've tried our best to keep you on, we really have. We'll wait a couple of months, and try again."

Contracting was obviously a nice way of saying laid off – again. My heart sunk. "Thank you" was all I could muster. My mouth was dry. I put the pen down. "Who should I get in touch with about contracting?"

My boss cleared his throat. "I'm your contact. I'll be in touch about the contracting."

"Great." It didn't feel great, and I heard him quickly hang up the phone.

So that was that. What about Jay's project? What about my documentary on the rocket kids? I could feel my face flushing. They didn't want me. What about my ideas for linking the inner world with the outer cosmos? What about improvisation as the key to innovation and communication? All my ambitions were evaporating as quickly as my boss had said "contractor".

So here I was, free to move in whatever direction I chose, but instead of spreading my wings and enjoying the soaring sensation, I felt glued to one point like an anchor: self-doubt. They didn't want me... I felt heavy with the thought. My pride was hurt. I had never failed at a job before.

Late in the evening, I lit some candles and set up my computer on the kitchen counter. I had been looking forward to my chat with Euan all day, especially given my rough morning. He had promised to stay up late tonight for an extra-long Skype session, and I was right on time, with three minutes to spare.

I heard the familiar whirring sounds as I started Skype. In bubble letters appeared the words "just breathe". Skype was better than my yoga teacher. As soon as the application opened, I heard it ringing and my heart leapt. Euan was anxious to speak with me? No. It was my parents.

Reluctantly, I clicked the green button, afraid if I missed their phone call they would be worried. In truth,

Jewish parents trump any screenwriter with the lengths to which their imagination will go. The ideas that come to their mind as to why I'm either not there or not picking up the phone would put any blockbuster to shame.

A screen popped up and two beaming faces appeared before me. My father was wearing his Pi shirt and my mom's beautiful eyes looked at me from behind her thin-rimmed reading glasses with concern. She could always tell immediately when something was wrong. We said our hellos and I reluctantly told them the news about NASA.

"It's their loss," my mother said. I wished I felt that way.

"Don't shake your head, Jessica. Your mother is right." My father's voice continued. I was distracted. In the left-hand column on Skype, I could see all the people online and Euan wasn't there. My eyes flickered towards the clock. It was already 5pm, 1am for him. He was an hour late. It was unlike him.

"It must be getting hard for them to justify hiring a storyteller," my father went on. "I wouldn't take it personally."

"She looks tired, Arthur. We should let her go." My mom said suddenly aware I wasn't paying attention. I instantly felt bad. My parents, two of the kindest people in the world, were trying to support me and calm my fears and I was mentally absent for most of the conversation. What was worse was that they could tell.

All I could manage was a half-hearted "Thanks, Mom, thanks, Dad," and I clicked "end" to our Skype conversation. The screen went blank.

I sat back into my chair, dejected. Two thoughts flashed across my mind simultaneously. I was a terrible daughter, and Euan hadn't showed up. I waited two more hours online, patiently sitting by my computer, then finally gave up.

The next day I had no emails from Euan, or calls. Another day passed and still nothing. Rose took me out to lunch at Greenblats and we sat in our usual booth, chatting. My hands kept on checking my phone, counting the hours until it would be too late to hear from him. I struggled to stay present through the conversation, my mind drifting to where Euan could be.

"What's wrong with you?" Rose's voice was offended.

"I'm heartbroken." I had meant it to be a joke but my eyes watered as I said it.

"That cake does look ridiculously good." Rose looked down as a massive piece of gooey, icing-covered chocolate cake was placed before us.

We laughed. "No, it's not the cake... I just miss Wigtown, I guess."

"Uh huh. Wigtown." Rose smiled. "How's Euan?"

I shrugged. "I haven't heard from him in a while."

"Do you love him?" Rose sipped on her soda, her blue eyes piercing through me.

"What?"

"You heard me."

"Well, it's not that. I... you think you already know the answer to that, don't you?" I crossed my arms, feigning shock at her audacity.

Rose smiled, then quickly changed the subject.

My usual quip to people that "we are always our own blind spot" echoed in my head. It was a phrase I liked to repeat when counselling friends, but I stupidly never applied it to myself, which proved the statement all the more. Like Narcissus, we all look into a blurry mirror of our own watery reflection, but rarely wonder why others seem clearer to us than we do to ourselves.

I did. I loved Euan. Shit.

"Well, why don't you get a calling card and call him?" Rose said.

"I guess I could."

"Stop feeling sorry for yourself and eat the chocolate cake instead. It's your fault I ordered it anyway." She was a woman of feeling, but also of action. I dipped into the chocolate cake and felt inspired.

At home, I took the calling card out of the bag and opened its plastic seal. What if he doesn't want to speak to me again? If he wanted to talk perhaps he would have called.

I sat on the edge of my bed, my stomach full of chocolate cake and butterflies, and nervously typed in his number. It rang twice, then a familiar baritone BBC accent answered. "Hello?"

My heart was pounding a mile a minute. "Hi, it's Jessica." I felt unsure.

Suddenly there was a burst of relief from the other end. "I have been trying to get in touch with you for days. I thought you were cross with me, that I had done something wrong."

Euan explained that Skype had been blocked, and his emails were being sent back. He'd tried my phone but it sounded out of service.

"I couldn't get in touch with you. I thought I'd lost you." He was stumbling to get the words out. "I love you."

"I love you, too."

There was a pause.

"I can come back, you know." I couldn't believe the words that were tumbling out of my mouth.

"Really?"

I tried to sound casual but my heart was racing. "We could do it for a month or two, see how it goes?"

"What about directing, your work?"

"I can make films from anywhere."

It was as if I could hear Euan smiling. "You've seen Wigtown at its best, you know. It gets deadly quiet in the winter."

"That's okay. I like quiet."

"It's a small town. You might get bored."

"I won't get bored. Euan, I don't want famous guests or exciting parties. I want to be with you."

Chapter 23

"...His heart skipped a beat involuntarily. In his 38 years on Earth Jack Theery had never felt such a sensation like that one. Later, when re-telling the story, he would attribute it to panic. However, you (and I) know better. It is commonly understood that only two sensations can stop the heart: fear and love. Jack, in that instant, felt both." – THE THEERY'S, GREEN SERIES, BOOK 1: *Children's section, out of stock.*

A knock on the door woke me. I had fallen asleep again, hitting the snooze button each time the alarm went off. My clock was useless on days like these, where I had nowhere to be and no reason for getting out of bed.

Through my sleepy eyes I could see a figure waiting patiently outside my front door. I slipped on a robe and opened it to see my landlord holding out a package.

"Here" – he quickly put it in my arms – "this just arrived. Someone must like you," and with that he headed back up the stairs.

The package was heavy and I got a jolt of excitement when I saw the return address: "The Bookshop".

The package slid easily from my arms onto the table and without hesitation I ripped the tape off. It was full of things. Euan had sent British films he thought I'd like: *Withnail and I*, *A Matter of Life and Death* and *Gregory's Girl*. Also, stuffed into the box were pictures of the town, books and my favourite sweets: Yorkie Bars, Maltesers and Jelly Babies. It was a proper Wigtown care package.

The jewel in this treasure trove, however, was a small clear box. In it there was an iPod and a note: "I hope you enjoy the treats. I think about you all the time – I put some songs on this that I thought you would like."

As I went to make some tea, I was still holding Euan's note in my hand. My gaze shifted over to the large bulletin board that was hanging above my desk. On it I had images, which inspired me, tokens from my tour with the Dresden Dolls, past productions and quotes. A yellow sticky note caught my attention. It was scrawled with my best friend Cole's handwriting, a quick note he had written and slid under my door when we lived together in New York. "Fox, remember," he had said, "you must do the thing you think you cannot do… love Eleanor Roosevelt."

Thank you Mrs. Roosevelt. I was going to do it; I was going to dive into Nietzsche's eternal yea and, like Joseph Campbell, say "yea to it all". I was going to return to Wigtown.

First, though, I had to think. If I was going to go back to Scotland, I would need time to move out of my apartment, move my car back east and to visit my family. Adrenaline started flowing through me. The thought of leaving Los Angeles thrilled me with possibilities. It was time to go. Tennyson's "untravell'd world whose margin fades/For ever and ever when I move" loomed before me and I felt the familiar fresh excitement of impending adventure.

However, it was not so much an untravell'd world to which I would be returning. I knew Galloway and Wigtown well enough, but it was the person to whom I was returning that held the question marks. Adventuring across different countries was one thing, but traversing the landscape of relationships was territory that terrified me.

"You set the wheels in motion," I heard a voice say. "Don't you want to see where they take you?" Melville was back, sitting on my living-room sofa, looking uncomfortably out of place. Oddly enough, he was dripping wet, his coat and boots creating what I imagined to be a massive puddle on the floor. He didn't look the least bit apologetic.

"Yes, of course," I said, watching him carelessly fling a piece of seaweed off his shoulder. "But I never really saw my life going in this direction. It's just…"

"Unplanned?" Melville interrupted me, "Now that's a true adventure."

"I thought you were only supposed to help me with my writing."

Melville waved his hand. "It's all connected."

A dog's distant barking disturbed my thoughts. All my senses felt incredibly sharp and aware.

I had two choices looming before me: buy a return ticket to Wigtown or consider my adventure with Wigtown and Euan over – complete and perfect unto itself – and move on.

Achievement or love, plans or adventure, my films or the unknown. I had been searching for a way to change the "or" to "and".

On the computer screen, I opened up a travel website and prices and dates for flights quickly appeared. Had I made the decision? Surely, yes. This was no time for self-doubt. Like Hamlet, I could theorise my whole life, caught in the whirlpool of my mind, and never act. Instead, for once I would trust the intelligence of the flow of impulses and instinct. Then again, was I mad? I clicked to the next month, November. The day after Thanksgiving, it was uncharacteristically cheap to fly to Scotland. The Day After Thanksgiving. I liked the sound of it. There was something symbolic about leaving the day after my whole family would be gathered together, like a natural send-off.

It also was a month away, giving me ample time to give up my apartment, sell my things and say a proper goodbye to Los Angeles. My eyes flickered away from the computer and scanned my studio. I had been so lucky to find this place, was I really going to give it up that easily? A pang of attachment sprang up in my heart – a feeling I was not used to. Los Angeles had been extremely good to me. While many have had their hearts broken in LA, it was the place that had healed mine – I had had my first taste of true freedom here, my self-confidence had been transformed, I'd made new friends, had a wonderful job and weather and food that made my heart sing. It was a city that had spoken to my self and my needs at that time, but I had changed, and now my outer world needed to change, too.

My arrow key moved over the date November 28th, and I clicked "purchase ticket".

I called Euan immediately. He answered the phone and I couldn't tell if his voice was filled with tempered excitement or fear.

"So, does the Fox return?" he asked.

"Yes." It was almost a whisper.

Chapter 24

"When you're young, you think everything you do is disposable. You move from now to now, crumpling time up in your hands, tossing it away. You're your own speeding car. You think you can get rid of things, and people too – leave them behind. You don't yet know about the habit they have, of coming back." – Margaret Atwood, THE BLIND ASSASSIN: *Fiction section, middle shelf, left of the window.*

"Happy Birthday!" A chorus of voices filled the air. Through the dim lights of the Mexican Cantina, with its red painted walls and paper hangings, I could see the inebriated faces of Rose, Max, Josh, Spencer and Anna smiling at me. I looked at my dear friends, cheeks flushed and beaming, and felt incredibly happy. We hardly ever got together as a big group, but this was a rare occasion, and I told them it was the best birthday present I could have imagined.

There was a crashing sound from the left, and a waiter, carrying a large cake, stumbled out of the kitchen. Everyone began to sing and a Mariachi band gathered on one side of our table. The sound of guitar and castanets filled my ears and I felt dizzy from the copious amounts of sangria I had been drinking. This farewell meal had stretched into the late hours of the evening. My bags had been packed, my apartment was empty and I was leaving for Boston the next day. It was my birthday, my last night in Los Angeles, and I was determined to enjoy myself to the full.

A white cake set aglow with sparklers was placed before me. I laughed and tried to blow them out, but the sparks kept reigniting. Rose leaned over to help me, and Josh took a camera from across the table. I folded my arms to hide my burrito-filled belly and smiled for the picture. A white flash went off and we quickly plunged back into the dark redness of the restaurant.

I handed a sparkler to Anna and Spencer, two good friends whom I had met during my first weeks in LA, when I had lived with Rose in West Hollywood. "I'm going to miss you guys," I said, wondering why we didn't have more gatherings like this.

Max, a dear friend and screenwriter, leaned over across the table and filled my glass.

"Less talk of leaving, more drinking, Fox," he winked at me.

It had taken a while for me to build the confidence to tell people I was returning to Wigtown. I had kept it a secret at first, mostly because I hadn't wanted to deal with anyone's criticism. For days after talking with Euan, the choice to return had felt like soft tissue, easily bruised and vulnerable to even the hint of a raised eyebrow. But, though I had yet to develop a protective outer shell, I was exhilarated, like the lady on the flying trapeze, without a safety net — or trapeze for that matter. I was flying through the air.

The first person I had told – out of necessity – was my landlord, exactly a month before my birthday. The news had been met with an anticlimactic nonchalance. Typical Californian.

"Go, go, of course, you must go," he had said. Not even an eyebrow raised. I had found his encouragement rather insulting. Having gone through such a rigorous interview process to get the apartment, I had thought he would have been more upset to lose me. "What city are you going to again?"

"It's not a city. It's a town. Wigtown's small, less than 1,000 people."

He had looked at me with a hint of disgust. "What will you do there?"

"Write, make films. Enjoy myself."

My landlord hadn't looked convinced.

"I fell in love with it... and with someone." I sighed, relaxing into the truth.

He suddenly smiled. "Well, that's rad."

It had taken my landlord one day to find my replacement. When he appeared with a woman at my door, I had packed my books and clothing, and was waiting for Anna to come and take away my bed. It had been painful to see the lovely furniture that I had worked so hard to buy vanish piece by piece. I had built a castle and now, for some masochistic reason, I was taking it down brick by brick.

The woman was tall, with blonde hair, and had the vulnerable air of someone who had recently suffered a trauma. Her cowboy boots clicked against the hard wood floor as she stepped into my now empty home and I tried to see the studio through her fresh eyes. The white clean walls looked airy and open with half the furniture missing, and the garden appeared particularly dazzling in the late-afternoon light. My favourite candle was burning, filling the room with a warm, spicy scent.

"So where do you live now?" I asked, trying to make conversation.

"Venice Beach – long-term relationship gone very bad." Her hand swatted the air as if to brush the significance of it aside. "I haven't lived on my own for ages but this... I can't believe I found a place with a garden." Her eyes lit up as she faced me. "It's been my dream for ages now to have a place of my own with a little garden."

In that moment, all my fears about leaving Los Angeles and the apartment and venturing into the unknown melted The Hindu concept of Dharma came to mind, what I understood to mean that we each have a responsibility to follow our own path – unique to ourselves, our interests and talents – for by doing so we give the space and opportunity for others to do the same. This woman too had a vision of her perfect home and it was my studio. By leaving to follow my dream, I was making room for someone else to follow theirs. It reminded me of Schopenhauer's views on will and fate, for it all seemed to work together like some mysterious choreographed dance.

The following day, with my confidence renewed and my apartment released to someone else, I started telling people I was moving. The greatest test, I thought, would be telling my family. As the youngest, "the baby", I was typically hypersensitive and, whether I liked to admit it or not, still had the childish desire to earn my parents' approval. Perhaps that's why I had felt so at home in Los Angeles – a city filled with inner children who were still searching for applause.

I called my sister first, knowing breaking the news to her would be easier than telling my father and mother. My sister, who had supported my move across the US to Los Angeles, was equally encouraging about me following my heart now.

"I'll miss you Jess," she said.

"Well, don't worry." I awkwardly attempted to make it sound okay. "It won't be for ever."

She sighed. "You don't know that." In the background I could hear a child yelling. "Look, honey," my sister scolded. "The batteries are in the left drawer. I told you to wait until I'm off the phone with Aunt Jessy." The yelling continued. "Jessica, I have to go. I love you."

Without hesitating, I hung up and dialled my parents' number. As the phone rang, my trepidation grew. I was going to give my mom more sleepless nights worrying about me. They didn't deserve a child like me.

The moment I heard their cheerful voices, I blurted it out. "I'm going to return to Scotland for a while."

There was a pause.

"It sounds more massive than it is, I promise. I'll actually be just as far from you there as I am here."

"We want you to spread your wings, and go wherever you feel is best for you." My mom's voice, though showing calm restraint, wavered slightly.

"Your mother and I just want you to be happy." My father chimed in, not to be left out.

"That's most important," Mom added. Their silent concern shouldn't have surprised me or unnerved me; my parents had a history of being heroic in their parenting. On my first day out driving with my new licence, my mom had returned home to find me standing in front of my father's totalled car.

"What happened, are you all right?" she had asked, heading towards me.

I had nodded. "Someone rear-ended me."

Banging had rung loud from the car. My mom had looked around confused. "Where is your father?"

I stepped aside and pointed to the trunk. My father was inside, curled up with a small hammer, trying to undo the damage himself. My mom had burst out laughing. My father, infinitely understanding, had insisted I get in the car the same day, saying even if you fall off you get back on the horse.

From an early age my parents had balanced their love for me with giving me the increasing freedom that I desired. Growing up, I never had a curfew, as long as they knew where I was and I had taken my vitamins. The first for my mother and the latter for my father.

"Will you have access to vitamins over there?" my father continued.

"I'm not sure, Dad." I couldn't help smiling.

"If not let me know because I'll have to order you some…"

*

The Mariachi band finished and the restaurant burst into applause. I smiled, quickly bringing my attention back into the moment. My birthday was almost over, and I felt sad, as if a really good carnival ride was about to end. I was 26 years old. So far I had toured with a rock band, made a film, started a company and worked for NASA. I had also had a major, disastrous relationship, dated infrequently and was stubbornly alone. I was "no spring chicken" any more, as Rose would say. It was clear that I needed balance in my life, and in three weeks I would be moving across the ocean, not for my career, but in the hope of honouring my heart.

A slice of cake was placed before me. "I don't think I can eat anything else. I already have a food baby."

"No problem." Anna's fork scooped up a chunk of icing.

"Picture, please." Rose stood up and offered her iPhone to the waiter.

I tried to protest. "Couldn't we have taken this before I started eating?"

Everyone gathered around my side of the table. It had been just a few weeks ago that I had told my friends I was moving. What I had thought would be the easy part of this process surprised me as being the most difficult.

"I can't believe you're leaving me. You're never coming back," Rose said.

"Of course I'll be back."

Josh had wanted to come with me. "No, please, Josh."

"Why not?" Josh looked offended.

"Because this is about me going on my own." I felt mean but I needed to be firm.

"Okay, okay," he had said half-heartedly.

Max had also been reluctantly supportive. I had broken the news to Max on a visit to one of my favourite spots in LA, the Getty Museum. It had been a glorious day, bright blue sky, the off-white walls of the museum looking stark and regal. "What about your friend Max? Did you ever think of him? What about our films?" We retired to the shade, sitting on a bench, and he put his arm on my shoulder. "Well, I hope you have a nice time. Stay a week or two, or three, then come back to us."

Later Max undermined his air of disapproval by handing me a book about a man travelling to a bookshop. "I actually think it sounds like a great adventure, Fox."

By the time my birthday arrived, I had told so many people about my decision to return to Wigtown that it almost felt like there were two versions: the narrative that existed on the outside, shaped by others' concerns and opinions, and the one that existed inside, still pure and belonging only to my own hopes, desires and worries. Although I told people I could fulfil my film dream from anywhere, it did feel like I was stepping off the treadmill. What would become of my dream if I was no longer in LA? Also, Euan, for all intents and purposes, was a certified bachelor. He liked his own habitat, his own space, and I was a meteor, bursting into his world, intruding on his privacy.

We had reached the end of the evening and, to my great pleasure, there had been no talk of Wigtown. The night had been full of LA stories, inside jokes, copious food and a river of sangria. We left carnage on the table and stumbled out into the cool Californian night.

The restaurant was half a mile from my home and I decided to walk back alone. We said our goodnights and people piled into cabs. In my drowsy, tipsy haze as I watched my friends disappear one by one, it didn't feel like a goodbye. I was waiting for some kind of seismic shift, but there was not even the smallest tremor. It all felt quite normal, like I would see them next week.

I turned up Santa Monica Boulevard and walked along the empty sidewalk. The graffitied concrete walls behind me ignited intermittently as the bright headlights of cars passed by. My last night in Los Angeles and I was on foot. That morning, a cross-country service had come to pick up my Toyota and drive it to my parents' house on the East Coast. It was driven up a ramp and into a double-decker trailer, surrounded by other homeless cars. The man gave me a pink slip as a receipt and drove off, leaving me vehicle-less on the side of the road under the Hollywood sun. Seeing it go had been a big deal, as the car was the last vestige of my Californian lifestyle. It had been like losing an identity badge. I was no longer a Los Angelino.

Chapter 25

"Entropy isn't what it used to be." – Anonymous, GREATEST JOKES OF THE CENTURY, BOOK 2 by Thomas Shubnell: *Humour section, across from Children's section on the left.*

The serendipitous meeting of like-minded souls is like a star's birth – forces compel the gathering of elements and in the vastness of space, flakes of gold touch each other, compressed and heated, creating something new yet unaware of the organic serendipity of their meeting. My collection of particles had yet to travel anywhere, however, whether across the vastness of space or over the Atlantic Ocean to Wigtown. It was now November 23rd and, while Euan was busy with the shop, I was back in Lexington, caught in the madness of pre-Thanksgiving grocery shopping at the local Stop & Shop.

Stop & Shop – a once small, ordinary, fluorescent-lighted food chain – had grown massively over the years as my small town had changed from a typical quaint, historical New England village to a posh and wealthy suburb of Boston. Town gossip and friendly greetings still echoed between the many shelves and it was clear to me that despite the cosmetic changes, Stop & Shop's aisles remained the local hub of social networking

Overhead, paper turkeys hung from the ceiling and Britney Spears droned away in the background. As we passed four shelves dedicated solely to olives, a dizzying selection of fresh mozzarellas and a whole wing of organic produce, I smiled, thinking how different this was to shopping at Wigtown's Co-op.

Following closely behind my mother, I took on a teenager's slouched stance, avoiding the glances from familiar-looking, middle-aged faces. I didn't feel like seeing anyone I knew. Looking up the aisle as my mother put another bottle of apple juice in her cart, I realised I had, unwittingly, regressed back to my childhood.

Gertrude Stein, on returning to her childhood home only to find it had been demolished and replaced by a parking lot, resolved that "there is no there, there". I beg to differ. I had been sleeping in my childhood room, living with my parents, and even something as harmless as walking behind my mother in a grocery store was confusing my sense of adult identity. Everything – all current reminders of my adult life – were gone or packed in boxes. Even the warm glow of my Hollywood tan had disappeared. I was in some liminal time between the past and present, neither here nor there.

My mother and I pulled into the shortest of the long lines and I looked at the young cashier who couldn't have been more than fifteen years old. She smiled at me and suddenly I became conscious that I had a scowl plastered on my face. I quickly smiled back. I needed to relax.

There was nothing I could do about being back in Lexington. In fact Homer, if he existed, would think it appropriate that I had returned home before my next adventure – a symbolic rebirth. Perhaps I had to re-enter the cocoon of my childhood in order to start a new life.

Chapter 26

"I am an outlaw, not a hero. I never intended to rescue you.
We are our own dragons as well as our own heroes and we
have to rescue ourselves from ourselves." – Tom Robbins,
STILL LIFE WITH WOODPECKER: *Fiction section, front room,
hardbacks under R.*

G rant was shorter than I had remembered him. But
memories could turn mice into giants. It was the
night before Thanksgiving, and I was shivering. We were
standing in the cold outside a movie theatre on Tremont
Street right across from Boston Common.

"The movie was pretty awful," Grant said, shoving his
bare hands in his pockets.

I snuggled into my down coat to escape the wind. "I'm
glad we saw it though."

Then we stood in silence.

Just as in myth when a donor figure equips the hero with
exactly the right thing to make his adventure a success, I
had asked the people dearest to me to offer something,
whether it was a word, a bit of advice, an object, a wish
– anything that I could take along with me to Scotland. It
had meant a great deal to me to have these tokens.

Cole had given me a string of photos, a book of matches
and a letter sealed tight in an envelope with wax. I was to
open the letter on the plane, he had instructed, not before.

My best girlfriend, who lived in South Africa, had sent me a quote and a picture of steep cliffs and the shining sea. I also had Euan's iPod with all my favourite songs. I was well equipped now for the journey into the unknown.

Grant was part of this ritual, too, though he didn't know it. We had left things on a dramatic note: no ending, no goodbye, just a lingering discomfort. I wanted to make sure the balm of healing was covering all past wounds before entering a new relationship with Euan. From Grant, I wanted the gift of closure.

In non-metaphorical terms, it was I who had brought Grant a gift. As a late birthday present, I had bought him a book that he'd said he'd always wanted to read. After a year of no contact I had thought it would be a nice gesture.

In the chilly silence lingering between us, I reached into my backpack and took out his gift, wrapped in shiny gold foil. Grant took the package and looked at it suspiciously.

"It won't bite. Take it. Please. It's for your birthday."

"Thanks." Grant took it under his arm. He suddenly smiled at me with a familiar expression. "Do you need a ride?"

"Oh um..."

His eyebrows rose and he glanced towards his parked motorcycle. He playfully smacked me on the arm. I couldn't believe it. After all that we had been through...

"No, I've got to get back."

"For what?" His intense eyes flashed with hurt.

"It was really good to see you though." I was trying to make him feel better. "I hope all goes well at work. It would be fun to catch another movie some time." This was the man who had broken my heart. Why did I feel the need to be such a girl scout?

"Yeah, sure." Grant smiled and turned so quickly that I instinctively began walking in the opposite direction. My feelings were suddenly all over the place. I was about to dissect them when I realised that I was walking entirely the wrong way, up Tremont Street.

Reluctantly, I turned and I could see Grant a couple of yards ahead of me. I didn't want him to think I was following him so I walked slowly. He approached a trash can and I watched as he dumped my unopened gift into it. I was dumbstruck.

After all the heartbreak and deep talks and reconciliation, he would still sleep with me but he had absolutely no desire to be friends. A gong rang loud and clear. I had my closure.

*

The following day my parents presented me with their gift right before the Thanksgiving meal. It was wrapped in blue tissue paper and I asked if I could wait and open it on the plane.

"Of course," my mother said and patted my shoulder. Mixed into the strange cocktail of emotions that had been brewing ever since I returned to Boston was guilt. I felt like I was leaving my family, tossing aside my loved ones for more exotic shores. I watched as my mom disappeared into the kitchen.

We were at my brother-in-law's parents' house, a beautiful period home right by the sea north of Boston. It was the ideal setting for a Thanksgiving meal, and I helped my niece and nephew set the table. They were instructing me where to set the plates, but I was distracted, looking through the doorway of the dining room into the hall, where my sister, her new baby, her husband and my father were chatting. My sister looked up and caught my gaze, smiling.

Instead of taking the time this November to enjoy my family, I had been removed, totally self-absorbed, by my upcoming adventure to Scotland. I instantly regretted having been so distant and was surprised by my feelings of homesickness for people who were just a room away. Whether I was on my way to Wigtown or the many other places in which I have lived, I perpetually found myself in self-inflicted exile.

The dining table was overflowing with food. Dishes were changing hands quickly as the Thanksgiving feast piled onto people's plates and I tried to grab spoonfuls of everything as it passed. Sweet potatoes, cranberry sauce, turkey, stuffing, gravy and green beans made a delicious collage, each colour dynamic with the tones of autumn – oranges, reds, browns – and the aromas were intoxicating. I was on sensory overload. The adults were trying to have conversations over the shouts and screams of the children. My sister looked at me and was about to say something, but the baby started crying and she became distracted.

The weather outside matched the liveliness within, with rain hammering down onto the pavement and the wind whipping the shutters with a howling intensity. Over the rooftops I could see the fog-covered ocean, a dull grey streaked with white peaks of foam. The rain made me nervous. I had become more and more scared of flying over the years and I hoped it would be better weather tomorrow.

My gaze drifted from the window to the middle of the table, where I suddenly noticed a massive starfish decoration. I peered closer and found it wasn't a decoration at all, in fact, but a real petrified starfish. It must have been very old because it was large, as if it had been pulled from a Victorian zoologist's collection. I wasn't sure how it fitted into the theme of Thanksgiving, but it was delicate and majestic and held a mysterious quality. What a magnificent thing, I thought, and suddenly felt grateful. Grateful for my family, for this meal, for the rainswept evening, for the giant starfish in the middle of the table and for my new life, which would begin tomorrow.

Chapter 27

"He folded his fear into a perfect rose. He held it out in the palm of his hand. She took it from him and put it in her hair." - Arundhati Roy, THE GOD OF SMALL THINGS: *Fiction section, paperbacks, left of the window under, R.*

I had a dream. I was in a stagecoach speeding along a bumpy road. My companions sat in shadow as the sound of horses' hooves echoed through the night air. Gunshots fired. A woman in front of me leaned forward into the moonlight. She was young, ornately dressed and terrified. Taking off her earrings, she quickly put them in her mouth. The coach suddenly jolted to a stop and men were yelling.

A shadowy figure next to me crossed himself. "Depart... We have to depart," he whispered.

I felt dizzy. The coach walls disappeared and I found myself, blindfolded, being forced to walk down a path with the sounds of the forest all around me. A long cloak hung heavy on my shoulders and the nose of a pistol dug into my back. Suddenly the gun exploded with a large bang and a warm sensation spread over my shoulders and up my neck.

The sound of a gate announcement dragged me back into consciousness. My eyes opened and the pistol in my back revealed itself to be the arm of an airport bench, uncomfortably poking into my spine. I was at Dublin Airport, trying to get some rest before my connecting flight to Glasgow. Euan hadn't seen me in two months and though I felt like I had just travelled part way across the world, I didn't want to look like I had.

I slid off my backpack and gave my shoulders a rub. They were sore. I had thought that second time around, the journey would be easier. I had left from Boston after all, not Los Angeles, which already cut my travel time down by five hours. I was also stopping over in Dublin, a much more manageable airport than Heathrow. The plane, however, had had trouble as we tried to land because of the wind. We had rocked dramatically from side to side as we had descended. Suddenly there was a massive thud and we had slammed against the runway. Everyone screamed. I had grabbed the arm of the woman next to me, who'd looked anything but sympathetic, then pulled myself away, apologising. We had bounced back into the air and, as a wind current scooped under the wings, begun ascending quickly.

"Sorry about that folks," the Captain's voice had said calmly over the loudspeaker. "The wind is making it difficult to land, but we're turning back towards the airport now. Let's hope in this case, second time's a charm."

Everyone had laughed nervously. I hadn't. I had been close to tears.

At the departure gate I stretched my arms and slid on my backpack, checking the time. It was still dark out of the large windows of the airport, which added to the illusion that I was in travel purgatory. It could be any time and I could be in any place.

I bought myself breakfast and found someone with a phone. They politely told me, in a wonderful Dublin accent, that it was 5:20am. I still had time before my gate opened. In exactly three hours I would be standing in front of Euan. My stomach was surprisingly calm. I wasn't nervous yet, just deeply excited. After leaving Los Angeles, then moving to Boston, all I had wanted was to be standing still in front of Euan's sweetly pensive face.

Now that I was on my own – after the decision to come had been made and I had dealt with leaving family and friends – I felt so much more capable and whole in myself. Eating my croissant, wandering around Dublin Airport, I was one-hundred-per-cent confident that I had made the right decision. In this moment, there was nowhere else I wanted to be other than Scotland. I had followed my golden guide and it had indeed put me on the pollen path.

*

In a blink of an eye, I was approaching the security check-point at Glasgow Airport. The butterflies in my stomach were now very much awake. Over the shoulder of the security guard, I could see the exit doors, behind which Euan would be waiting.

Like a repeat of my first trip through Heathrow, they asked why I was visiting the country. I wanted to shout, "Because I am following my feelings." But instead I said quietly, "To visit my boyfriend."

"It seems like you were just here." The guard said, eyeing my passport suspiciously.

"I was, for a quick visit. This time I hope to stay longer."

The guard did not like this answer. "Do you have a return ticket with you?"

"No." My heart pounded. "I didn't know I'd need to show one at security. I hope to stay through Christmas."

The guard softened and stamped my passport. "Next time, you need one."

Relief ran through me. I was approved. I was through. I was walking towards the doors. They opened and I could see Euan.

I saw him before he saw me. Euan's curls bobbed above the crowded lobby, full of people waiting expectantly for their visitors to come through the doors. He was wearing his brown coat, holding what I thought were flowers. I began to run, dragging my suitcase behind me.

Euan suddenly saw me and his face lifted into a smile. He moved through the crowds until we were a couple of yards away from each other, then just one yard, then a couple of feet. My heart was thumping so loudly that I was convinced he could hear it. We stood awkwardly smiling at each other. The flowers in his hand revealed themselves to be his newspaper.

"Hello," I said. There was an awkward pause. I stared at him and he at me almost in disbelief. The last time I had seen Euan we were just friends and any evolution of that relationship to one of lovers had happened over a great distance apart. It was as if the waves in the air between us were retuning, finding a matching wavelength to connect two realities. All this was new – but wonderful. Suddenly, he grabbed my hand and I felt myself grabbing his; whatever calibration had suddenly occurred was now complete and the awkwardness melted away.

Euan wrapped his arms around me and we kissed. Every cell of my being aligned and, after so many weeks apart, I finally felt happy.

*

"How was the flight?" Euan held my suitcase in one hand and my hand in the other. It was still an unfamiliar feeling, his large hand in mine, but warm and perfect. I began to relax.

"It was good. Very bumpy," I said, suddenly nervous again. He was taller than I had remembered him. As his hand tightened around my own, I wondered how he could feel like a stranger and a dear friend all at the same time.

We headed towards the doors in silence and as they opened, I could see the familiar red van parked before us.

"Now I should tell you, we're not going straight home." Euan strode quickly through the airport parking lot. He smiled and looked at me intently through his glasses. "I thought we'd have a little adventure."

Chapter 28

"Neither in 'Snow White' nor in 'Cinderella' are we told about their life... living happily with their partner. These stories, while they take the heroine up to the threshold of true love, do not tell what personal growth is required for union with the beloved other..." – Bruno Bettelheim, THE USES OF ENCHANTMENT: *Psychology section, front room, middle shelf on the right.*

Euan had done better than flowers. He had planned a three-day whirlwind trip for me around the coast of west Scotland. Not wanting to give much away, he said we were going to one of the most stunning places on Scotland's western side, Glencoe, the seat of the MacDonald clan. From there we would head to a ferry and stay overnight on an island. On the way back we were to visit the birthplace of Robert Burns and the home of Sir Walter Scott.

Euan looked over at me to gauge my reaction.

"That sounds wonderful." I beamed and Euan, satisfied, looked back to the road. I was home. I was finally home. Though excited, my eyes fought to stay open. The van was warm and as it rumbled along, it rocked me into a drowsy hypnosis. The green fields stretching beyond my window faded in and out of grey as my eyelids drooped.

"Jessy, you had a long journey. It's okay, you should sleep." Euan patted his shoulder and I shifted up to lean on him, my head sat perfectly next to his collarbone. I quickly fell into a deep slumber. The last thing I remember was Euan's warm hand still holding mine.

When I woke, the scenery outside looked like a different world. The clouds were so heavy they touched down in places close to us, making it impossible to see beyond a couple of yards ahead. Every once in a while I would glimpse rust-coloured barren and bracken-covered moors. The bright-red van must have stood out in this neutral landscape like the ruby nose on Rudolph.

"Ah, she's awake." Euan smiled, and turned on Radio 4. He had been driving in silence this whole time to allow me to sleep. "I'm sorry it's such a crap day. You wouldn't know it but we're surrounded by highlands. This is Glencoe."

My eyes adjusted and rested on Euan. Any lingering notion that he felt like a stranger had dissolved. I looked at him closely, happily, enjoying the sensation of being completely in love.

Euan caught me staring. "What is it, you strange American?"

"I didn't dream you up. You're real. And I'm actually here, in Scotland."

Euan laughed. "Yes, unfortunately you are."

I smacked his arm. I wondered if any strangeness he might have felt had disappeared as well.

As night closed in and it grew dark, the van pulled into a small gravel drive. The fog was still thick but I could see the twinkling of lights coming from a massive stone house before us. Euan slid the van easily into a small parking lot and I quickly opened the door. After hours in the warm van, the cold night air that greeted me shocked me awake. Goosebumps rose on my skin. I hadn't expected it to be this cold. My breath appeared in great white puffs before me and, as I pulled my suitcase out of the van, I could hear the nearby sound of rushing water. In the dark, I had no sense of scale or distance, but by the way the sounds were echoing, it felt like we were in some kind of canyon.

I placed my suitcase on the ground and tried to grab Euan's as well. It wouldn't budge. Euan stood there impatiently as I fiddled in the dark. "Ah, I forgot about Fox help." He pushed past me and prised his old leather suitcase loose.

I made a face.

Soft orange light and warmth burst forth as we entered the foyer of the hotel. A stuffed bear, as tall as the ceiling, arched over me as I stepped in. As my eyes travelled along the walls, I felt I had stepped back in time. The small, Victorian reception hall was covered with stuffed exotic animals. A peacock stood shyly in the corner, near a hat rack, above which sat a squirrel. The faded ornate wallpaper acted as a backdrop for stag heads, mounted birds and paintings of hunts.

Euan approached the reception desk and rang a brass bell, around which a stuffed mongoose wrapped itself menacingly. He turned, and shook his head at my delighted expression.

"I thought you'd like it."

We spent the rest of the evening in the firelit pub, drinking beer and having dinner. Talk ranged from the history of Scotland, to movies, to friends. We were almost tripping over each other to discover how far our similarities went. I felt like I had known Euan all my life and was taken aback whenever we uncovered points of disagreement, as if such a thing couldn't be possible.

"I would never do that," I said, scooping up the last bits of sticky toffee pudding. I was surprised by how hungry I had been. After a full portion of Guinness pie, I had downed three beers and polished off an ice-cream-covered pudding on my own.

"Do what?" Euan asked, half drowsy now from the long drive and copious amounts of beer. He had been telling a story about a friend who had recently given her boyfriend an ultimatum about getting married.

"Well, I would never make a guy choose like that. It's highly unromantic," I said. My fingers pushed my plate away and I sat back, happily content. "I wouldn't want to have to force someone to marry me. They should want to on their own volition."

"But some men need a bit of a push," Euan said and quickly avoided eye contact. The conversation suddenly felt delicate, like I was holding an invisible bubble with a thin membrane, almost bursting with meaning. Was he giving me some kind of cloaked instruction? The beer and food were making me hazy, and I wasn't sure who we were talking about any more.

*

The following morning I woke up to someone in my bed. Having slept alone for the past couple of years, the surprise of finding a tattooed arm lying across me jolted me awake. It was light in the room, and quiet. I followed the arm to a muscular shoulder and a mop of curly hair chaotically spread across the pillow. There was a loud rumble from under the mass of curls. It was Euan, fast asleep.

We were a contrast in almost every aspect, from our age to our upbringing to our genealogy. The difference between his strong, light-haired, tattooed self and my slim frame, pale skin and dark hair pleased my senses. It felt new and exciting to wake up next to such a person. I slid up slowly against my pillows, so as to not to wake Euan, and my arms were now exposed to the cold bedroom air. It was freezing and I wondered how early it was. I looked at the clock, which rested on a table on Euan's side. It was just a couple of minutes after 7am.

Standing at the window across from our bed, I gently pulled back the curtains. The view took my breath away. What the fog and darkness had cloaked the previous night was the most spectacular vista of the Highlands. They were right in front of us, like a sheer wall of steep rock and craggy waterfalls, topped with snow and clouds. The scale was dizzying. I could see four early-morning hikers half way up Glencoe right in front of me, no bigger than ants. They would have faded into the side of the mountain altogether if it weren't for their brightly coloured parkas.

My entire body was buzzing. I could imagine these highlands would affect people in one of two ways. Either you would feel dwarfed, crushed by the sheer magnitude of size and drained of all energy while looking at the fortress of nature all around you. It would be enough to make someone feel insignificant, and caged in. Or you would feel invigorated by the challenge to conquer the seemingly impenetrable dominance of Glencoe, each sheer face a red flag to a bull, a challenge set by nature saying, "Come on, human, show me your spirit." The effect on me was the latter, and being in such a dramatic environment almost gave me a physical high.

I whirled around and jumped on top of Euan. "Wake up, come on, we have things to see."

Euan moaned and wrapped me in his arms. "Calm down, Jessy." I could see he was smiling.

After a day of hiking up a waterfall and finding the hidden valley – an opening between a cluster of highlands where the MacDonald clan would hide cattle – we left Glencoe for the ferry.

The ferry arrived on the Isle of Mull just before twilight, and we drove along its enchanting one-lane roads to the other side of the island before it got dark. Because it was late autumn, the trees were bare and the landscape was shadowy in tones of black, grey and brown. It reminded me of something out of a fairy tale, with twisting knotted trees and copper hills, a slumbering land, waiting for a hero to come and whisper the words to wake it up.

For half the drive, we had an extra passenger, a blonde hitch-hiker Euan had picked up as we embarked from the ferry. It had annoyed me that our romantic solitude had been interrupted, especially by an attractive young blonde. I couldn't fault Euan's kindness, however, so I said nothing but seethed quietly.

We had stopped at a deserted sandy beach to stretch our legs, and I had drunk in the endless rocky coves, grey water and isolation of the Isle of Mull. The blonde woman, who had gone off to have a joint, had returned to talk non-stop for the next 40 minutes. We listened to her wax lyrical about Reiki healing and how she could tell someone's soul by the aura of colour around their head. I had started to like her more because I could see how annoyed Euan was becoming.

"Oh you know, Euan hurt his knee on our climb yesterday," I mentioned cheekily.

The blonde woman widened her glassy eyes. "I can heal it, I can." Despite Euan's protests, she proceeded to pray over it as he drove.

"Is it better?" she asked earnestly.

"Yes, I think so, thank you." Euan smiled but shot me a glare. I was delighted. Once we arrived at her hostel, he looked more relieved than I to see her go.

As we rounded a massive hill, Euan announced, "This is Tobermory."

Almost on cue the sun emerged. I looked ahead and below us I saw a never-ending row of vibrant, painted houses lining the main street and a gem-toned boat-filled bay. It was as if all the colour of the island had been drained and re-routed to this seaside-port town. As we drove downhill, the pavements became increasingly crowded and busy.

Euan quickly parked and we grabbed fish and chips from the famous van, parked on the pier. The seagulls were massive and ferocious, dive-bombing any tourists in hopes of dropped leftovers. Sitting on the pier watching the water, we waved them away with one hand while eating with the other.

Euan had again showed a lot of thought with his choice of hotel, this time a little grander, with views of the sea. "This is the nicest hotel we're staying in," he announced, almost in apology.

"Please let me help you pay for things," I protested as we headed up the stairs to find our room. "How about dinner tonight?"

Euan looked offended. "Don't worry about it, Fox. You came all the way here from America. All I want you to do is enjoy it."

*

It rained the next day. Our departure from the Isle of Mull back to the mainland was less eventful than our arrival. Stretches of fog-covered roads appeared before us and after a soaked visit to Sir Walter Scott's home, as we were preparing to head back to Wigtown, Euan had got a call. A man had a load of books he wanted rid of immediately, not too far from Glasgow.

Euan looked at me apologetically. "Do you mind? It's on the way."

"Of course not. I can assist you, load things." Having been so well treated, I was pleased to be of some help.

"If there is anything to load. It could be a pile of crap." Euan's mood today had darkened. I wasn't sure if it was because our holiday was ending, or because of something I had done. My heart pounded, and a mean little thought crept into my mind – perhaps he had already tired of my company.

We drove in silence for two hours, with Radio 4 echoing in the van. They were tumbling over the same news stories and I was getting irritated. Every 20 minutes they would repeat themselves: more distress in the Middle East, the NHS falling apart, hospitals failing us. It got to the point where I could lip-sync each depressing piece of news, which, to my American ears, with its perfect diction sounded eloquently detached.

My sense of discomfort was growing, too. Euan's sudden moody silence was a small hammer, driving cracks into my confidence.

"How do you feel about the NHS?" I asked after Radio 4 rolled around again to the story on neglect in the major hospitals.

"What do you mean?" Euan said, annoyed. He obviously wasn't in the mood for conversation. The quieter he became, the more my mind filled with reasons for his silence, each more extreme than the last: he liked listening to the radio without interruption; he was worried about work; after three days he was tired of my company; a certified bachelor, he was regretting inviting me, and worse, he had realised he didn't love me at all.

Outside, the fields shrank to make way for more houses. We were entering a larger city and in the twilight I could just make out people walking dogs, attending to their gardens and shopping. The roads became more confusing, jutting off into different directions, and Euan leaned forward to adjust the satnav, which was attached to the windscreen.

"Do you want me to be navigator?" I felt myself going into girl scout mode.

"No." Euan sighed. "I already texted the guy for better instructions."

When I first started working at NASA, they had made us take personality tests for group training and development. The test had specifically keyed in on how, as individuals, we approach conflict. It had never occurred to me that we differed so greatly in this area or indeed could even be classified into predicted systems of conflict behaviour. After reviewing all our answers in an exposed room, the differences had become perfectly illuminated.

I had fallen into the group Green Yellow Red. This meant, apparently, that at the first sign of tension I quickly went into problem-solving mode, doing anything I could to avoid further conflict by resolving the issues at hand.

The test had then gone on to say that if having gone "Green" did not work, I shifted to "Yellow", ignoring any type of conflict in the hope that it would go away. If conflict still continued, I went "Red", battling my corner to the bitter, bitter end. I had looked at my results with a sense of self-recognition that included pride. It held the same satisfaction as meeting a long-lost relative or seeing yourself for the first time in a clear mirror; it was self-affirming.

Most of the people in my group had been classified as Red Yellow Green, meaning if their stapler had been taken, the first course of action they'd take would be to argue for it back. How helpful would it be, on a first date, for couples to take this test? Euan, who I guessed to be Yellow Green Red, would probably not have mentioned anything was amiss with the stapler but simply gone out to find another.

As the silence reached a defeaning crescendo in the van, it occurred to me that I might not know Euan as well as I had assumed. At the festival, I had seen him only when he had wanted to be seen. Now, we were together all the time, revealing every mood and hiccup in our personalities. Nothing was hidden. This was a new way of seeing each other, perhaps less romantic, but all the more exciting as new bits of the person you loved were revealed. From Euan's pensive expression as he drove, I wasn't sure he felt the same way.

I looked at my own reflection, refracted, water-like, in the window of the van as we sped along. I wondered if self-awareness really changed things for the better. Look at the Lady of Shallot – the moment she gained perspective "the mirror cracked from side to side, the curse is come upon me cried". And then she died alone. Of a broken heart.

Euan's phone beeped. He eyed it but the phone was far from his hand, resting on the seat between us. "Here, can you answer that," he asked, "and tell me what it says? I hope he's sent better instructions."

Reluctantly, I grabbed his phone and saw "One Message" appear on the screen. .

"Well, what does it say?" Euan looked at me.

"I'm thinking of you too darling X". A lurching sensation rose in my stomach. I became flustered. "I don't think it's the bookseller guy." I handed him the phone.

Euan quickly viewed the message and then looked at me concerned. "Oh, um, no, definitely not the book guy."

I wished I hadn't seen the message. What did that mean, "I'm thinking of you too", and who would be calling Euan "darling" with a kiss afterwards? No matter how benign, it was now stained into my brain, and I couldn't think it away, as if it was an "out, out damned spot" of doubt.

Euan turned onto a small road and I could feel the car slowing down. He was searching house numbers.

"So who was that?" I asked, feeling awkward. Was it rude to ask? After such a lovely three days, the last thing I wanted to do was sound paranoid.

"One of my exes," Euan answered and stopped the car. I waited for more of an explanation but none came.

"You text her? You're still friends?"

"No, not really."

The satnav's "you have reached your destination" blasted loud and clear. My heart was thudding.

"I just wanted to make sure she was okay." Euan added, not looking at all concerned.

"Why wouldn't she be okay?"

"Because you're here."

I followed Euan out of the car as we approached the house. It was dark now, and the light from the small cottage lit our way as we walked up a handful of steps. Adrenaline was flowing through me and my stomach was performing acrobatics. I really hoped the person selling books wouldn't answer the door. I needed answers.

"Look, Jessy, she broke up with me years ago. It's not a big deal."

"Okay," I breathed but my brain kept on tripping over a missing piece. "But why would she be upset?"

"I don't know. It's none of her business. It's not anyone's business, really."

"Wait." Suddenly the number of questions swirling in my mind doubled. "What do you mean, not anyone's business?"

"Well ,why should I have to tell her, or anyone, that you were moving in with me?"

The sound of a door latch opening interrupted my thoughts and an elderly man appeared, blinking through thick spectacles. Euan spoke to him for a few minutes while I lingered in the background in a cloud of confusion.

Euan turned back towards me and looked concerned when he saw my expression. "What? What's wrong?"

"I don't really know where to begin," I mumbled. I could see Euan rolling his eyes as if to say, *please God, don't let her unleash a monologue.* "Well, first," my cheeks flushed, embarrassed, "are you still in love with her?"

"I'm not sure what you mean." Euan looked confused by the question. "I still care about her. I still care about everyone I've dated. Once you love someone, you love someone." Euan ran his fingers through my hair. "Silly Fox, come on."

I stood outside, numb. Grant would have said the same thing. I felt my heart ache. I had made another, terrible mistake. So much for lessons learned. What was wrong with me? Why did I have a hidden talent for picking the poly-amorous needle in the monogamous haystack of men?

"I'd like you to take me to Glasgow Airport," I shouted suddenly. "I'm not interested in being part of your harem."

"What?" Euan stopped and turned, looking genuinely surprised. "What are you taking about? What harem?"

"You seem to have a roster of women interested in you…"

Euan laughed. "Jesus! If only. There's no roster of women, Jessy. What gets into you sometimes?" He walked back towards me shaking his head.

"I don't want this to get more confusing." I fumed, completely disoriented.

"More confusing? I'm not confused." Euan, concerned, wrapped me in his arms, looking directly into my eyes. "There's no one else for me but you. I was lucky enough to find my strange American and I'm not going to let you go." He enveloped me in a hug.

As I sunk into his arms, I started to get my bearings again. I had overreacted, I knew it, but I couldn't help myself. My emotions were all over the place. Perhaps I was experiencing a wave of delayed panic. I had just moved across the ocean to a new country to live with someone I had known only for a couple of months. There should be a grace period for acting irrationally. Making sure I was all right, Euan kissed me, then turned and disappeared into the house.

I was suffering from emotional jet-lag. There had been a reason I was single for so long in LA. No matter how much I had prepared otherwise, all the anxiety I had experienced in my relationship with Grant was coming back now as I faced this new relationship. Grant had never closed the door on any woman who wanted him and his lack of loyalty had crushed my sense of self-worth. Euan was different; he was motivated by kindness, not self-gratification. He truly cared for the people whom he had dated. They were so different, in fact, that I couldn't believe I was confusing the two in my head. After all that Euan had done for me over the past couple of days, I was mortified. I looked down at my empty hands and was surprised by the amount of hidden baggage I had brought with me.

Euan's voice echoed from the well-lit basement as I descended the narrow flight of stairs. I gently negotiated the steep wooden steps and looked up to see Melville, leaning against the banister in front of me. He had a walking stick in one hand, and proceeded to use it as a pointer, targeting it at my heart.

"That is not as indestructible as you think, you know," he said.

"I thought our capacity to love was endless." I crossed my arms. "I'm sure you've said those very words to me before."

He shook his head. "That's disinterested love. In this case, you're interested." Melville tapped his walking stick on the stair.

"Jessy, is that you?" Euan called.

"Yes, it's me," I shouted, leaning over the banister. When I looked up, Melville was gone.

As I descended the stairs, I could see the basement open up, full of books. The walls were covered in bookshelves and the floor was filled, like a fledging forest, with small stacks of old hardbacks.

"Anything good?" I asked, trying to sound apologetic.

Euan was kneeling next to a wall that had a massive heraldry shield and a piece of a stained-glass window hanging from it.

"Yes, I think I'm taking the whole lot," he said without looking up. I looked around the room and realised the books had to be moved from here to the van, via the long, narrow flight of stairs. Though the man who owned the house was quite old, he sadly wasn't Rumpelstiltskin, and there would be no magic solution other than for Euan and I to schlep every book out of there ourselves.

"So you'll be needing my help then?" I knelt down and started to box up a handful of books by the door.

"Ah yes, Fox, help." Euan smiled at me. There was no need to sound apologetic; he had obviously forgiven me, if he had been angry at all.

Ten boxes of books later, and 20 trips up and down the stairs, we were done. As we climbed into the van, I found myself tripping over something Euan had said earlier.

"You really didn't tell anyone that I was coming back?" I asked.

Euan started the van.

"Nope."

"Not even your parents?"

"Especially not my parents."

I smacked Euan's arm. "Really no one?"

"No one." He was grinning but I knew he was serious.

My head shook in exasperation and I looked out the window. It was completely dark now, and all I could see was my own reflection, clearer this time, staring back at me. Despite myself, I was grinning, too.

Chapter 29

"...when I was swimming far out, or lying alone on a beach, I have had the same experience, became the sun, the hot sand, green seaweed anchored to a rock, swaying in the tide... like the veil of things as they seem drawn back by an unseen hand. For a second you see, and seeing the secret, you are the secret. For a second there is meaning! Then the hand lets the veil fall and you are alone, lost in the fog again, and you stumble on towards nowhere for no good reason." Eugene O'Neill, LONG DAY'S JOURNEY INTO NIGHT: *Drama section, Garden Room, second building out the back.*

No drowsy jet-lag to greet me when I woke on my first morning back above The Bookshop. Our trip around the west of Scotland had quickly acclimatised my inner clock. I had expected to smell lavender, hear the faint horn-like sound of mooing and open my eyes to white walls with oatmeal curtains framing the view of the rooftops of Wigtown. Instead, I woke to bright-yellow walls and the faint smell of Euan's cologne, which still lingered in the air. As I listened, I could hear the kettle flick on downstairs in the kitchen.

I rolled over in the large bed, enjoying the solitude. I was cushioned between marshmallow-white pillows and a massive duvet. The mattress seemed to extend for ever, compared to my small bed in my parents' house. The air was crisp and I stretched lazily; cosy and safe inside my Scottish cocoon. In front of me I could see the indentation on the pillow where Euan's head had been, and beyond, the clock came into focus. It was just before 9am. The shop would be open soon.

The faint echo of footsteps sounded from downstairs as Euan made his way into The Bookshop. I willed myself to sit up. I did not want to start my first day in Wigtown in an idle fashion. I had a chance to begin my life here with good habits. I would get up, go for a run, send out flyers to start a yoga class and finish my consulting work before my collaborators on the East Coast had started their lunch. Then, I would have the rest of the day to explore.

The wooden floor of the bedroom was ice cold under my feet, and I quickly hopped to and fro as I unpacked my things. Euan had more of a Laura Ashley touch than I would have expected from a typical bachelor. Everywhere I looked he had painted, renovated, decorated and demonstrated better taste than most people I knew. He had moved an extra small wardrobe into the bedroom, and had also emptied half of his closet, a gesture that meant a great deal to me. This was his home, after all, his man-cave, and even if he had just shoved his shirts to one side, he was carving out a space in it for me.

I hadn't packed much. I carefully took out my dresses and hung them one by one in the closet. They looked sweet next to Euan's plain, button-down shirts. Although dresses and tights were fine in a Los Angeles winter, I was now experiencing late autumn in Scotland. I was also living inside a large stone refrigerator of a house, with no heat and seven outward-facing gables. The clothes

I packed would barely keep me warm even if I stayed surgically attached to the wood-burning stove. Emptying the rest of the suitcase, I wondered if I shouldn't have packed more. My clothes only took up the first two drawers of the bureau. I would use the third drawer on the bottom as a laundry hamper, I decided. There was something highly satisfying in figuring out where everything should go.

I turned to a stack of drawers, like a little nightstand, near my bed, searching for a good place to put my face cream and hairbrush. The top drawer was a little sticky, so, with a good yank, I prised it open. Inside the top drawer, there lay – dust-covered – a pot of anti-wrinkle night cream, some hairclips and perfume. I guessed these items weren't Euan's, rather remnants of a former girl-friend, or lover. Why hadn't he thought to clean these drawers before I came? Maybe he didn't know they were still there. The sense that I was special quickly drained away.

I took out the bottle of perfume, examining it. In some haunting way, I felt like an archaeologist, finding evidence of prior civilisations, with feelings and stories that had lived before I existed. Everyone had a past, I reminded myself, although it was altogether different to stumble upon physical evidence of it. I scooped up the contents of the drawer in my arms and stood above the rubbish, unsure. It was not my job to clean up his past, but they were my drawers now. The lines from the folktale "Mr. Fox" echoed in my head: "be bold, be bold, but not too bold". I lingered over the rubbish, debating the issue in my head, the moral implications of the scenario, but this was my day to start good habits. I dumped the contents into the bin without another thought.

As I walked through the shop, clad in my running gear, heading towards the door, Euan gave me a quizzical look.

"What?" I asked, smiling.

"My God, what are you wearing?"

"My shorts? You know I always go running in them." I looked down.

"But this is Wigtown – and it's midwinter. You'll cause car accidents." Euan was incredibly amused and wrapped his arms around me. He was built for the climate and though he too was wearing shorts, he was radiating heat. "Crazy American."

Wigtown was as beautiful as in my memory. Perhaps even more so. Under a bright-blue, cloud-filled sky, I ran along the main road, down past the church across from which held my favourite view over the fields, wetlands and the sea. Every cell of my being felt like shouting, I'm back, I'm home.

The early December air was cold, invigorating. I had debated bringing music along with me, to keep the beat as my sneakers hit the road in a slow rhythm, but for this run I wanted to hear just the sounds of Wigtown. I heard birds, and cows in the distance. I could also hear a horse neighing in a nearby field and the noise of houses waking up: doors opening, dogs being called in, morning greetings.

Curving down a bend in the road, I ran fast and breathlessly, my lungs stretching and singing in the clean morning air. The road then quickly levelled out and opened to expanses of fields. It was the most exquisite landscape imaginable and the distant haze softened everything like an Impressionist painting. My pace slowed and I tried to drink it all in – an impossible task. Even if every particle of my body was on fire with feeling, how could you truly appreciate the majestic?

A mile down the road I thought of L.M. Montgomery and her book *The Alpine Path*. In it she talked about how she always felt there was a world of ideal beauty, just beyond this one, and that between herself and that world there existed a veil. Sometimes, when the wind blew, the veil would lift and for a moment she'd glimpse that world and be transported. Ed Ricketts would call that moment "Breaking Through", an overwhelming feeling of connection and awe. Here in Wigtown, there was no invisible curtain to veil the ideal; it was the most beautiful place in the universe.

Thus, bewitched, my mind seemed to empty. I wondered what this landscape would do to my writing, my need to create, for that impulse had always been fuelled by dissatisfaction, by *shpilkus*, and the restlessness that the crisp New England air inspired. Here, I didn't feel dissatisfied. I didn't need to be transported elsewhere. I hardly needed to create a film. I felt I was already in one.

I was nice and warm by the time I returned to The Bookshop. A handful of customers eyed me as I slipped past them on my way upstairs. There was no separation between my life and the shop, I suddenly realised. If I came home sweaty from exercise, I would have to face customers. If I came in from shopping, arms full of groceries, I would have to pass them as I struggled to make it up the main staircase. Every time I returned it would be like I had entered a play and only when I reached the first floor would I finally exit the stage, and be at home.

After a quick shower and change into jeans and my warmest shirt, I came down into the shop for the second task of the day. I had a schedule after all, and I wanted to keep busy. It was important to me. Euan had only known me when I was relaxed and on holiday, and I wanted to make sure he didn't think that was all there was to me. I was hardworking and determined, and was not here to abuse his generosity. My drive was not for Euan alone, however. Underneath my excitement I was terrified. The big empty space called my career loomed before me. If I did enough things, and occupied myself with a fabricated list of to-dos, perhaps I wouldn't feel my ambition waning, its gravity as inescapable as a black hole.

"So what else would you like me to write on it?" Euan asked, viewing the computer with some concern.

"That it begins in the fall."

Euan's eyebrows rose.

I had asked Euan to print out flyers for a yoga class that I would lead. On my way back from the run, I visited the town hall library and agreed to rent out the smaller of the two social hall rooms upstairs. I had remembered the room from the events at the festival and thought its high ceilings, wooden floors and large windows looking onto the sea would be the ideal space for a yoga class.

Wigtown had never had a yoga class before, and the women at the library had looked at me with equal measures of curiosity and suspicion.

"What kind of yoga is this?" one of them had asked.

"Vinyasa Flow, for all levels," I had said, not convinced this answer would illuminate anything.

Euan handed me a stack of freshly printed flyers. I looked one over, happy with the result. "Wigtown Yoga, Thursday nights from 6:30 to 7:30pm, Supper Room, Town Hall. Come and enjoy the benefits of this weekly practice: greater flexibility, strength, stress reduction and an increase in overall wellbeing."

"I'll put one up in the window." Euan took one from my pile. "You're going to have us all connecting with ourselves and talking about feelings before you're done."

"That's the plan," I said as I kissed him on the cheek. "Thank you."

Euan's eyes darted around the shop, making sure no customer saw the public display of affection. "You're so American, Jessy."

"Shocker." I smiled.

Papers in hand, I walked up Wigtown's small high street. The sun had finally come out and the pastel stone houses were looking cheery, as strangers walked up and down the street, visiting the bookshops. The excitement of the crowds, marquees and events from the festival were all gone, but I preferred this version of Wigtown. It was quaint and soft, but there was still a buzz.

On my way up the street I saw familiar faces from my previous visit, and got a new thrill as they recognised me in turn. There was the impeccably dressed elderly gentleman, with his suit neatly pinned where his arm was missing. He was in the phone booth and smiled as I passed. Ahead I could see the hearse double-parked outside the Co-op, and the goth-dressed woman emerged. She leaned into the back seat of the car and pulled out her beautiful young baby. I had entered the Scottish version of a Fellini film.

My heart filled with a deep love for this quirky town, and I, perhaps the strangest among them, felt right at home. My pace slowed as I reached a small, peach-coloured house to my right with the name Mackerel's painted on the top. "The Biggest, Littlest Store In Town" was written in bold, italicised letters underneath. Every inch of the windows was covered with community flyers and posters, and outside, sitting on the window sill and blocking the door was a handful of Wigtown youths, dressed in tracksuits and armed with crisp packets and Irn Bru. I slipped by them and entered "the biggest, littlest store in town".

Inside should have been dark but instead the walls of the shop were lit by electric lighting, soda fridges and a colourful gambling machine, which played music. A couple of young teens followed me in and raided the fridge, putting a fistful of coins on the counter. Gathered on the small shelves were a grab-bag variety of items. You could get everything from firewood and newspapers to candy, plus drop off your clothes to be dry-cleaned. I could see why it was the biggest, littlest store – it was the Tardis of shops – and it was here that I knew I had found the beating heart of the town. Standing behind the counter of this small, disorganised, cement-floored convenience store stood the man behind the curtain, Mackerel himself.

Mackerel was softly-spoken, and middle-aged. His father had owned the store before him, and the candy, frozen at 1950s prices, was famous with children of many generations who had grown up in Wigtown. Mackerel himself was unassuming, but not to be underestimated. In exactly a year's time he would vanish for two days, the town's concern escalating at the sudden disappearance of its most integral member. However, the concern wouldn't last for long. Mackerel had won an MBE for his dedication to his community, and had made the round trip to London to meet the Queen via two overnight buses within a 48-hour period, just so that he could open the shop the following day.

"Hi, Mackerel," I said, walking up to the counter. "I was wondering if you could put this flyer up on the window?"

"Let's have a look, ma dear." Mackerel put on his glasses and read over the benefits of yoga. "I'll get that dun right no," he said and walked over to the window.

"Thanks." Being tone deaf, I was surprised by my ease in understanding the various local accents. "Any chance you'll join us?"

Mackerel immediately blushed and laughed. It hadn't meant to be a joke, but I quickly laughed too and slipped out of the shop onto the street.

Up the road, I came to Wendy's Frame Shop. It was painted a beautiful deep-green colour, and the windows were decorated with great care, showing items for the home, cards, jewellery and artwork.

As I passed through the door, a small golden bell rang and a well-dressed elderly woman, with playful eyes and silvery hair, appeared behind the counter. She tilted her large glasses in my direction.

"Can I help you?" she asked, eyeing the flyers under my arm. "We don't take those."

I searched for the right thing to say. "Oh, I just stopped in to say 'hi'. I'm Jessica," I said, walking towards the counter. Wendy's expression melted into a warm, big smile.

"So you're back at The Bookshop are you?" Wendy's eyes twinkled. "How is my boyfriend with the Titian locks?"

"He misses you, of course. Says you broke his heart."

"I like you already," Wendy laughed in pure delight. "Now tell me all about yourself, my dear."

After a long chat, I headed, one flyer lighter, diagonally across the street to the post office. I felt warmed by

Wendy's feisty spirit and smiled, thinking that perhaps in addition to Deirdre, I had found my first true friend in Wigtown.

Inside the post office, there was a long line, but all eyes were on me as I appeared in the doorway. So much for my short-lived anonymity.

If Mackerel's was the heart of the community, then the post-office was its eyes and ears. It not only transferred information in letters and packages, but in chatter, too. It was the knowledge-sharing hub of Wigtown. I chuckled to myself thinking that even NASA's knowledge management department would be envious at the speed at which information travelled, intact, here from the post office to the rest of the town.

I waited in line and finally handed my flyer to an unhappy teenager behind the counter.

"We don't have room," she said, handing the flyer back to me.

"Well, do you mind holding onto it in case something opens up?" I politely handed the piece of paper back to her.

"Yoga? What's that?" she asked, as if yoga was a dirty word. Suddenly a voice called from the back of the post-office.

"Yoga? That must be Jessica." Doris, a kind-looking woman standing behind a pane of glass, in the packages and parcels department, waved at me.

"Hi there, Doris. Yes, it's me." I walked over and would have given her a hug if it weren't for the wall of glass, so I waved awkwardly instead.

"I'm happy to see you, darling. I had no idea you were coming back."

"Neither did I, until recently."

"Euan didn't say anything, the dark horse. I hope he's making you feel at home?" Before I could answer, she winked. "I'll have a word with him." The words of Hillary Clinton, "it takes a village", suddenly came to mind.

Heading back to The Bookshop, I felt disappointed at the number of flyers still left in my hands. It was Tuesday, and in a week I doubted whether I could drum up enough support to make the rental of the hall worth the effort. As I entered the shop, I saw Deirdre standing there, grinning. My fears about what people would think when I suddenly returned all but evaporated in the intense warmth that greeted me.

"I'm so happy to see you, darling," she beamed. "Euan, the monkey, said absolutely nothing about you coming back."

"Mum," Euan began in protest from behind the counter.

"And look at you, hitting the ground running." Deirdre picked up one of my flyers and began to chuckle. "Yoga will start in the fall."

"Is something wrong?" I looked from Deirdre to Euan.

"It's called autumn here, dear. Everyone will think you have injured yourself."

I moaned. "Euan, why didn't you warn me? I'll change it."

"Don't change one bit." Deirdre put her arm around my waist. "You are delightfully American. I absolutely love it."

Chapter 30

"Two birds, beautiful of wing, close companions, cling to one common tree: of the two one eats the sweet fruit of the tree, the other eats not but watches his fellow." – Sri Aurobindo, THE UPANISHADS: TEXTS, TRANSLATIONS AND COMMENTARY: *Religion section, Garden Room, second building out the back.*

The beautiful old house, nestled above the shop, felt much larger than it had before with just the two of us rattling around inside.

Today would mark the end of my first week in Wigtown. We had kept ourselves to ourselves for this time, not going out or socialising. In contrast to my busy days filled with driving, fast food and friends in Los Angeles, I was enjoying the solitude with Euan: the long rambling days, the home-cooked meals and our nights sleeping in the blissful silence above the shop.

The routine of life here had become clear within that first week. I would wake up in Euan's arms each morning, and enjoy a lazy moment with him, warm in bed, before greeting the chilly day. He would smile sleepily, then at the first sound of the alarm clock, would jump up, throw on his clothes and disappear. I hated that alarm clock.

My mornings were taken up with writing, finishing consulting work and, if I was really motivated, a run or walk in the cold winter air, drinking in my fill of ice-capped mountains, green-brown fields and the silver sea.

In the daytime Euan would have his assistant join him, and depending on how busy the shop was, we would leave to go out on adventures. Adventure is a relative term, mind you, for anything we did in this new world felt like an adventure to me, from grocery shopping to going to drop scrap furnishing at the dump. It reminded me of a time in childhood where outings, no matter where or with whom, were filled with possibility and opportunity for excitement.

On my first Sunday, with the whole afternoon to spend together, we had hiked through the woods to see a water-fall. It was a beautiful walk; the waterfall wasn't very high but it was thundering, swollen from the rain of the previous night. We raced down the path and Euan won, by miles, it would seem, and we then drank out of a stream. What a thrill to be thirsty, heart racing, and to gulp down crystal-clear mountain water. This was a luxury that a place like Los Angeles could never have afforded. This was happiness to me.

As the sun set we visited a beach with an ancient grave-yard and church set into the cliffs. The church was crumbling, and the gravestones were marked with images of skulls, wings and hourglasses. In the orange light, Euan and I made our way down the beach path and onto the long stretch of soft sand. It was low tide and the beach was deserted. I couldn't believe that in a place such as this, we were the only ones to enjoy the views. Steep, dramatic cliffs faced us on one side, and sand dunes on the other. It felt like our own private island. The calm ocean was full of contrasting sunset shades: soft blues and peachy oranges. In the distance, Euan pointed out the Isle of Man, shadowy and mysterious on the horizon. This was a place that would satisfy even the most romantic of souls.

Another day, still blessed with good weather, we climbed Cairnsmore, following the steep mountain path through pine forests, which opened up into brown fields. It was a rigorous climb and I would need frequent breaks, pretending to be taking in the view but really catching my breath.

We sat at the windblown top, sipping soup from a thermos. Euan had been particularly quiet that afternoon. Searching his wistful face, I wondered if he was thinking of someone else, perhaps the last woman he had taken on this hike. I knew his facial expressions by now, and whatever was occupying his thoughts was taking him worlds away. Before descending, however, Euan took a picture of the two of us, smiling into the sun with the ever-stretching view behind us. New memories, I had thought. We had each come with a past and it would take time to tip the scales of newness; but, slowly, we were building up memories of our own.

My favourite days were less grand. On these, Euan would often check in on me through the day to see how my writing was going or ask if I'd like to come along on an errand. One particularly rainy day, he and I headed off to the dump, which may not sound inherently exciting, but in this part of the world any excursion involved driving through small country roads – an experience that I still found exhilarating. We listened to Count Arthur Strong as the van rumbled along, laughing out loud, before he tuned the radio to a recorded reading of A.E. Housman poetry. It was the first time I'd heard his verse and I was swept away by the lyricism and language. The green fields rolled by as I lost myself in "A Shropshire Lad" and Euan glanced at me, thoughtful.

At night, after the shop closed, Euan would spend every daylight hour left in the garden. At the back of the shop, he had created a mini-paradise. Like The Bookshop itself, the garden seemed to go on for ever, with paths that twisted and turned, taking you through beds spilling over with flowers and plants. He would be in a trance while working in the garden, beer in hand and Radio 4 droning away. I'd try to join in, and be "helpful", often feeling out of place, lingering awkwardly with nothing to do. My tasks were always reluctantly given; on most days I would go back inside, feeling as if I was interrupting his sacred time alone.

Euan teased me for being lazy or having nothing to do, which he thought was hilarious, but in truth it had started to annoy me. My future was completely blurry, with little income and no clear sign of what to do next. I was exploring, I had told myself: this was a brave thing to do.

When the weather wasn't cooperating, which was often, and blankets of rain dramatically covered Wigtown, Euan would spend the evenings fixing and improving the house, beer still in hand, and Radio 4 still droning in the background. These were solitary evenings that I'd spend alone. I had to remember that Euan was in the shop all day, surrounded by people, and he was used to having his evenings to himself. I was overly conscious that I was having to fit into the life of a certified bachelor, whose rhythms and routines dominated mine, for I was younger, more flexible and the visitor.

To mark the anniversary of my first week in Wigtown, Euan made haggis for dinner. He was establishing himself as the chef, because, as he would often tell me, he felt my American culinary skills left much to be desired. The comment was more than justified. I had tried to cook meals the entire week, from Mexican dishes and my grandmother's matzo ball soup to American hamburgers, but each ended in a spectacular disaster.

The Co-op had provided little in the way of ingredients for a Mexican burrito and I had had to improvise, soaking beans myself, which were not ready by the time dinner rolled around. My second attempt was more tolerable. To create matzo balls for the soup, in lieu of mazto meal, I'd had to hand-grind crackers with a mortar and pestle, an act of devotion that should have won me some kind of Jewish Nobel. It had taken so much energy that I had lazily used chicken stock cubes instead of real chicken stock, and Euan quickly turned his nose up. My old faithful canned soup was not going to cut it, obviously.

Finally I had tried the classic American hamburger, with a make-shift bun, although I had been lucky enough to find ketchup in the Co-op, and topped the evening off with a home-made brownie sundae. The meal had, at first, been a success, but Euan couldn't sleep that night as a result of indigestion and an overdose of sugar. Two things Americans are immune to, apparently.

So with my cooking duties discharged for the evening, I sat expectantly, trying to look gracious, as Euan placed the haggis before me: a brown lump closely resembling the kasha my mother used to make, swimming in gravy, under which were mashed potatoes and black pudding. I was learning, quite quickly, that although many of the foods Euan presented me with seemed foreign – Branston pickle, haggis, black pudding – most felt oddly Jewish: pickled herring, smoked salmon, kasha, boiled veg and potatoes in every shape, size and consistency.

I scooped some haggis onto my fork and took a bite. A meaty, nutty flavour of roughage swirled in my mouth;

it was delicious, salty and quirky, with smooth and rough textures mixing together. Every forkful was incredibly filling, like swallowing heavy mud. I cleared only half my plate and Euan looked disappointed.

Despite his solitary habits, Euan had been particularly attentive that week, cooking in between my efforts, taking me out to do things, filling the firewood basket and sharing his home. I didn't want him to think I was unappreciative of all his effort.

Taking a deep breath, I rallied my appetite and pulled the plate closer, scooping up large mouthfuls of dinner until the other half was finished.

Euan tilted his head, amused. "So you like haggis?"

"It's delicious, I just have a food baby." I put my hand on my belly, now swollen. "I don't think I can eat for another week."

Euan's eyes darkened, suddenly pensive. "You know, you're the first woman who really has lived here, I mean, full-time."

"Oh." I said, shifting uncomfortably. I wondered if "full-time" wasn't said with a hint of trepidation. "Well, I'm really liking it."

Euan took a sip of wine.

"Are you liking having me here?"

"Of course," he replied, nodding, and quickly stood up, clearing my plate. It was an unfair question; what else is a kind, polite person going to say?

I watched as Euan leaned his tall, slim frame against the sink and wondered why I had been the first of his girl-friends to make a home with him above The Bookshop. Was it the isolation? The lack of heat? The wrong time, place, person? Or was there something more complicated hidden under Euan's calm surface?

"It must be a big change for you, having me here?"

Euan shrugged. I watched as he poured himself another glass of wine.

"This is an experiment, you know," I continued. "You're not stuck with me. If ever you felt it wasn't working, I'd leave."

Euan laughed. "I know you would – 'take me to the airport, Euan'," he said, feigning a high-pitched girly tone, and I rolled my eyes. He walked over to the table, slowly, never taking his eyes off mine. "But it's just not that simple for me, Jessy."

"Why?"

"Because I'm a ditherer."

Silence quickly descended between us. I wasn't completely sure what he meant, but whatever a ditherer was, I felt as if Euan had just handed me a big piece to a puzzle.

My eyes searched the room. Outside the cold dark night was creating ice-crystals on the window, making the dimly lit kitchen look bright and warm. Over on the refrigerator, I spied a new picture of Euan and me on top of Cairnsmore. He must have put that up a couple of days ago but it was only now that I noticed it. It was held on with a small magnet, and I could see our smiling faces staring at me. Looking at it, I couldn't help smiling back. The kitchen, in that moment, no longer felt like his kitchen, but ours. I had my bit of string added to the nest.

Chapter 31

"Beauty before me, beauty behind me, beauty to the right of me, beauty to the left of me, beauty above me, beauty below me, I am on the pollen path." – Navajo saying interpreted by Joseph Campbell, THE HERO WITH A THOUSAND FACES: *Folklore and mythology section, front room, second bookshelf on the right.*

Feeling at home in a new place is not just about loving the landscape or understanding the language, but is also accomplished, as superficial as it may sound, by establishing important creature comforts: a hairdresser, a good place for waxing and, being Jewish (and American), a good doctor. This holy trilogy, symptomatic of my middle-class Bostonian upbringing, was at the forefront of my mind as December extended its chilly fingers and I stood, shaking with cold, attempting to trim my hipster fringe in front of the mirror, between great white puffs of breath.

In Los Angeles I had made an effort to feel fabulous, a valuable lesson from Rose that I did not want to lose just because I was in a remote corner of Scotland. I especially needed to feel fabulous today. I was not only teaching my first – and Wigtown's first – yoga class, but tonight I would be going to my first dinner party. Hosted by clients of Euan who would often give him first editions of anthologies to sell at auction, it was black tie only and our first big social engagement as a couple. In the unlikely event that word had not yet reached those attending that I had returned, tonight they would be in for a surprise.

The invitation had come on cream-coloured card with fancy silver lettering, and to my delight, I had seen my name included next to Euan's. I had not yet become acclimatised to calling Euan my boyfriend, but seeing us together on paper reminded me that we were already linked, at least in some of the community's eyes. Drinks were to be served from seven till eight, at which point there would be dinner, then dancing. Though I hadn't seen exactly what posh meant (a word we didn't have in the States), this invitation looked like the definition of it. The highlight for me was that it was to be hosted on an estate, with ruins in the grounds dating back to medieval times.

My hands wouldn't stop shaking as I held the scissors up to my forehead. It was useless to try and cut my own hair. With a day already full of appointments, perhaps I could fit in a haircut too. If the local barber could see me this morning, I'd have just enough time to make it to the doctor's office down the road, and then Euan had agreed to drive me to my waxing appointment. It had felt strange asking Euan to take me, since you always wanted a new boyfriend to believe that your manicured beauty was entirely natural – not the result of hours of painful waxing and tweezing. However, not having a car had limited my options and offered many perks too. The hassle of parking had disappeared, along with the petrol bills; and not spending a quarter of my day stuck in traffic was still a novelty.

The only spa in an hour's radius that claimed it could do a full wax was a tiny little place 40 minutes away called Kelly's Studio. Set in a sleepy little village, the studio offered all kinds of treatments and alternative therapies.

Kelly herself had answered the phone. "And what kind of treatment would you like?" She had a thick local accent.

"For my bikini," I had whispered, covering the phone with my hand. "I'd like a Brazilian."

"What's that?"

A Brazilian was standard in LA, like getting your car washed or picking up your eco-friendly dry-cleaning. I quickly looked around. I had used the phone at the front of The Bookshop, within earshot of other customers. Leaning further over the counter, I turned my back towards them, and replied, barely audibly. "That's all of it off, you know, everything."

"Oh yes, we call that a Hollywood," she said. I had found that point of difference entertaining. "I'm the only one here certified for that kind of wax, dear, so let's say late afternoon?"

"Great," I said, relieved. "Could I also book a massage as well?" I had decided to treat Euan to a massage for having driven me all the way there.

Ice twinkled in geometric snowflake formations on the glass of the bathroom window. I put away the scissors. Abandoning hope of maintaining my chestnut-brown shag of a haircut myself, I ran down the stairs and found Euan.

"How much does Harry charge?" I asked, only now noticing how fitting his name was for his profession. Euan was stooped over a pile of books near the computer. He was researching prices, looking up the name and date of publication of the books to find if any were listed on AbeBooks or Amazon. From his expression, I could tell there weren't any treasures so far.

"I don't know for girls," Euan said without looking up. "Maybe five pounds?"

"Five?" That sounded incredibly cheap to me. I started to become worried. "Well, how much does he charge for your hair?"

"Three pounds," Euan said.

"Oh my God," I mumbled.

The smell of the doctor's office hit my nostrils the moment I opened the front door of the surgery. Standing in the dark hallway, I waited in a short line for reception, then was told to sit in the small, brightly lit waiting room. I suddenly felt exposed. In LA it would be highly improbable for me to see anyone I recognised at the doctor's, but in Wigtown it would be impossible for me not to see someone I knew. In line with me were familiar faces from the Co-op, and sitting next to me was a woman I had seen during my morning runs.

Feeling like a beetle in a petri dish, I looked around anxiously. I wasn't at the doctor's for any sordid reason, but I realised I might raise an eyebrow or two by being there so soon after my arrival.

"Jessica Fox for..." the piercing voice echoed from speakers above and tripped over the next words, "general check-up, please see reception." They had been reading from my information form. So much for anonymity. Everyone stared as I made my way to the front of the room. I was Jessica Fox and I was here for a check-up.

Next to the reception window there was a small sign which said: "If you'd like to discuss your problem in private, please ask."

There seemed little point in that now. I waited for the young woman on the phone behind the desk to look up. The medical odour was stinging my senses and deep in my subconscious the dark, shadowy sloth of self-doubt started to move. I began to wonder if finding a doctor here might not be worth the effort.

The receptionist opened the glass shutters of the desk window.

"Now, Jessica, it says you are here for a 'general check-up'?" she asked, looking quizzically at my form.

"Yes. I was hoping to find a doctor."

"Well, you've come to the right place. Are you on holiday?" She peered at me and then suddenly her smile widened. "Wait, you're the American living at The Bookshop?"

I nodded. So word had already spread this far.

"Is this a permanent thing?"

"Uh," I stammered, unsure if this was for her form or out of general interest. "I think so." I hadn't expected such a simple question to be so hard to answer.

"Well, Jessica." She looked at me with concern and pulled out a couple of forms. "You're sick already. Not surprising with this weather. That bookshop will be freezing.

"No, no, I mean yes, it is, but I'm not sick." I paused and she looked confused. "I just wanted to see a doctor."

"Why, dear?"

"For a check-up." I shoved my hands in my pockets. My American stars and stripes were showing. "You know, and to say hello, to a doctor."

"Oh." She smiled, confused. "Well, thanks for saying hi then."

Behind me, I felt intensely aware that I had the attention of everyone in the waiting room.

"Come back if you're not feeling well, okay? And tell Euan I hope he's keeping that icebox of a house warm for you." The glass shutters closed.

I stepped out of the surgery onto the street, blinking into the sunshine. Well, that was a bit of a disaster. Euan had tried to warn me.

I had only two blocks to walk before reaching Harry's salon. Given how things were going, perhaps I should pass on that idea, too.

It had taken me ages to find the right haircut and hair-dresser in LA, but once I had, it had been the key to giving me a fresh start and a new-found sense of confidence. All that had come at a pricey one hundred and fifty dollars, and, though hair was just hair, I found myself standing outside Harry's five-pound barbershop in trepidation. With its unassuming faded-blue sign and pictures of models from the 1980s in the window, I felt as if I was Samson facing Delilah. My grown-out locks wielded a type of power: they were a reminder of my old, single, happy life in California. By losing them, I would be losing the last vestige of my Los Angeles identity.

*

My reflection stared back at me as I sat, legs dangling, in a comfortable swivel chair. The mirror was framed by dark wooden panels, and below was a shelf cluttered with mismatching clips, hair dryers and brushes. Harry was like an oak tree and he stepped behind me, spreading a sheet over me with his branch-like arms.

"Nothing really drastic," I said, hoping it didn't sound rude. "I just want a trim."

"Ay," Harry squirted a water bottle and mist landed on my hair, making it look thin and matt.

I searched the room for a distraction. My eyes landed on a basic, colourful map of the world, pinned to the far wall.

"Do you travel much, Harry?"

"Ay, but not for awhile, ken." His massive hands held a fine comb and brushed my hair gently.

"Is your family from here?" I asked.

"Lived here all my life, ken, but my sister lives in Aberdeen." Harry addressed my reflection in the mirror, running his hands through my hair to plump it up.

Some part of me thought that if I kept him talking, I'd avoid the inevitable and keep him from cutting my hair. "Do you visit her?"

"Na."

"Never?"

"Never even been to Glasgow. I don ever get over that far," Harry said with a smile.

I contemplated this answer for a moment. Here was someone with the map of the world on his wall, who was tall enough to see Glasgow if he stood on his tiptoes, but his long legs had never taken him farther than this small corner of Scotland.

"Well, I travelled all the way from Los Angeles to get my hair cut by you," I teased, starting to enjoy myself.

Harry's smile faded. Beads of sweat appeared on his forehead as he continued combing.

"I'm teasing."

"I knew that, like." He laughed nervously, quickly snipping away with a sharp-looking pair of scissors. I watched as the first pieces of hair fell like dark snow to the floor. Embrace it, I thought. Nothing you can do now. As more cut hair began to flutter towards the ground, I no longer felt concerned, but liberated.

*

Euan stared at me as we entered Kelly's studio. "I can't believe you were so worried. You look just the same."

My hair did not smell of sweet florals nor did it shine from copious amounts of product. In a flurry of movements and cutting, Harry had trimmed my fringe and hipster shag in only ten minutes. It was shorter, neater and, though terrifyingly fast, Harry had cut it well, leaving my identity still intact, if not a bit renewed.

"I got you a backrub with Kelly," I mentioned as we walk through the door.

"You didn't have to," said Euan with a blush, either touched or embarrassed.

In a studio of scented candles, new-age music and cream colours, Kelly stood waiting for us behind a long black counter. The studio felt sparklingly new and cutting-edge, an oasis of indulgence in a land of farmers, stone cottages and wellington boots. Here was my bit of Los Angeles in Galloway.

"Euan, hello." Kelly stepped out from behind the counter, revealing her snug black uniform. She was in her late forties, and her hair was long and curly, with a black coal-like sheen. She hugged Euan and turned to me, obviously thrilled.

"Now you must be the Hollywood? Come with me, dear." Confidentiality didn't seem to exist in Galloway. She took my hand and led me down a hall.

Thirty minutes later and I was still lying on my back in the small treatment room, staring up at a plastered white ceiling. Though I wasn't an expert, I thought Kelly was exhibiting signs of being a certified sadist. I was in serious pain as her long, manicured nails tried to unearth the rock-solid wax from my skin. Every time I cried out, I quickly apologised, embarrassed. Kelly just laughed. She looked delighted.

This wasn't the way I had thought a Hollywood wax was done. My entire "area" as Euan's Irish cousin liked to call it, was covered in hard wax, like an eco-friendly chastity belt. Kelly struggled to rip even the smallest piece of it off me.

"I might have put the wrong wax on for this." Kelly looked at my "area" with fascination. There was no sense of apology in her voice.

"Oh!" My nerves were fraying.

"To be honest, I haven't done one of these in years."

"Seriously? What are we going to do?"

"Right," she said. "We're going to give it a hard yank."

Kelly grabbed hold of the wax just below my belly button. "You ready?" I started laughing. It was an awkward defense mechanism, one that always came out at the most inappropriate moments.

Euan sat in the next room, trying to relax as his back was being pounded by one of Kelly's assistants. Suddenly, a blood-curdling scream shot through the wall.

Apart from that first visit for the book festival, Euan and I had never had the pretence of a courtship period. We had lived together from the moment we met so there was no veil of mystery. No sense of dating Oz only to learn in disappointment that there was a man behind the curtain. To Euan this had felt as if we were doing things backwards but to me it had felt innovative. We were our daily selves, not the idealised version, from the very beginning. So the fact that he was now banging on the door of my waxing room, shouting to see if I was okay, was not quite as embarrassing as it should have been.

"She's fine, Euan," Kelly yelled, grinning ear to ear.

Small beads of sweat were slowly dripping down my forehead. "Yes, fine," I echoed. "We're almost done."

Euan's footsteps retreated down the hall.

"That's optimistic, darling." Kelly patted my shoulder.

I looked down to see a patchwork of skin and wax, with Kelly's fingers pulling off small little bits of each at a time. A hundred wasps stings would have felt better.

Kelly pushed my legs open wider to get to the more sensitive areas. "Well," she said, "I can tell you've never had kids."

My mouth dropped open.

*

The van sped along the sunset-lit single-track road back towards Wigtown. Clothed, but still covered in wax, I repeated the words Kelly had said to me. Euan burst into laughter.

"There was absolutely no way I could endure more. She was a total sadist."

"Well, what are you going to do?" he asked, wiping a tear that had formed under his glasses. I took great pleasure in making Euan laugh. He laughed with his whole body; his shoulders would rise and even his fingers looked as if they were shaking in delight.

"Soak in the bath for an hour, hoping the rest will come off before yoga class," I said, unable to cross my legs. "Can you imagine trying to do downward dog with a middle as stiff as a Barbie doll?"

Euan burst out laughing again. "God, Kelly's so bad." He revelled as only an angelic child would in others' bad behaviour.

"It says here she is trained in the healing arts of Reiki." I looked down at the glossy brochure for Kelly's spa. Despite the horror of the afternoon, I found myself chuckling with almost a fondness for Kelly's competing fetishes for inflicting pain on the one hand, and fulfilling her entrepreneurial desire to create a business that genuinely heals and pampers people on the other.

Though I didn't exactly feel fabulous by the end of it, the afternoon afforded another sense of beauty. My love for Wigtown, if possible, had grown. I glowed in appreciation of its kind and complicated characters and its exquisite uniqueness. Euan wrapped his hand in mine as we drove. A feeling of happiness and ease filled the silence between us and I felt beautifully content.

Chapter 32

"Sthira Sukham Asanam. Asana is a steady, comfortable posture." – Sri Swami Satchidananda, THE YOGI SUTRAS OF PANTANJALI: *Health section, front room, left of the cookbooks.*

Holding a wooden box clinking with coins to my chest, I walked back home in the dark from the county buildings. Euan had made it to store my donations from yoga. The box had a small slit at the top, and six solid compartments and now housed a handful of coins, not enough to cover the rental of the hall but enough to jingle a metallic tune.

I had arrived at the hall early, lit some incense and paced around the room, clearing both the air and my thoughts. I was unusually nervous. I hadn't taught in a while and though I'd been practising a new routine aimed at beginners, I felt unprepared. I didn't know how many people would appear, or what they'd be like or what they expected. In Los Angeles, the students were generally seasoned yoga connoisseurs, borderline yoga snobs. They knew as much as or even more than their teachers and the yogic stakes were high. Here it would be different. No one, I guessed, had any preconceived ideas of what yoga was or should be. Teaching these beginners would be profound. The weight of responsibility to give them a good first yoga experience was sitting in a perfect lotus position on my shoulders.

Teaching yoga had never been a conscious ambition, rather I was called to it by convenience. My yoga training had begun in New York, three floors above a restaurant in a tiny sunny studio nestled in mid-Manhattan on the West Side. The studio was on the way home, blocks from my work at public television, and gave me an excuse to unwind and connect with my body after days full of staring at television and computer screens. I had attended so often that it didn't take long to find myself joining the teacher certification programme. With a group of women, of various ages and from various walks of life, I'd meet regularly for lectures in physiology and philosophy – mostly on the yoga sutras.

"*Loka samasta sukhino bhavantu*," one of my teachers had said, "let's begin there."

A beautiful middle-aged Manhattanite, with the perfect body of a personal trainer, had shot up her hand. "May all beings everywhere be happy and free."

"Exactly," my teacher said.

I had felt my mind tripping over something, unable to lose itself in the flow of peace and wellbeing that seemed to fill the room. I put my hand up too.

"Yes? Jessica, something to add?" My teacher said, smiling.

"Well, I like the sentiment a lot, but what if my experience of happiness and freedom starts impeding on someone else's sense of happiness and freedom? I may feel free running around the room, for example, but at the same time I could be making someone else feel uncomfortable."

A cloud descended over my teacher's face. "If you don't like it, Jessica, you don't have to be here."

Apparently the sutras were not up for discussion. We were supposed to appreciate, not argue, and for the rest of the training I had struggled to quell my desire for deeper investigation so as to not impede on my teacher's, or anyone else's, sense of happiness.

In the end, four people attended Wigtown's first yoga class. I hoped the evening had gone as well as I thought it had. I omitted only two things: hands-on adjustments and saying "om" at the end. The former was because when I had sat gently on one of the women's backs during child pose, my first hands-on teaching of the evening, she and her friend had started laughing hysterically. The moment I touched any of the four practioners, in fact, their muscles would seize up. Quickly it became clear that the safest way to spend the rest of the class was at the front of the room.

I also felt it was important not to spring "om" on a beginners' class. I appreciated that these four people were trying something new and the physicality was enough of a foreign experience without my adding to it, yet. I hoped, if these classes continued, I could do more levels and get deeper into the yoga philosophy. Wigtown yoga could lead to – who knows – Wigtown meditation.

"Why not?" I said to Euan, who had looked at me with incredulity. "The young people here already wear track-suits all year round; they won't even need to change to come to a yoga class."

*

Euan placed his hand on my knee as the cab rumbled along in the dark. A bottle of wine, a gift for our hosts, rested in his kilt-clad lap.

I had never seen a man in a kilt before, or Euan so well groomed. I stared at him admiringly – he was looking quite handsome, his curly hair resting just above his crisp white shirt, which was tight on his broad shoulders and tucked in at the waist. I glanced at his strong legs. There was something so attractive and thrillingly masculine about a kilt. It was surprisingly erotic.

"You clean up well," I said, but Euan wasn't listening.

I searched his expression to see if I could discern who or what was occupying such intense energy. A knot formed in my stomach. My mind began to connect a series of separate events and feelings from earlier that day, linking them together until a pattern emerged, like a dot-to-dot puzzle.

When I had returned home from yoga that evening, I had found Euan in the darkness of the large sitting room, with a glass of wine and his phone in his hand.

"Are you all right?" I asked. Euan just sat there without responding, looking upset. Had I done something? How could his mood have changed so radically since this afternoon?

Euan continued to sip his wine. I had taken the hint that he wanted to be alone and gone upstairs, spending extra time getting ready for dinner in the hope of banishing the past two awkward interactions with Euan from my mind. With the wax happily removed after a long soak in the bath, I braved the night cold of our bedroom to slide into a form-hugging red-and-gold vintage halter dress, with a dramatic slit up the side. I felt good, on top of the world again as I came down the stairs, transformed, with my hair done and make-up applied. Euan, at the bottom of the stairs, looked through me.

"How do I look?" I asked, determined that if he wasn't going to instigate compliments I would get the ball rolling.

My hooking for a kind word did the opposite of what I intended. Euan only liked fishing when it applied to salmon, apparently.

"Civilisations could be built in the time it took you to get ready," he said, and grabbed his jacket.

In the cab, as he stared broodingly out of the window, I searched his expression. Things were still so new between us, our connection was still forming, still vulnerable. My heart had started to ache at every odd interaction, curt word or mysterious mood. We had taken a huge risk diving into living together and I wanted things to be perfect, but we were still getting to know each other; the soft tissue of the relationship was still growing.

A cloud of panic spread quickly through my mind. The idea that Euan wasn't happy with me weighed down heavily, threatening to crush my inner optimism. Perhaps we were sitting in silence because he didn't know how to tell me that he was regretting having me here. Euan wanting me to leave had always been a possibility, though deep down I thought, hoped perhaps, that he'd never feel that way.

Living most of the time in my head, however, I was used to doing mental yoga. All I needed to do to get out of this rut was to do downward dog of the mind, to look at both sides of the situation. The panic Euan's mood was triggering could be old anxiety. Just because Euan was moody or quiet, didn't mean he was sick of me and it certainly didn't mean he wanted me to go back to America. As I had already deduced, Euan was not Grant. He wouldn't love me one moment and break up with me the next. In fact, epiphany of epiphanies, Euan's mood might not even be about me at all.

Stop being the Hercule Poirot of other people's feelings, I thought to myself. You two live on top of each other all day – give the poor man some privacy to think and feel without a full mental investigation. If further down the road the relationship doesn't work out, or he decides he's not in love with you, so be it. But that's in the future. You cannot pre-emptively protect yourself – what kind of life is that? Do not ignore your instincts, but try to take what he says and does at face value. If you want to grow and truly be in this relationship, you have to trust him.

"A warrior's approach to life is to say yea, yea to it all," Joseph Campbell would say. I am a bold and confident woman, I repeated in my head. Act like one. Suddenly I felt lighter.

In the dark, the cab turned off the main road. I peered out in front of me, watching as its headlights revealed a steep drive, with large gates at the end. We eventually passed through the ornate iron gates and approached the courtyard of a small stone castle. In my mind, I replaced the battered blue estate car for a gilded carriage. I was in my element, no longer Jessica but a cross between Morgan le Fay approaching Camelot and Elizabeth Bennet arriving for a ball at Pemberley.

While most children wanted to be Cinderella or a princess out of a Disney fairy tale, my fantasies were always more unusual, to be Jane Eyre or even Sherlock Holmes. Perhaps an odd combination, especially for an American girl, but I have finally come to the conclusion that it is the BBC's fault.

At six years old, when asked on a Wednesday evening if I wanted my father or mother to put me to bed, I had known enough to choose my father. He would then give me two options. I could either chat to Clara the Rabbit, a loved but disgruntled anarchic puppet who complained mostly about bills and the government, or I could ask my father one question – any question – about the universe.

On a Wednesday night I would choose the latter because I knew that if I asked a difficult enough question, and followed it up with several clarifying whys, then my father would eventually fall asleep in his chair; a victorious moment for any six-year-old but imperative on a Wednesday night.

And so the Wednesday night ritual would begin. "Why are things getting farther away from us?" I propped myself up against the pillows, settling in.

"Because the universe is expanding," replied my father, leaning back in his chair.

"But how can space expand?" Thrilled, I hugged Chuck Chuck, my stuffed elephant, to my chest. My father continued to talk about space having qualities and looking at light waves to see how, when they travel, they could shift red and blue.

"If it is expanding, what is it expanding into?" This still counted as one qualifying question. I would usually, at this point, feel more awake than ever as my poor father blinked hard to keep his eyes open.

When he had explained that it wasn't expanding into anything, I had started to get upset.

"But what's outside the universe?" my six-year-old self demanded. This was getting out of the territory of follow- up questions. I hadn't been sure he'd answer that one but as I waited, only snores came back in response. He had fallen asleep. I slid out of the bed, triumphantly. I had done it again.

Downstairs my mother would be watching public television, as they aired the latest BBC period drama on Wednesday evenings. I would sneak behind the sofa and watch with her, until my giggles alerted her to my presence.

"Oh, your father!" she would sigh and welcome me onto the couch next to her. By the age of eight I had watched and loved every period drama the BBC had aired on American TV, from *Jeeves and Wooster* to Jane Austen adaptations. As a child I had felt more connected to the past worlds I had seen on the television, the lands of costumes and countryside, than I had the modern American suburb in which I found myself.

This sense of dislocation manifested itself in a number of awkward and unsuccessful teenage attempts at self-expression. At thirteen, for Halloween I dressed up as Emily Dickinson, a reference that was lost not only on my teenage friends who were more interested in being sexy vampires or playboy bunnies – yes, playboy bunnies at thirteen – but on the adults who handed out candy as we went door to door. Other teenagers learned song lyrics by their favourite bands, I memorised Tennyson, Longfellow and Blake. Even during college I still kept my costume box, but had finally learned to channel that angst, that homesickness for a place and time that I couldn't touch, into my films.

That schism, between the past and the present, was perhaps just another genetic inheritance of a grandchild of Holocaust survivors, where the tragic past was ever present, my lost relatives being mentioned only in heavy echoes or never mentioned at all, leaving gaping spaces in conversations that echoed even louder. Or perhaps the schism was common to all filmmakers; perhaps we all long for worlds and lands beyond our own and to fall in love with people we've never met. Perhaps, as the psychologist Bruno Bettelheim states in *The Uses of Enchantment*, my fascination with make-believe was because I was "too disappointed in reality to trust its rewards". But most likely, as stated before, it was the BBC's fault. Having exposed an American girl early to dramas and good manners and castles, they carved a longing in me that lasted throughout my childhood, teenage years and into adulthood.

Now in Scotland, whatever the reason for its existence, that rift was resolving itself. I felt as if my inner world was finally matching the outer one, the expanse of rolling hills, the ruined castles and the sense of mystery hanging in the air like the haar which drifted in silently from the sea.

"Thanks so much," Euan said to the cab driver. "If you could pick us up around eleven?"

The cab slowed, and the light inside popped on. The cab driver nodded as Euan handed him money.

I stepped out into the cold air and looked up at the looming castle before us. The courtyard echoed with laughter and music from inside, and I took a deep breath as I followed Euan through an unassuming side door. On it was written in a child's hand: "Guests please this way".

*

Highland dancing was not as complicated as it might first look, but a word to the wise for the complete novice: first wear comfortable shoes as there is a lot of hopping. Second, pick a person of the same gender who looks fairly competent and copy their movements exactly – eventually the dance repeats itself and you'll learn quickly. Third, and most important by far, wait until everyone has had at least five glasses of wine and champagne before you dance, and then no one will notice that you have no idea what you're doing.

The ballroom was bursting with light and energy and I, Elizabeth Bennet, sat observing everything and everyone around me. Deep-red walls gave the grand room, lit by sparkling candles, a warm glow. All around us paintings and portraits hung in gilt frames. Beautifully dressed people passed by, twirling and dancing. The ballroom matched perfectly my BBC-inspired romantic notions of what a ballroom should be like. However, to my disappointment, the witty banter I had seen so many times in *Jeeves and Wooster* was not present. Instead, the conversations tended to be polite and local, about the weather, fishing, Euan's parents, family and mutual friends. Underscoring the chatter at the front of the room, a band, playing Highland tunes, held sway.

After two rounds of embarrassed attempts to Highland-dance, I took a break on a chair, which looked so dainty and delicate that I was afraid it might be for decoration rather than use. My feet were killing me. Even before the dancing there had been a lot of standing. When we first arrived in the castle's grand hall, we were served drinks below a massive staircase, surrounded by deer heads and old tapestries, and familiar and unfamiliar faces. We had chatted for what seemed like hours, until my stomach had started to growl and the cold of the castle seeped into my bones, turning my lips a faint blue.

"So, Euan," an elderly man, with bright salmon-coloured trousers and a green jumper – obviously ignoring the black-tie-only instructions – had said, walking up to us, "who is this lovely American?"

"This is Jessica," Euan said, rigid and polite. He looked nervous. "My special friend."

The words grated on my ears. Special friend? Euan was clearly so ill at ease with me by his side that I was beginning to feel equally out of place. Once the elderly man found a bowl of crisps, which interested him more than our company, I turned to Euan.

"Special friend?" I tried to tease, but the words came out angry.

"Well, you are special." Euan shifted. "I know, I'm sorry. I didn't know what to say."

"How about your girlfriend?"

"Of course, yes, okay." Euan squeezed my arm.

"Everyone knows I'm living with you," I said, pulling my arm away. "So what's your problem?"

"I don't know."

"You've gone all cold and formal."

"Sorry, it's just, you know, a change." Euan smiled sheepishly as if he had just dodged a bullet. "Would you like another drink?"

At that moment, I could no longer dream myself into Elizabeth Bennet. Standing in the large grand room, I felt more like Eliza Doolittle, ruefully aware that this was Euan's world, not mine. He knew almost everyone there – they were his friends, parents of friends and friends of his parents – and arriving with me was his first full and open declaration that we were a couple. For someone who hadn't even been able to tell his own friends that I was coming back, this night was clearly a reason to be uncomfortable, like a social baptism of fire.

As if my thoughts were amplified by the old medieval stone walls, the host of the evening, a widow in her late sixties, silver-haired in a long black dress, came slinking through the crowd. She smiled when she saw Euan returning with drinks, and intercepted him accordingly.

"Euan, dear, I've been meaning to talk to you all night." She pushed past a cluster of Euan's friends, ignoring them completely, and stood on tiptoes, kissing Euan on both cheeks.

Euan smiled politely. "Fiona, I'd like you to meet Jessica, my girlfriend." Euan looked at me and I smiled.

Fiona's eyes flickered over me for a second. "You must come and have a look at my library one of these days," she continued, turning her attention back to Euan. "I've been doing some winter cleaning of my late husband's books and it could all be junk, but I'll leave it to you to figure out what's what." Fiona put her arm through Euan's and laughed as if she had made a joke.

"I'd be glad to," Euan said as he unhooked his arm to grab another glass of wine passing by on a silver tray.

I looked at Fiona, and said, "Thank you so much for inviting us."

Fiona hadn't yet made eye contact with me and I could practically feel icicles forming in the air between us. The reason for her instant dislike for me wasn't obvious, however, and it made me more curious than offended.

She smiled coldly.

"I've never been in such a beautiful home before," I continued with complete honesty, having decided to either melt her disdain for me with sincerity or kill her with American enthusiasm. "Actually, the night is full of firsts because I've never been Highland dancing either."

Fiona's smile quickly turned to a scowl but I had succeeded in getting her attention. She hooked me with her gaze. "Where are you from exactly?"

"Originally? Boston."

"Oh Boston, lovely city." Her smile forced its way back. "Where did you go to school?"

"The local high school in my town. My mother was the art teacher there." Fiona waited for more. It then occurred to me that her dislike hadn't stemmed from the fact that I was Euan's girlfriend, rather that I was an American from an as yet unknown background. In other words, she couldn't tell if I was posh enough for her social empathy. "Christmas sounds exciting. Will you celebrate here, Fiona?"

"What do you mean, 'sounds exciting'?"

When I told her I had little experience with Christmas, she said nothing, but slowly stepped back as if to distance herself from whatever foreign disease I might carry.

Before I could continue, she waltzed away to speak to other guests and I turned to Euan.

"I don't think she liked me."

Euan shook his head. "You're too sensitive, Jessy. Of course she liked you."

It was a relief when it was announced that dinner was ready. Apart from Fiona, who had values as ancient as the furniture that surrounded us, everyone was lovely, generous and very accepting. I especially loved seeing two couples, Euan's friends, whom I had met during the festival. After dinner they were determined to teach me Highland dancing, dragging me onto the floor before anyone was sufficiently drunk, which was why I was now sitting on one of the most expensive chairs I had seen outside of a museum, rubbing my aching feet.

The music started up again. The ballroom, though grand, was so filled with people that there were many half-drunk collisions. The dancers switched formations, from rows of six to circles of eight people holding hands.

Though not as quick-witted, or light on my toes as one of my period-drama heroines, the child in me, who had spent every Wednesday night enraptured with the BBC, started to glow in flushed delight. Perhaps not everything was as it should be; I had a dithering Darcy after all and a chilly echo from Fiona's frosty reception, but I decided to give her the benefit of the doubt – I was in her debt after all for including me in this experience. Social hiccups aside, I had actually been dancing in a castle.

Across the room, I could see Euan dancing next to Fiona. As they held hands, the circle changed directions, then collapsed in on itself, and expanded again, like a living, breathing organism. Euan had a near miss with the circle behind him, and he caught my gaze, smiling. Next to him, in the corner of the room danced Euan's friends, who when they saw me sitting, started yelling at me to join. I could hear their shouts over the music and my heart swelled. Like the brass bell, which rang so sweetly in front of The Bookshop, a little ring of recognition sounded within me. Despite a day full of sadists and ice queens, there was an abundance of kindred spirits in Galloway, and I was now lucky enough to call them friends.

Fiona's dog, a friendly chocolate Labrador wearing a Highland hat, secured by elastic around his chin, lazily wandered over to me. He looked as dazed as I felt. Perhaps he was also overwhelmed by the swarm of people, the increasing heat of the ballroom and the constant music. Looking at me, he opened his purple jaw and yawned. I smiled. If Fiona was not an attentive host, her dog seemed to be. His lean front legs stretched out in front of him, and he arched his back into a perfect downward dog.

Chapter 33

"The country here is very special and very picturesque,
everything speaks, as it were, and is full of character...
one sees blackthorn hedges around the gardens, fields and
meadows here. Lately, with the snow, the effect is that
of the black lettering on white paper, like pages of the
Gospel." – Vincent van Gogh, DEAR THEO: *Correspondence
section, gallery, first bookshelf on the left.*

Snow dusted the rooftops of Wigtown, and through the
dark window I could see the frosty marsh extending
to a silvery, white-capped sea. The morning light had
hardly reached the bedroom and I stood, my teeth chattering, looking at the familiar grey sky. The days, as we
reached late December, had become unbearably cold. The
Bookshop's thick stone walls acted like a giant refrigerator,
and I was surprised to find it was often colder inside than
it was outside.

It had been especially hard to get out of bed this
morning. The thick duvet, electric blanket and Euan kept
me toasty warm until the alarm rang. On waking, I noticed
my face was stiff from cold and it was hard to yawn.
My breath puffed out before me and I watched it like a
warning of what I would soon be contending with outside
the covers. It wasn't that the cold was worse in Wigtown
than in New England, which boasted harsher weather and

conditions. However, I had been used to 24-hour heating in Boston, blasting through the snowy winter, keeping the house roasting and the cold outside.

As usual, Euan got out of bed without complaint or hesitation; years of boarding school had made him hardy, and he met the painful exit into the cold morning like he did most other unpleasant tasks: he just did it. I'd clutch his arm, hoping he'd be uncharacteristically lazy and lie back down in bed. The struggle would only last a minute, with him leaning over me, kissing me on the forehead and laughing, telling me that he had to open the shop.

With Euan gone, I would flash out of bed, hopping from one bare foot to another on the frozen floor, and throw on whatever I could find. It didn't matter how I dressed, for it would soon be a base layer on top of which would be piled jumpers and jackets.

I had tried, for a while, to stay fabulous and wear dresses with tights, or more form-fitting clothes, but there was nothing sexy about being cold. After sporting blue lips for a couple of days, I reluctantly retired my Los Angeles shirts and dresses into a box and tucked them away under the bed. I could almost feel Rose's look of disapproval, so I had tried long skirts to still feel feminine and keep the chill at bay. Nothing worked except for wearing three pairs of trousers at a time, layered with two shirts and a massive jumper and my heavy hiking boots with thick socks. My only fashion accessory was my white ghostly breath, which followed me wherever I went.

Wigtown was more beautiful than ever, though, the hills and fields, still surprisingly green, often covered in a delicate blue frost. The orange winter light cast long shadows as the sun stayed low, no matter the time of day, on the horizon. Though it got dark increasingly early, when the sun was out, hanging low in the sky, it was constantly magic hour; the time of day that filmmakers lived for, where each view, whether it was the sea, mountains, the town or farm-land, was a picture-perfect, frozen postcard.

There was a romance about this time of year, which kept the depressing aspects of it at bay. The colder weather meant Euan was diligent about lighting the fire in the snug, a small carpeted sitting room at the back of the house where I had set up a little desk. Every morning he would silently carry a basket full of logs up the spiral staircase and I would watch as he knelt by the stove, carefully sliding in one log at a time until there was a roaring fire. He was my knight in shining armour brandishing baskets of wood, taking it upon himself, like a sacred duty, to keep me warm.

The winter also afforded sledging. Euan and I would go out at night, under a full moon, to the golf course down the road and slide down the hill beneath the shadowy trees, drinking in the sharp, clear cold air. Winter was the season of hot Winter Pimms, warm stews, evenings curled up on the sofa in front of the fire, a quiet bookshop, time to write and dangerously delicious mince pies – with brandy butter, of course. Though the cold and I were at odds, Euan and I had developed a blissfully happy rhythm together.

Winter also brought Christmas. I faced the prospect with intense pleasure and a healthy dose of Jewish guilt. Celebrating Christmas in my own home was an exciting new adventure. No matter how much I tried to justify that Christmas was a pagan tradition, I was keenly conscious that I was throwing away generations of tradition and joining in for what was essentially Jesus's birthday party.

I knew a lot about Christmas. I knew some of the carols from school. I knew about the presents, candy canes and Santa, and I knew that Jesus was actually meant to have been born in the spring, but during medieval times, priests had moved the holiday to coincide with the pagan winter solstice. Many cultures, including my own, had a festival of light at the darkest time of year. The common ritual seemed to be a glorified distraction from the lack of vitamin D, the cold and dwindling food resources, and it worked. As the days were getting shorter, instead of feeling depressed, there was an excitement and buzz in the air for the impending celebrations and I was swept away by it.

Deirdre had kindly dropped off Christmas decorations, which I carefully put up around the shop. To add to the growing collection, Euan and I had foraged for holly and other foliage to create wreathes during one of our free Sunday afternoons. It had been a joy to my starved winter eyes to see the greenery indoors. The Bookshop looked like a cosy Christmas wonderland.

"Euan," I said as I shuffled into the front of The Bookshop, wrapped in a blanket and sporting hair that hadn't been washed in three days. "Aren't you excited? Christmas is only two weeks away."

Euan shook his head like Eeyore. "Everyone gets to enjoy Christmas, while I still have to work."

"It's not all bad, you know?" I replied. As I was throwing myself into the Christmas spirit with gusto, Euan was growing increasingly despondent and grumpy. "At least the shop is busy." A handful of customers, as if on cue, entered the shop. The familiar sound of the bell jingled with what to me seemed like holiday cheer. Christmas was a rare, much-needed retail window in an otherwise slow, quiet winter in Wigtown.

"You should have gone to Ireland to celebrate with my evil cousin. Eve would have loved having you there." Euan glared at one of the customers who dropped a tissue onto the ground and left it there. "She wrote to me saying something about a Catholic getting extra God points for getting a Jew to go to mass and eat bacon at Christmas."

I laughed. "Euan, seriously. It's my first Scottish Christmas. You could make some effort."

Euan shrugged and sipped on his tea. "Like what?"

"Maybe you could do a holiday window?"

"I never do a holiday window." Euan turned back to his computer. It was his not-so-subtle hint that he wanted to be left alone.

That night, Euan cleared out the larger window display, and hung a single "humbug" sweetie from the ceiling.

*

Euan was asked to play Wigtown's Santa at the annual Christmas Fayre and, when he politely declined, I volunteered in his stead. Surprised that they agreed, I practised continually and Euan's reaction filled me with dread. He would double over in tears of laughter as I rehearsed cloaking my high voice in low "ho ho hos". The rehearsing did little to prepare me as I was still unsure of what Santa's voice sounded like or what he said. My hope was that the children's unshakable belief in Santa would blind them to the fact that I was Wigtown's first Jewish, American, cross-dressing Father Christmas.

I arrived five minutes early for my post, equipped with a massive duvet. The Santa on the shift before mine, a middle-aged gentleman with a generous tummy, sauntered out of the coat closet, which apparently doubled as the Christmas changing-room.

"There are a lot of them out there," he said, looking exhausted, and handed me the now sweat-drenched, red-and-white Santa suit.

Joy, a tall, silver-haired and appropriately named volunteer, helped me into my costume. The duvet worked a treat, providing me with a rotund, if lumpy, belly, which a black belt held in place. My feet easily slipped into the large Santa boots but I shivered when the damp, sweat-soaked hat was placed on my head. The beard was the tricky part, my head's circumference being smaller than the lineage of Santas before me. Joy, who was talented with safety pins, secured it to my hat in such a way that, if I held my chin low, the beard would stay in place.

"You look great," she said, patting me on the shoulder.

Her calming presence allowed my confidence to grow, but I squirmed, feeling the wet hair around my mouth, imagining all the germs crawling in the hat and dripping off the hairy beard. Just don't breathe, I reassured myself, and you'll be fine.

Sitting in the winter throne, surrounded by my elves, candy canes and presents, I felt like I imagine Santa would have felt: important and itchy. After countless children on my lap, I was growing uncomfortably warm, and the duvet, plus the Santa suit, which I now felt certain hadn't been washed in generations of use, were scratching my skin.

There were two big baskets of presents next to me, one filled with boys' toys and one for girls. Blinded by my extra-large hat and beard, I couldn't see which was which. One boy, on being given a girl's gift, had walked away crying. When I ran after him, dragging my lopsided belly with me and clutching a gift from the other basket, he cried harder.

The children of Wigtown stared at me; some in horror, some with adoring faces that would have made the iciest of hearts melt and some with cool indifference. One nine-year-old, who had found out the whole thing was a hoax but knew he'd get presents anyway, sat po-faced as I did my best with belly laughs and baritone "have you been a good girl/boy this year", and photo-smiles through my sweaty whiskers. Joy, ever present, would quickly adjust the plastic albino beard as soon as she saw it going awry.

The only time I was close to being outed was when one clever six-year-old girl asked her mother in a piercing voice the whole room could hear, "Why does Santa have woman hands?"

Joy leaned down and whispered, "Next year, we'll have to get you gloves."

All in all, no one seemed bothered by the American accent, the ever-roaming beard or my small head. My Santa shift passed quickly and I soon found myself taking off the soaked costume and handing it back to Joy. I emerged from the coat closet, having shed half my weight, and felt not only ten degrees cooler, but renewed.

The elderly man for the next Santa shift after mine arrived.

"There's a lot of them out there," I said and happily handed the sweat-soaked costume over to him, relieved that it was now all over.

Perhaps embodying Santa had filled me with delusions of grandeur, or an abundance of festive cheer, but if Euan couldn't get excited about the holiday, I thought perhaps I could teach him about the spirit of Christmas. From the Christmas Fayre, I went to the post office and bought three colours of twine, a handful of his favourite chocolate bars and a book on cycling routes around

Galloway. I found the nicest bottle of red wine that I could afford at the Co-op, and went home with my bundle of treasure.

*

"I have a surprise for you," I said to Euan just as he closed the shop.

Euan moaned. "Oh God. Have you cooked?"

I rolled my eyes and put my hands on my hips. Sometimes I wished I had the witty words to throw back at him. "No, it's not food, come on – follow me."

"God, you're so bossy." Euan reluctantly followed me up the stairs.

The sitting-room door was closed, with a piece of paper taped to it which read "Christmas Treasure Hunt".

Euan sighed and then opened the door to see his period sitting room transformed into a maze of colour. I had hidden each gift, and to it attached a long piece of coloured string, which I had wound like an intricate web around the room.

"Jesus!" Euan looked horrified. "What the hell have you done to my sitting room, Fox?"

This was not the reaction I was going for. I stepped into the room and tried to demonstrate. "See, you follow the colour, until it leads you to a prize. I thought it might be silly fun – you know, for Christmas."

Euan tried to smile and I watched as he carefully followed the blue string around chairs, window shutters and door handles. His back was so stiff that he struggled to lift his legs even five inches off the ground over the maze. Poor Euan threw himself into it with as much heart as I had put in to playing my role as Santa. Better than the Christmas spirit, Euan was showing his love for me by enduring quite considerable amounts of pain as he traversed my coloured web, clambering around his priceless furniture and antiques.

"Found one!" Euan said, straightening up and holding a bar of chocolate in his hands.

I tried not to laugh. "Great, five more to go."

Euan shook his head and started following the yellow string. I leaned against the wall, promising myself I would never ask Euan to take part in forced winter cheer again.

*

Flicking on the kettle, I walked over to the ice-covered kitchen window and ran my finger along the twirling patterns of frost. The tips of my fingers suddenly burned with cold and I was surprised to find that this beautiful display of nature was actually growing on the inside of the glass. A cold bedroom and bathroom were a challenge, but as I stood there trembling, anxiously waiting for the kettle to boil, I decided a cold kitchen was unbearable.

If my transformation into Santa had been my baptism of fire into the holiday season (which sounded like a particularly cosy phrase as my teeth chattered over my tea), then Christmas shopping would be my first test.

When Wigtown became Scotland's National Book Town, two other towns were awarded titles of their own in the hope of creating a triangle of venues, south-west Scotland's Venus flytrap for tourists: Kirkudbright, a beautiful, medium-sized town on the coast, boasting new artists and influential past residents in the Scottish Colourist Movement, was named the Art Town. Castle Douglas, filled with restaurants, cafes, upmarket butchers and food festivals, was designated the Food Town. Euan and I were heading into the latter, Castle Douglas, a village much larger than Wigtown and closer to the city of Dumfries, to visit their shops.

Euan and I piled into the van. As he started the engine, he grinned at me.

"Someone's happy," he said.

I was. I was getting out of Wigtown for the day.

Though I loved it, Wigtown had become an island for me without either a car or a house to call my own. So much of who I had been in LA, an independent woman rocketing up the career ladder, or who I thought I had been, a yet undiscovered director, had radically changed these past months. I was now housebound, dependent on Euan, far removed from the production world and with ample time to myself. Though it still held the excitement of being on holiday, I was getting a bit stir-crazy and I couldn't wait to have an adventure outside Wigtown's invisible walls.

I hadn't been writing my films of late either, a massive shift – though predicted – from my angst-driven urge to create and emote. Part of me felt, perhaps as many women fear, that I could have only one success in my life – a relationship or a career. Why did I think I couldn't have it all? Surely, the notion that love and career were on opposite sides of a balancing scale was not an inherent fact, but rather the result of my inability to dream of a better balance.

My lack of ambition, I quickly decided, was the cold's fault. My brain was as frozen as my hands, and it was impossible to concentrate when you couldn't sit still. Sitting in the snug, fire roaring, I would finish consulting work and instead of dreaming up projects, I would enjoy the prospect of an afternoon with nothing ahead of me. I hoped this shift was time-limited because a little voice inside had started whispering, "If you don't use it, you lose it."

Neither Euan nor I were ones for lists, so as we arrived in Castle Douglas, a panic set in. There were gifts for his family, gifts for his friends, gifts for my friends and gifts for my family to buy. Already I started to feel the down-side of Christmas. While Santa had elves, we did not, and getting gifts that everyone would like was going to be not only stressful, but expensive. How did people do this every year?

As if we were embarking on a mad scavenger hunt, Euan and I headed off down opposite ends of the street, splitting the load of presents to buy for his family and friends. The main street of Castle Douglas, a long shop-lined road which ran straight uphill was buzzing with energy. Holiday music pumped out of the cafés, there were Santas ringing bells on every corner and decorations hung between houses. I felt a stranger in a strange land as each sense – sight, hearing, taste, smell – was bombarded with Christmas cheer.

The allotted two hours passed quickly and I stumbled back to the van, arms swinging with fresh purchases. My hunter-gatherer instinct had gone berserk and I had bought a seemingly endless list of cashmere hats, scarves, wallets, pens, calendars, candles and jewellery. I dropped my bags next to the van, completely exhausted. In the distance, I could see Euan approaching, his arms empty. My shoulders slumped. This meant we would have to go onto Dumfries, round two of the sadomasochistic art of holiday shopping, with more mind-numbing music, more crowds and more gifts.

*

Two days before Christmas, Deirdre arrived holding a package. Inside was a knee-length hand-knitted Christmas jumper. It was a crowning jewel from the 1980s, with a massive Christmas tree under which were presents and a giant teddy bear. Any hipster from Los Angeles would be proud to wear something so retro.

"Deirdre, thank you, I adore it," I said, holding it up and loving the long, lean shape.

Euan walked into the kitchen and stared in horror. "What God-awful thing is that?"

Deirdre put her hands on her hips. "Euan, that is my Christmas jumper." She turned to me. "I hardly wear it now, though, Jessica, so it is all yours if you like it."

"I love it."

"Really?" Euan refilled his tea.

"Yes." I glared at Euan. "Thank you, Deirdre – do you mind if I add some bells and whistles to it?"

"You mean that literally?" Euan raised an eyebrow.

I did. In my mind I pictured adding light up LEDs or jingle bells.

"It's yours to do what you like with, my dear." Deirdre smiled her kindred-spirit smile. I looked at her admiringly. There was a wonderful sparkle and magic to Deirdre, making me feel that anything and everything was possible.

As if wound up like a tight rubber band that was about to snap, the anticipation for Christmas was mounting. Days passed quickly, and when I woke up on Christmas morning, watching my breath appear before me and hearing neither the jingle of Santa's sleigh nor the distant cries of "Merry Christmas" – like they do in the movies – I felt deflated that Christmas was as ordinary a day as any other. Though we had slept late, Euan shot out of bed first as usual, and with my crucial heat source gone, I reluctantly followed.

Hopping on the ice-cold floor, I quickly slid on trousers and my now flashing-light-adorned Christmas jumper.

"That is hideous." Euan looked at me, delighted. He seemed privately to revel in my unselfconscious attempts to embrace new things, watching with school-boy eagerness as they led often either to disastrous consequences or accidental transgressions in propriety. "Are you actually wearing that to church?"

"Why not?" I shrugged. "It's festive."

*

From inside the church, I watched as the snow swirled outside. Snow blanketed the rooftops, trees and pavement, downy and thick.

Opening The Bookshop door on to Wigtown's main square that morning had been an unexpected Christmas present. I had changed my black flats for knee-high wellies and enjoyed tramping through the snow hand in hand with Euan towards Wigtown's Catholic church. We were late and had walked more quickly than I wanted to. I'd like to have had more time to savour the landscape which had been transformed from dark stone and grey skies to a fresh bright white, as if Wigtown were smiling and flashing its pearly teeth.

The sound of a page turning roused me from my thoughts. We were about to sing another carol. I was sitting on a wooden pew, surrounded by people. Euan and the couple next to me suddenly kneeled and I followed, never having knelt at a worship service in my life. I felt humbled and extremely uncomfortable. Everything about the service and my surroundings felt new and foreign.

In my childhood synagogue, most of the service had been in Hebrew. This, I now realised, had been essential to my spiritual welfare because the less I understood the less I had to disagree with. Now, in church, understanding every word as the priest read aloud in English, instead of feeling the touch of the divine, I felt a touch argumentative. The tunes were beautiful, though, haunting and dramatic. As I blurred my listening to this lovely soundtrack, my eyes fixed on the handful of statues gathered around the pulpit. Worshipping graven images is strictly forbidden in Judaism and going to synagogue for me was always a cerebral experience with words, ritual and song serving an abstract concept of a God, one you can neither see nor even begin to picture. In the Catholic church it seemed to be something very different. To me this was a powerfully emotional experience, with iconography, readings, ritual and song giving a concrete concept of God, one that I could see, right before me.

On taking my first steps ever into a Catholic church I had come face to face with a large statue of Jesus, his bloody wrists and ankles nailed to the cross and his forlorn eyes looking up to heaven. Across from him stood a statue of Mary, cloaked in blue robes, holding a baby surrounded by candles and flowers. The archetype of a woman holding a child flew past my consciousness and into my subconscious, igniting emotions that were not spiritual, nor intellectual but deeply visceral. It was mysterious and primal, and it was a feeling I associated with theatre, or with the time I had seen a Native American powwow enacted. This was the realm of myth, as defined by Joseph Campbell – a journey that is universal but deeply essential to us as individuals, like a depersonalised world dream. I understood the awe and desire to worship the divine relationship between a woman and a newborn baby; it was one of the great mysteries of human experience.

After church, Euan and I sat together in the warmth of his parents' sitting room, with his sisters, their husbands and children. Wrapping paper covered the floor and the contented silence of post-gift-giving filled the air. We had demolished an extraordinarily large Christmas feast not moments before, and I leaned into the cushions of the sofa, my stomach throbbing with rich food. My massive stocking, now empty, lay at my side, and a vast pile of presents was stacked neatly before me. I was both touched and embarrassed by the way I had been spoiled by Euan's family and so warmly included in their Christmas rituals.

Euan's phone beeped and he looked at the message, quickly leaving the room. I had seen him send out a handful of Christmas cards weeks before, many to female names I did not recognise. A now familiar jolt of panic rose within me. I tried to ignore it and instead watched Deirdre demonstrate her new Christmas gift. Henry, Euan's father, an engineer and brilliant inventor, had transformed a hard hat into an eyeglass cleaning machine. Gears were carefully positioned so that two toothbrushes hung perfectly in front of Deirdre's eyes. When she switched it on, a battery-powered bird at the top spun and moved the gears and made the toothbrushes move in a windscreen-wiper motion.

Applause and laughter filled the room. Henry, satisfied that his invention worked properly, quietly slipped outside to smoke his pipe. The children clamoured up to Deirdre, each begging for a turn.

A hollow longing appeared like a sink hole in my chest. I felt so at home here and yet still so far from my own family. Surrounded by Euan's old childhood pictures and holiday decorations, and with my belly full of foreign delicacies, I realised that I had thrown myself into the Christmas spirit with such reckless abandon that I had all but forgotten my own identity.

Chapter 34

"*Got hot bashafn a velt mit veltelekh* – God created a world full of small worlds." – YIDDISH PROVERB.

What do you mean just us?" Euan was standing behind me in the kitchen. His eyes followed my hands as they rolled out three long strips of dough and delicately folded them into a braid.

"No one else could come," I said, trying to hide my disappointment. I slid the lopsided, braided challah bread into the oven.

It was three days after Christmas and Wigtown was about to have its first ever Hanukkah. Part of the fun of living in a different part of the world, I had decided, was not just embracing the new culture, but bringing your own to it. For the party I had hung decorations that my mom had sent over on the kitchen mantelpiece, silver dreidels with blue confetti. I set out a traditional table, with an eight-pronged candle-holder known as a menorah (for the eight nights of Hanukkah), which I had made out of an egg carton.

"What's that?" Euan asked. He watched as I crushed thin crackers with a stone mortar and pestle.

"It's supposed to be matzo meal for the matzo ball soup – remember? I made it for you before."

Euan winced. I handed him the pestle. "Feel like having a go? We have to do the whole packet."

In my imagination, all of our friends, and their children, would have come so I had cooked enough for an army. I had prepared traditional latkes, fried potato pancakes, and my multi-course meal was almost all complete, including a slow-cooked beef brisket in beer, spices and vegetables. In the end, though, everyone was busy and even Euan's parents had committed to other plans.

"Jessy, why don't you rest in the snug? I've lit the fire," Euan said, handing me a glass of champagne. "I can take it from here."

Euan, to my delight, was enjoying the idea of celebrating Hanukkah. His enthusiasm had come as a surprise to me because of his disdain for Christmas cheer, and the fact that he seemed to be suspended in a state of perpetual culture shock. As if in a sitcom, he could be heard sighing, "I never thought I'd date an American" after I did anything typically foreign. When I'd hug his friends goodbye, he'd groan, "You're so American, Fox." Or when, overwhelmed with a feeling of warmth and happiness, I told him I loved him, he would reply, yet again, "Jessy, you're so American." But now, in contrast, Euan seemed to be revelling in my Jewish identity and his affectionate interest in my different background warmed my heart.

I grabbed my glass of champagne and kissed him on the cheek.

"The matzo balls should be put in right as the guests come," I said, watching as he ground the crackers into a fine powdery dust.

"I get it." Euan looked insulted. "Go, please, relax."

"Okay, chef."

The door to the snug was shut to keep the warmth of the fire in, so I struggled with my glass and the bowl of crisps in one hand as I turned the knob with the other.

Inside, I found myself face to face with Eve. I shrieked and dropped my drink onto the carpet. She was perched happily on the sofa, drinking a glass of wine as if she'd been there all afternoon.

"Happy Hanukkah, you American," she said with a grin.

I scooped up my now empty glass and sat down on the couch and hugged her. Fumbling for what to say, my mind raced, quickly putting together the facts that she had come all this way, that she must have crept up the spiral stairs when I was cooking in the kitchen, and moreover that Euan had orchestrated it all.

"Surprise."

"I can't believe you're here."

"You certainly look shocked. If not horrified." She smiled and refilled my glass from a massive bottle of champagne that had been keeping her company on the table next to her.

"I'm thrilled you're here." I hoped my voiced showed how deeply I meant it. "I just can't believe you came all this way."

Eve shrugged. "Euan and I thought it would be fun as a surprise."

I had always supposed expecting something was half the pleasure of experiencing it and had subscribed to Anne of Green Gables' philosophy that "anticipation is as glorious as soaring through the sunset and almost worth the thud". I was so wrong. Seeing Eve in the snug was a complete joy. Surprises were better.

"I can't stop smiling. I just can't believe you're here." I squeezed Eve's arm affectionately.

"Well, believe it." She took a sip of her drink. "Who knows what else is in store?"

Soon afterwards, to my delight, more surprise guests arrived. Euan had told everyone to come in fancy dress with the theme "American". Besides our neighbours' daughter, who dressed as the Statue of Liberty, and Eve, who dressed as an annoying Irish American tourist, everyone else came as an obese person. Laura and her boyfriend showed up, each with a duvet stuffed into their trousers. Callum arrived sporting a massive pillow-padded belly and a suit whose buttons looked about to burst, while Euan came downstairs, looking all too comfortable in a dress of mine, which annoyingly fit better over his hips than it did my own.

"Happy Hanukkah!" they all shouted in clashing accents, looking a little like an American freak show.

The crowning moment of the evening, as everyone indulged in juicy brisket and poked curiously at the sweet noodle dish called kugel, was when Euan's parents arrived. Deirdre not only entered the kitchen singing "Hava Nagila", but Henry brought a menorah that he had made in his workshop. He had found a picture online and copied it exactly, carving the wood to make eight perfect candleholders.

I quickly replaced my egg-carton attempt with his beautifully carved one. This evening was the perfect antidote to my post-Christmas homesickness, and as the candles burned brightly, and I half listened to the friendly chatter around the table, I felt my sense of longing fall away. I suddenly was at home in Wigtown, not because it was Hanukkah, but because the holiday was an opportunity to show me that, despite my different background, and the fact that I was unfortunately "so American" – from the land, apparently, of the obese – I was surrounded by true friends.

Chapter 35

"When she woke up both Prince and castle were gone
and then she lay on a little green patch, in the midst of the
gloomy wood." – Peter Christen Asbjornsen, EAST OF THE
SUN AND WEST OF THE MOON: *Children's section, left side,
along the window sill.*

January passed in frozen time. The house was at its
coldest, with nowhere to escape the icy chill. Some
mornings I would start crying, frustrated by the intensity
of the cold, my teeth constantly chattering at the impossible task of staying warm. I made endless cups of tea,
challenging it not to grow cold before I had had a chance
to drink at least half.

December had been a good month for Euan and me,
and I thought we had hit our stride. But then my first
Hogmanay was, to my horror, spent unplanned and
disregarded – despite my efforts for the contrary. I had
hoped we'd go somewhere romantic, either Edinburgh
or Paris, but we stayed in the snug, like any other
evening, with the fire roaring and the TV on. I watched
the fireworks in Edinburgh, live on the screen, below
which stood crowds of families, friends and couples
enjoying themselves. In the distance I could hear real
fireworks coming in short bursts from somewhere in
Wigtown.

I thought of my friends, celebrating in Los Angeles or enjoying the First Night activities in Boston. Didn't Euan realise how much I was giving up to be here with him? Why wasn't he doing everything he could to sweep me off my feet? The snug felt lonely and quiet as he helped himself to more wine, with no desire to sit near me or make conversation. Every now and then I'd catch him looking wistfully into the distance, as if he were in another place and time entirely, and I felt inadequate and worried about where his mind had wandered off to. The lack of romance for my first Scottish New Year hurt me deeply and, over the ensuing weeks, as winter's damp cold days settled in over Wigtown, my mood also sunk into something cold and dark.

Frost blanketed Galloway's hills in a crisp blue line. Windows were covered in ice and the cars in the town square stood half frozen, with a dewy side that faced the sun as it rose and a frozen side that stood in shadow. I shrank from writing my scripts. I couldn't even seek out work. With no visa, my hands were tied, and the yoga classes did little to fill my pocket or sense of ambition. My parents were worried about me, and so were my friends. They knew that I had a single ambition and passion to make films, and watched flabbergasted as I turned more and more work down to remain in Wigtown. Soon, offers of work dried up, and then stopped completely.

For the best part of a month, Euan spent his evenings alone fixing something in the house, equipped only with his beer and portable radio. The only time we spent together was when I insisted on lending a hand. As we painted, or chipped away at plaster, through the evening we would soften, and begin to enjoy each other. Laughter and a warmth would again grow. At these moments, it was a mystery to me why they had ever gone away, and why it became so easy for unhappiness and resentment to manifest themselves between us.

A panic was growing inside me, and would often rear its head (which looked identical to my own except with wide, anxious eyes), but still I forged ahead into the Unpath. This was a land where childhood ambition, plans for the future and past explorers' maps had no place. This was the wilderness of listening to your instincts, of trying to see what's before you and the Zen art of fully facing one day at a time.

Perhaps I was trying to convince myself there was an art to being lost. The truth was, I didn't want to write. I didn't want to make films. I couldn't picture a future past the week I was in. My only leading passion was to be in Scotland and for some mysterious reason, no matter how rocky things became, to be with Euan. All my self-belief, the magic of making things happen, all the effort that had at one time launched my visions and career, was now being used to keep my dream of Euan and Wigtown afloat.

Chapter 36

"Cloudy today, wind in the east; think we shall have rain...
WE? Where did I get that word – the new creature uses it."
– Mark Twain, ADAM AND EVE: *Fiction section, front room,
left of the window.*

In The Bookshop window, aglow with fairy lights, was my Valentine's-themed display. Red fabric carpeted the floor and clouds hung from the ceiling (cotton balls I had sewn together), along with flying cupids. Carefully placed on multiple levels rested my favourite romantic works: Shakespeare's *Antony and Cleopatra*, Tom Robbins's *Still Life with Woodpecker*, Bridget McNulty's *Strange Nervous Laughter*, *Pride and Prejudice* by Jane Austen and *Vampire Loves*, the graphic novel by Joan Sfar.

Outside, the rain pelted down and the windows rattled in the wind. Two ladies, hidden under an umbrella, carefully made their way across the dark road. They approached the window, leaning into the glass, and peered in at the display.

I sat at the computer behind the counter, bundled under jumpers and hugging a portable heater, which sat at my feet. With the house now to ourselves, and the shop ghostly quiet in the daytime, I had become used to being on my own listening to a silent soundtrack. There was ample time to play the well-worn record of my circular thoughts: career, life, love, career, life, love, never getting anywhere but with every turn feeling as if I were seconds away from an emotional epiphany. It was always a surprise to me when a customer did stumble into the frozen silence of The Bookshop, and I tended now to greet them with the grumbling indignation that I had once teased Euan for displaying.

The two Scottish ladies appeared, dripping wet, listening to the soft bell as it jingled in the cold silence.

"We're visiting from Aberdeen," the tall one announced, as they walked through the front gallery slowly, arm in arm. They whispered loudly, agreeing it was the largest bookshop they'd ever seen; the shorter one grunted, it was also the coldest. They hesitated near the Maritime History section, next to the front counter.

Listening to them was like hearing a scene from a Pinter play and I smiled. It was a while since I had last been at the theatre.

"My son says we were never bombed."

The smaller lady scanned the shelf, obviously not hearing. "Well now, I wonder, is the 1960s considered Maritime History?"

The taller lady crossed her delicate arms. "What, I say to him, so I suppose it was oranges and apples they were throwing at us."

"I don't see it here."

"You were never bombed, he says." She shook her head. "Now where did he read that?"

The smaller lady shrugged. "I worked at a school down in Dumfriesshire and they taught the children all about the Holocaust."

"I think he may have looked it up on the computer. He just thinks he's right."

"I'm glad they did, aren't you?" The smaller lady took off her glasses. "That's something that should never be forgotten."

"Who says it never happened?"

"There's a man. I think he's English."

"Oh dear."

I had been eavesdropping so diligently that I didn't hear the fresh sound of footsteps next to me. In my mind, these two women were on stage, framed by a small proscenium, perhaps in a black box theatre with minimal set and stark lighting.

"Excuse me," a soft, posh accent said behind me. "I was wondering if you could help me."

The footsteps stopped. I turned to see a woman waiting expectantly for me, her umbrella tucked under her arm and dripping onto the floor. I had, on first arriving at The Bookshop, been eager to help customers, interested in what book they wanted, and I had respectfully listened as they ultimately explained why they wanted it. The excitement had worn off quickly and now I only saw needy customers as an unwelcome intrusion into my otherwise idyllic deserted bookshop island. Other Americans especially annoyed me, as they ruined my "Local Hero" fantasy of being a stranger in a strange land, far away from anything familiar.

The list of offences customers caused was endless. Many were rude and obtuse, with a penchant for demanding discounts on books that were already under five pounds. Working with the public did little to encourage your faith in it. I had one customer demand a bulk discount as he shoved three books in my direction. Another approached the counter, complained he couldn't find "a damn thing he wanted" and proceeded to sneeze on me. One woman, who used the child on her back like a weapon, knocked over an antique vase and let it crash to the ground before turning to me accusingly and asking, "Well, what happened here?" Of course there were nice customers, but they were in the majority and far less interesting. The nasty ones, who spewed bile or germ-infested sneezes, left their sticky fingerprint on your memory. They also left finger-prints elsewhere, like the elderly woman who had asked for books on sermons and when I had pointed her in the right direction, had slapped my ass.

"I was hoping you could help me find a book," the woman said again, staring at my blank expression. She wore a dull-brown blazer suit with a cream silk shirt that matched her short white hair. The happy wrinkles around her eyes indicated she must be 70-something. There was nothing sharp about her, and, no matter how pointedly I stared, she seemed always to be just out of focus.

"It's by an author," she continued, her voice as soft as her presence. "I just can't remember the name."

A book by an author... what a novelty! I felt the quick trigger of annoyance being pulled. In moments like these, I could see why Thoreau went off to live in a cabin by himself. Only in true isolation could he come up with an inspired vision of humanity. I challenge him to be so enlightened while working in customer service.

I tried to be polite. "Do you know the book title?"

"Well, it's a series."

"I can't really help you unless you know either the author's name or book title," I said and pointed across the room. "The Fiction section is there, so you might want to have a browse."

The woman didn't move.

"Is there anything else I can do?" The words were polite but my tone was not.

"I do actually know one title," she said in almost a whisper. "It's called *Blue Diamond*."

I turned to the computer and typed in the title. On the computer screen the author's name quickly appeared, and I wrote it down on a piece of paper for her. "You might want to try the Fiction section, listed alphabetically by author."

"I'm not sure it will be there," she said quickly. "It's an erotic novel."

I tried to keep my facial expression neutral, and wondered if I was succeeding. "Oh, well, in that case it would be in the Erotica section, left of the spiral staircase, right next to the Mystery section."

"They're very good novels," the woman said gently. "Really well written, you see. Have you read any?"

"I'm afraid I haven't."

The woman suddenly chuckled. "When you're my age, people don't think you have those feelings, but you do. Perhaps the French can get away with it, but something happens in this society that when we hit our mid-sixties, old ladies like me, we start becoming invisible."

I smiled sympathetically though I felt terrible. I was at fault for having treated her just that way. Her inner life was showing itself to be complex and colourful, far more so than I had imagined on first appearance. It's so easy to lose sight of the truth that, as Vincent van Gogh writes to his brother, when you look on people with patience "one discovers their Millet-like side". Then and there I promised myself to do my very best to keep my patience with customers.

"I was happy to find that *Blue Diamond* was part of a series," she continued, "Really well written, it took me to the tropical beaches of the Caribbean. Put some colour in my cheeks. Reading her novels, all those feelings come rushing back – I feel alive again."

"I really hope we have some of her novels for you." As I looked at her, I pictured myself in the future, her age, and wondered how I would stop myself becoming invisible.

"It doesn't matter really, dear." She took my hand and patted it. "I enjoyed talking with you."

The conversation stayed with me for most of the day, a lingering uneasiness that only began to fade as the shop neared closing time. As the last bit of sunlight crept away from the shop window, the familiar jingle sounded and Euan appeared carrying a box of books. I jumped up smiling, not having seen him since the early morning.

"How was the deal? Did you get anything good?" Euan brought a gust of cold with him from the outdoors and I shivered.

"It was okay. The house was beautiful and massive. You would have loved it." He shoved the box onto the counter. "I noticed your God-awful window display, by the way. Annoyingly festive. I usually do a D-Day window for Valentine's."

"That's surprising." I rolled my eyes and watched as Euan flipped through the mail. In his coat pocket, I noticed there was a wrapper. My heart fluttered. "You are a romantic, aren't you!"

Euan followed my gaze and laughed. "Nope," he said, "unless you want this." Euan's large hands dug into the pocket and pulled out a Big Mac wrapper from McDonald's.

"I'm already invisible," I mumbled. Euan watched as my shoulders slumped.

"What do you mean invisible? Jessy, I told you, I don't do Valentine's Day."

I made my way back behind the counter. "I just thought after New Year's…"

"Well, why do I always have to be the one to do something?" Euan grabbed the box off the counter, smiling. He was in a particularly good mood.

I thought about that for a moment. Why did I always expect the man in my life to be the romantic one? Surely Euan deserved to be wooed as much as I did? It didn't exactly adhere to the classical idea of courtly love and chivalry, but then again, it's a sad day when one looks to the medieval era for an enlightened way to behave.

"Fine. I'll cook you dinner."

"No!" Euan's plaintive voiced echoed back as he headed out the back. "Anything but that. Please. I'll do something."

Smiling, I turned my attention back to the computer. This was one way of getting what I wanted.

The following day I took a bus into the neighbouring town of Newton Stewart to visit the butcher. I was still determined to make Euan a Valentine's Day meal that would sweep him off his feet, though the day had already begun better than I had imagined.

I had blinked awake, wrapped in Euan's arms. It had been one of those perfect waking moments, where Euan had woken first and I found him looking at me, his expression pensively affectionate.

"You're so pretty." He gently stroked the side of my face. "I do love you, Jessy."

The alarm clock, my second arch-enemy after the cold, had rung and interrupted the blissful moment. Euan had leaped up and I had struggled to follow, and he laughed watching me half sitting up and half unwilling to get out from under the warm covers. "Look under the bed, Fox."

I rolled over and hung myself over the edge. Under the bed, a massive Valentine's Day heart filled with chocolates and a present sat waiting to be opened. Delighted, I scooped them up and opened the wrapped box. Inside, there was a necklace with a little fox dangling from the end, plus a book of pictures of Euan and me over the past five months.

"This is... just wonderful, I love it all." I jumped up and kissed Euan.

"Calm down, Fox." He looked overwhelmed but very pleased. "I wanted you to have a good Valentine's Day."

In turn, I handed Euan a small heart-shaped box. In it, there were two silver cufflinks with his initials engraved on them. "Jessy, that's so thoughtful," he said. "You really didn't need to get me anything. They're lovely."

"Well, I thought I was supposed to woo you." I smiled. "Just think, you still have dinner to look forward to."

Euan moaned. "Jessy, if you loved me, you'd stay far away from the kitchen."

In the butcher's, I was overwhelmed with choice. In a long glass counter that went on through the shop, I found local meats of all kinds, a pinky-red pallet of flesh and fat. Unsure of what to get, I looked for the most fancy-sounding. "Beef olives" sounded quite posh and looked tasty to my untrained eye. I peered through the glass at what looked like rolled beef stuffed with fancy olive pâté, basil, garlic and spices. I proudly asked for two.

"Is this for anything special?" The butcher eyed me curiously.

"Valentine's Day, of course," I smiled. "Do you have any recommendation of how to cook them?"

The butcher looked confused. "No, just the usual way, in the oven."

On the way home, the beef olives sat cold on my lap. I dreamed of making a large salad, perhaps with cooked potatoes, and I would get some nice champagne to have with it as well. We'd eat in the big room, by the fire, and Euan would feel spoiled. Then he would have to take back his evil comments about my cooking skills, or lack thereof.

As I walked through the door to the shop, Euan started laughing. He was sitting behind the counter, eyeing the brown paper bag dangling from my arm.

"Is that my dinner surprise?" Euan asked, looking pleased with himself.

"Yes, if you must know." I stiffened and quickly made my way through the shop and up the stairs. Euan followed behind.

In the kitchen, I slid the brown package into the fridge and Euan filled up his mug from the kettle. He was laughing uncontrollably.

"What, exactly, is so hilarious?"

"Beef olives, Jessy. Beef olives?"

My mouth dropped open. "How did you know? Who told you?"

"My mother just called."

"How did she know?"

"She went into the butcher's right after you and called me from home, before you arrived back on the bus." Euan was beaming. "What possessed you to get beef olives?"

"Well, I thought it sounded nice." I sighed. Nothing was secret in this part of the world. Even innocent Valentine's Day dinner surprises were impossible to keep. "Don't you like them?"

Euan laughed harder. "Jessy, I was forced to eat beef olives at boarding school. They're like cafeteria food, cheap meat stuffed with God knows what."

"Maybe these are gourmet versions?" I flushed, embarrassed.

Euan tried to stifle his chuckles and wrapped his arms around me. "I'm sure they'll be delicious."

That evening, after a picnic dinner in front of a roaring fire, enjoying our beef olives and champagne, Euan took me down to the Martyr's Stake. As we walked along the boardwalk, I felt as if I was finally making a long-overdue visit to a friend.

The stone monument, lit by moonlight in the frosty field, stared at me as we approached. As Euan undid the small gate, and we stepped into the solitary circle around the large stake, I could clearly feel a vibrating magic. Something about this spot was special, whether it was the openness of the landscape, the vast sky above or the single, humble stone itself. The energy tingled my skin and I stood there, well aware that I alone might be feeling this sensation. I looked at Euan, who stood smiling down at me, seemingly only aware of my presence and the wind.

Euan took out a red folded lantern from his bag, and let the thin paper fill with air. As it ballooned, to my delight, it took the shape of a heart. He reached into his pocket for a lighter.

"Where did you get this?" Iasked, feeling properly swept off my feet.

"From some website. I thought after New Year, I could perhaps put some effort in." Euan looked at me knowingly.

I couldn't help smiling. This relationship had not been as smooth as some from my past, nor as rocky either. It was more as if we were running a marathon. Sometimes we hit our stride together, only to find at other moments we were out of step, struggling to keep pace with one another. Perhaps this was how things worked. We were still learning about each other and trying in earnest to meet each other's needs – what else could you ask for from a relationship? As Euan struggled to keep the lantern lit in the wind, I felt incredibly happy.

Euan let the paper balloon fill with hot air, then let go. He grabbed my hand, and we watched anxiously as the lantern lifted a couple of inches off the ground, swinging towards the monument, then sinking into the long grass.

"I think it's going to crash." I could hardly look. "Please, please go up," I whispered, worried the grass would be set alight. The lantern teetered and the burning centre blinked tentatively. Then a gentle breeze suddenly reignited the flame and the red heart glowed brightly, pausing mid-air, and slowly rose into the night sky.

And we have lift-off. My mind travelled back to the last time I had seen a launch, on the sunny, hot shores of Florida. I shivered, looking around the dark, cold night in Galloway. That trip to Florida felt like another world, so different and distant that it could have been a dream.

"I love you," I said, leaning into Euan, and waited for the predictable "you're so American'" to come back to me. Instead, I felt his arm wrap around my shoulder.

We watched, our necks craned, as the lantern shrank to no more than a spec above us. My eyes closed, and as if about to blow out a birthday candle, I made a wish. I wished for everything to turn out well, because in the labyrinth of my feelings, I wasn't sure that it would. Despite my current happiness, there was an undeniable crack between Euan and me, which had first appeared this winter. It was as small as a pea, but just like the princess who slept atop the layers of mattresses, even a pea can be enough to cause incredible discomfort, for there is always the potential that it might grow.

I opened my eyes, but wasn't convinced that they were open for all I saw was the cold, inky-black night sky. I peered deeper into the blanket of clouds. Behind them would be a myriad of twinkling stars and the thick band of the Milky Way. I searched the sky for light, but nothing. The lantern was gone.

Chapter 37

"...a director cannot help projecting his own state of mind on to the stage." Peter Brook, THE EMPTY SPACE: *Drama section, the Garden Room, second building out the back.*

Vincent was a tall, thin man, whose gentle manners were better suited to a knight in shining armour than a mechanic in blue overalls. He was stooped, like a willow tree, after years of bending over cars, and the effect was that he looked like he was constantly taking a humble bow.

I adored him. The screenwriter in me wanted Vincent, the golden-hearted bachelor and Cambridge graduate, to be a spy – perhaps a sleeper agent sent into the backwoods to be the eyes and ears of the country. And yet the possibility that Vincent was south-west Scotland's James Bond was as unlikely as pirates still existing in Wigtown's now drained bay. Piracy and political intrigue in Wigtown were things of the past – as deep and buried as The Bookshop's foundations – and belonged to a time when there were troubles in Northern Ireland or even further back, when the Isle of Man had a notorious reputation for smuggling.

Vincent silently guided me around his garage, the side garden of which was littered with cars from various eras. I explained that I needed to find an automatic car to rent or a cheap one to buy – something that made Vincent lean back onto his heels, and ponder.

This was a harder mission than it sounded. Automatic cars were not easy to come by, especially in Wigtown, so Euan had tried to teach me how to drive stick shift, using his red van. My driving had been like riding a bucking bronco, until finally I had hit my stride going three miles per hour. Tears had streamed down my face. I'd been terrified. This was Euan's work vehicle, critical to his livelihood – what if I damaged it? On the right side of the van, a man who had been walking his dog passed us.

"A pedestrian just overtook you." Euan hadn't known whether to laugh or cry himself.

"What if I hit them?" My heart had beat out of control. "I want to get out, I hate this."

Euan had started laughing. "You're doing fine, Jessica. I bet you can put it into a higher gear."

The car stalled again, and lurched forward. The burning smell of transmission reached my nostrils. My voice increased in volume, hysterical. "I'm going to wreck your van. This is stupid."

"No, it's not, the van is fine. Try again. Try driving home." Euan was patient, encouraging.

"I hate this!" I shouted back.

I turned on the engine and started off slowly.

"You're doing so well. Now bring it into a higher gear."

The main road into Wigtown loomed before us. Left. Left. Left. I had kept on chanting, not trusting I'd know which side of the road to pull out on.

"Now you'll stop before pulling out, okay, Jessy? And put on the handbrake." Euan started to relax but I stiffened. The road up to Wigtown was a steep hill, and I pictured myself stalling, slipping backwards, unable to stop and squashing anything in my path.

When we approached the crossroads, the car slowed and stalled. We lurched forward again and Euan screamed, "Handbrake!!" My right hand grabbed for the handbrake and instead I got the door-handle. Euan jumped to the rescue, and lifted the handbrake himself.

"I told you," I said, quickly turning off the engine, and leapt out of the car.

"Where are you going, Fox?" Euan shouted out of the window. "Come back, try again!"

"I'm walking. It's faster!" I yelled, and found a tree to sit under and cry.

Vincent shoved his hands into his pockets, leaning against a car, half overgrown with grass and rust. "So, you're living in Wigtown permanently then?"

"I hope so, as long as I stay far away from Euan's kitchen." I smiled. His expressive eyebrows rose.

When I told Vincent about my various cooking disasters, his usually neutral expression melted into a large smile. He laughed, his sloping shoulders bouncing in amusement. "Now don't worry about that," he said, patting me on the back. "Euan should be making you candlelit dinners every evening."

As Vincent wandered ahead to inspect a small blue car for me, I looked after him affectionately. Suddenly I knew exactly what Vincent was – this shy, bachelor who lived quietly in a cottage outside town wasn't a spy at all: he was a romantic.

*

Being the daughter of an engineer, it was thrilling for me to just pick out a car and drive off without the lengthy headache of checks and research and inspection. My hands proudly gripped the steering wheel of my not-so-new dark blue Citroen Saxo, the heat blasting in the cramped front seats and a cold chill coming in from the sun roof, which didn't shut all the way. Vincent had suggested he inspect the car before I road-tested it, but I said no, despite my father's voice echoing words of caution in my head. Gail Sheehy, in her book *Passages,* would say that those parental voices, as we mature into adulthood, should be replaced by our own judgements as we learn from experimentation and experience. Buying this potential blue death trap was my experiment – my belated teenage rebellion – and it felt fabulous.

I had fallen in love with the car the moment I laid eyes on its small retro frame. Besides having a sun roof, it was automatic, a hatchback, and had a new CD player, plus the most important feature: it was inexpensive. Vincent had generously said I could rent to buy, offering a price that was affordable as long as my bits of consulting work continued in the States.

Wigtown's winding streets challenged my little Citroen Saxo, and it shook as it gripped the steep curves. I had decided to test-drive my new car with a celebratory shopping mission to Dumfries and was now regretting the ambition of my first Scottish drive. Dumfries, the largest city near Wigtown, was about an hour away.

I slowed, chanting "left, left, left" as cars to my right passed at terrifyingly close distances. Driving on country roads was unlike anything else I had experienced. There was barely enough room for two small cars to pass each other, and it was a mystery to me how Euan's van, like an American football player training in ballet, could so easily manoeuvre the close impasses with grace.

At my first roundabout, my heart thudded so loudly in my ears that it drowned out any noise. It felt counterintuitive to follow the cars clockwise. My muscle memory was resisting driving this way and my shoulders were tense.

"Left, left, left," I chanted as I gripped the wheel and sped around three quarters of the circle. The car carefully followed the outside kerb and pulled out onto the A75 exit. To my relief, the road quickly widened here and became comfortably straight. I was driving abroad, in my own car and, after panic, I felt a wave of pride. With the long stretch of highway before me, I considered this mission practically over and a roaring success.

The sound of a phone buzzing filled the car. I looked down and saw Euan's old mobile, which he insisted I carry with me, flashing. I scrambled to reach it while my eyes were glued to the road. I grabbed it, flipping it open.

"Where are you?" Euan's voice echoed from the phone's small speaker. He sounded concerned.

"I'm on my way to Dumfries," I gushed. Euan had left for a book deal early that morning and hadn't been privy to my trip to Vincent's, or around when I returned with my new blue car.

"When you say 'on your way'," Euan said slowly, "do you mean in a car, and you're on the road driving?"

"Yep."

Euan's voice became louder. "In what car?"

"In a car I just bought off Vincent."

"Oh God."

"Look, I can't talk, I'm driving." I emphasised the last word for dramatic effect.

"Okay, fine, but please call me if you need anything."

I hung up quickly and dropped the phone onto the neighbouring seat. My fingers fiddled with the dials on the radio, and BBC Radio 4 finally blasted out loud from my new garish speakers and subwoofer as my car made its way along the A75.

*

I was down the road from the major Dumfries roundabout when I heard the explosion.

I had turned off the radio and slowed, preparing to enter a supersized roundabout. This would be the first of many in short succession, and I had taken a deep breath. When there was a break in the traffic, I quickly pulled out into the first of the four lanes, and began circling around the track, unable to remember where I was supposed to exit. Euan and I had done this route many times before, and I had tried to pay attention, knowing one day I'd end up in this situation, but now everything felt different. Finishing one circuit slowly, with cars beeping behind me, I panicked and pulled out into the nearest exit. Luckily, this exit turned out to be the right one.

That's when the explosion happened. It came from underneath the back of the car – like four guns going off – the bang so loud that I screamed and let go of the wheel. My limbs felt weak, my mind blanked and I could feel a tingling sensation in my gums, something I hadn't felt since I was eight years old and frozen in stage fright at my first piano recital. I tried to keep on driving but the engine now sounded like an angry lion and I could hear the dull scrape of metal against concrete. Cars whizzed by, honking, and I realised I was on the wrong side of the road.

Another small roundabout was now just feet ahead of me. I pulled out from the wrong lane and would, like a bowling ball, have taken out several cars had I not luckily found the circle empty. Heading anti-clockwise, I took the closest exit and hung onto the car as it sputtered and leapt. Another small explosion sounded, this time closer to the front of the car, and automatically I pulled into the driveway of a McDonald's, a fact that still today makes me feel slightly grateful to an otherwise loathed food chain. As I headed over a speed bump, just inside the parking lot, the car slowed with a painful loud grunt and died.

It was only in the silence that followed that I realised I had been crying. I sat there shaking, thinking it could have been much worse, as my mind filled with the angry faces I had witnessed on the drivers. I had only once been in an accident previously, when I was sixteen, and that wasn't even close to the near catastrophe this could have been.

It had been my first day driving with my brand-new licence and to celebrate the occasion my father allowed me to drive his car to school. In the late afternoon, I had felt so cool walking out of Lexington High School, keys in hand, telling my friends I would see them later because I was driving home. My boyfriend had run up to me and asked for a ride. New drivers, as I well knew, weren't allowed to take passengers, unless accompanied by an adult. But my boyfriend had often taken me home in his car and, though nervous, I felt it was only fair to reciprocate.

Not wanting to be caught, I offered him a ride home on the condition that he hid in the back. Surprisingly, he accepted. As I pulled out of a side street on my way to his house, into a four-way intersection, I suddenly panicked. Cars flew by on both sides, passing faster than bullets. No one slowed to let me through, and as I inched my way into the middle of the road, cars swerved around me. Shaking, I put the car into reverse. And then, backing up onto a side street, without looking in the rearview mirror, I crashed.

I had turned to see a massive white SUV sitting there, waiting to pull out onto the main road.

The SUV had been fine, not a scratch on it, while the back of my father's car was dented and his light was broken. The driver had waited as I got out, crying hysterically, and had tried to calm me down. His empathy had turned to shock when he looked up to see a young teenage boy jump out from the crushed boot and run down the street.

My trembling hands adjusted the Citroen's rearview mirror. Tears poured down my cheeks and I tried to quickly wipe them away. I glanced behind me to see if any cars were waiting impatiently to get their fast food. The driveway was empty, but, to my horror, strewn across the McDonald's parking lot and on to the road, were pieces of my car.

It was as if the innards of my car had instantaneously burst and splattered across the road. I walked along the sidewalk, passing pipes, bolts, cylinders and odd pieces of metal. Across the way, a large man in a hooded sweatshirt came running over. He was unfit and panted as he approached, speaking in a friendly, thick local accent.

"You okay, pet?" he asked kindly.

My mouth was numb. I could hardly speak. "I don't know how this happened."

"Here," he said, bending down to grab one of the pipes, "I'll help you." He wrapped his large hand around a piece of metal and screamed, throwing it back down and yelling obscenities. "It's hot, it's fucking hot!"

Two more men came over and carefully lifted bits of car onto the side of McDonald's carefully mulched and manicured lawn. Though my car had let me down, my faith in Dumfries and Galloway only grew in the next few hours. I was so well looked after by these strangers on their way to work that I ran inside and bought them each an Egg McMuffin. My heroes gratefully accepted their rewards and reluctantly, I called Euan.

"My car exploded," I breathed.

There was a pause. "What do you mean, exploded? Where are you?"

As I told him what happened, he gave me Vincent's phone number through fits of laughter.

"I'm glad you're finding this all very amusing."

"You're obviously fine, Jessy. Adventure seems to find you. On the bright side, you can still go shopping. There's an auction house right down the road from where you are."

When I walked into The Bookshop later that afternoon, it felt as if I had been gone for months. Vincent, my knight in shining blue overalls, had picked me up in Dumfries and promised to have my car sorted in days. He was horrified that I had driven it to Dumfries without getting it properly looked over.

"Then these nice men helped me put the bits of my car on the sidewalk," I said, standing in the cold kitchen, leaning against the table as Euan slid a roast, covered in onions and roasted potatoes, into the oven.

"Pavement. You mean pavement, not sidewalk." Euan shook his head. Whenever Euan was annoyed about something, he would turn into Henry Higgins. His corrections of my speech were like pulling the plug on a bath: all the energy drained from what I was saying, leaving me little desire to continue.

"What's that sound?" I asked, wandering over to the window. Outside, in the darkness of the garden, I could hear an other-worldy low rumble.

"Frogs," Euan replied, handing me a stack of warm plates. "In the pond."

I had never heard a sound like it – like a gurgling baritone chorus. "I thought it was the pipes in the bathroom."

"The bathroom? Do you have a bath in the downstairs loo?"

"The restroom then."

"Do you go there to have a rest?"

I sighed. I couldn't win. Boot not trunk, pavement not sidewalk, autumn not fall, acclimatised not acclimated, courgette not zucchini, aubergine not eggplant.

When I had first arrived, I had already known enough not to use the American "fannypack", something that inspired hysterics from Euan's employee Hannah, but I had learned the hard way about trousers. One snowy December day, I had horrified both Euan's parents by declaring that I hadn't packed enough pants.

"Two countries divided by a common language," Euan teased me, but I didn't smile back. Today, with my adventurous ride to Dumfries, I felt like I had survived an important right of passage. I was living, eating, speaking and now driving in Scotland, and starting to truly feel at home in Galloway. However, in one sentence Euan had reduced me back to alien status. The only person I had been fooling into thinking I was acclimated, excuse me, acclimatised, was myself.

"So finish the story," Euan continued, handing me a cold glass of red wine. Everything in the kitchen was frozen, and Euan would often tell people, without exaggeration, that in the winter we put things in the refrigerator to "warm them up". "What happened after people helped you pick bits of your car up from the pavement?"

I glared at him. I had never wanted to accept the idea of something called "The Cultural Divide", believing that people were people. Any failure to relate to another culture, I thought, showed a lack of flexibility and curiosity of the mind rather than a real disconnect. However, living with Euan was beginning to convince me that "The Cultural Divide" was not some fictitious national landmark, but represented a true impasse – a gap between us as vast and impressive as the Grand Canyon. "The Cultural Divide" meant there were things I could never share with Euan; it meant misunderstandings and bickerings. It also, to be fair, meant we avoided the rut of relationship boredom and predictability. On good days it kept us fresh and interested in one another. "The Cultural Divide" kept us on our toes.

Instead of finishing my story, I helped Euan slice carrots in silence. I had always – eventually – grown antsy in my past boyfriends' company, knowing them so well that familiarity had bred contempt. Instead of feeling as if there were two people in a relationship, the relationship had taken over and it had come to feel like one shapeless, bland experience with no mystery or sense of excitement lingering around the corner. I would feel trapped, as if I had joined the Borg, my identity lost in the amorphous cloud of me, him, us. Euan was different. No matter how much time we spent together, there was something uncoupling, distant and separate about him. Perhaps being with Euan would always feel like that – a mix of familiarity and distance. Perhaps the distance I felt was "The Cultural Divide" and instead of keeping us apart, it would by nature of its separateness, keep us together.

*

"Why are we having so much food for dinner?" I asked, chewing on a raw carrot and peering curiously as Euan lit candles, placing each carefully in the centre of the table. "Are we having people over?"

"I thought you'd have worked that out by now, Jessy."

"You said Callum, Rebecca and the kids are coming." Opening the door to the oven, I peaked at the massive roast inside. "But this is enough to feed them for weeks."

"Well, a friend of mine is staying over too. I'm sure I told you. And Olive may be joining us."

"Olive, as in the woman you used to date?"

"Only a couple of times. She rang to tell me that she had moved into the area so I thought it would be nice to invite her over to dinner."

"…with your girlfriend?"

Euan was silent.

"Does she know I'm here?"

"Yes, of course. I mean, I don't know, I assume so."

"Jesus, Euan, honestly. You're totally clueless sometimes."

Euan's face darkened, hurt.

"So who is this other friend, then?" I sighed, trying to relax into the night ahead.

Euan passed by me, trying to get to the oven. "Her name is Heather. I knew her at uni but haven't seen her in ages. She's over from Dublin to visit her parents in Dumfries."

"Does she know about me?"

"Yes, she knows about you."

"It's a fair question." I shook my head, abandoning my cold glass of wine, and went out into the hall. A fire was growing inside my belly as the doorbell rang.

*

Euan and I lay in bed, not speaking. The evening, predict-
ably, had been a disaster. I had opened the door to find
Olive waiting patiently outside, dressed for a romantic
night for two, wearing heavy eye make-up and a slinky
black dress, and holding a bottle of wine. She had looked
bewildered to see me.

"Is this where Euan who owns this shop lives?" she
asked, pointing to the sign and cocking her head.

"Yes, come on in, we're expecting you." I had tried to
sound gracious and took the bottle of wine. Confused, she
followed me upstairs, her tight dress making an irritating
rubbing sound as she slinked close behind me.

In the kitchen, I quickly got her a glass of wine, feeling
that she might need one as well, and introduced myself as
Euan's girlfriend. Her face sort of froze in the no-man's-
land between politeness and sheer panic. Before she could
say anything in reply, the familiar, happy voices of Callum,
Rebecca and the children sounded from down the hall.
They entered the kitchen all smiles and "hellos", cancel-
ling out the bizarre developing energy. Euan's uni friend,
Heather, arrived soon after.

Heather was tall and blonde, in her mid-forties and stun-
ningly beautiful. Olive no longer concerned me. Rather, I
looked on curiously as Heather held onto Euan's arm as
she laughed, and brushed her hair aside as he handed her
a glass of wine. For two people who had just reconnected,
there already seemed to be a private library of inside jokes
and knowing glances that I was not privy to. Throughout
the meal, the spark of energy between Heather and Euan
was palpable, and I wondered, in hurt embarrassment, if I
was the only one who had noticed.

I wasn't. It didn't take long for poor, confused Olive to find an excuse to leave, and I envied her her swift exit. For the rest of the evening, Callum shot me glances, his eyebrows raised, looking concerned. Wanting time alone, I suggested Euan take the others into the sitting room while I cleaned up. Unfortunately, Heather hung back to help me with the dishes. Instead of helping, she leaned her long, thin body against the kitchen worktop, watching me curiously as if I were some exotic animal in a zoo.

"So you're Jessica." She said my name as if it was difficult to pronounce.

My blood suddenly boiled, hotter than the water filling up the tub in the sink, which was now scalding my hands. I turned off the tap and pretended to be very interested in washing the dishes. She might as well have said, "Euan never mentions you". What could I say in response? I didn't want to look simple, ignorant of their relationship, whatever that might be. Nor did I want to seem defensive in any way. So instead I took a page from Euan's book, and said nothing.

This seemed to irritate Heather, who came closer. "Euan's lovely, isn't he?"

Again, I met her loaded comment with silence. I didn't know how one created a stony silence but I hoped mine was befitting a glacier. I straightened my shoulders, trying to keep my expression serene, as I stared at the dishes floating in the sink.

"I have no idea why he doesn't think you're the one for him," Heather continued in an almost conspiratorial whisper. "I think you're gorgeous." She poured herself more wine. Realising I wasn't going to play ball, she stood for what felt like cavernous minutes, before at last leaving the room.

The bedroom's air was icy cold, but did nothing to distract me from remembering Heather's words, "he doesn't think you're the one for him", which ran on a masochistic loop over and over in my mind. Euan rolled towards me, bringing much needed warmth to my side of the bed.

"I'm really sorry, Jessy."

"You told her that I wasn't the one for you." My fairy-tale dream of Scotland, and my bookshop owner, started to crumble in my mind in cloudy puffs of dirt and rubble.

"I don't know why I ever said that. It was ages ago. I guess I felt that way then, but I don't now," Euan's sleepy voice sounded concerned and sincere.

I was getting a lot of practice at creating stony silences.

"There is no one else for me but you." Euan said dreamily. I let him snuggle up next to me, despite my mounting anger.

I half believed him. Euan was not deceptive, just indecisive. I now knew what being a ditherer meant: someone who was confused. His feelings kept being dragged back into the past by the shadows of ex-girlfriends, or being pulled into the future towards new people he had not yet met, but they only rarely seemed to reside here in the present, in this relationship, with me.

I have never liked the term a "thin line between love and hate". Feeling angry towards someone I deeply loved has always felt less like two sides of a coin and more like two opposing forces, anti-matter meeting matter, a negation of realities. It's like Bruno Bettelheim's observation that for a child to express anger towards his or her mother, a duality needs to occur, splitting her into the good witch and the bad witch, or the fairy godmother and the evil stepmother. Unfortunately, I was old enough to know that people are complicated and no matter how angry I was, there were not two Euans, the good and bad – but one. Truth existed not in separation but in contradiction. This was Euan. I was furious and I didn't want to be, for there was nothing to be furious about – I had fallen in love with the totality of him, all the dithering sides of him. However, it didn't mean I had to like how conflicted he was, or live with it.

I felt I was losing some imaginary battle over the forces of fate and love. My vision, as visions should, brought with it a journey whose rewards were things I deeply needed but never had anticipated: a place of perfect beauty where I found a sense of belonging, peace from *shpilkus*, a break from ambition, new kindred spirits and most important of all: love. Everything was working so perfectly so I couldn't understand why the biggest piece of the puzzle, Euan, was falling out of place.

Euan ran his fingers through my hair in a sleepy, careless manner. "I wouldn't know what to do without you." His words were heartfelt but fuzzy, as if he felt that way but wasn't confident about why.

In the darkness of the bedroom, I stared up at the ceiling. I had left my life in Los Angeles, I had changed my job, my routine, my friends – everything. I had embraced the change fully, going with the flow of what felt right, so why wasn't it working? The pea was sprouting and the crack was widening.

The answer suddenly became clear. I had been the one making all the decisions. My face flushed with embarrassed recognition as I saw how my directing instinct, without films to channel the energy into, had gone berserk on my own life. I was the one who had made all the small and big decisions to make our relationship happen, and perhaps it was because of, not in spite of, all the risks I had taken to get here that I was so committed. Euan, however, had never really had to make any decisions at all; everything had happened to him and the result was a massive imbalance.

This had been my dream, my adventure, and Euan had never had the privilege of having that kind of ritual to create his future. He was just a willing accomplice in this scenario. I suddenly saw it from his point of view. He had been descended on by an enthusiastic American who was supposed to stay for a couple of months but had ended up taking over his house, changing his routine, invading his social circle and never leaving. What had started as a trial run had suddenly turned into a long-term, permanent relationship and no matter how happy he was or content he felt, he probably didn't feel as if he had had any part in making it happen. Where I thought he should feel lucky, he very likely felt bewildered.

My mind tried to come up with an appropriate plan of action, but like James Lapine's Cinderella when she decided to leave her shoe for the prince to find on the palace steps, "I knew what my decision was, and it was not to decide". It was still just a glimmer of an idea, not a fully formed thought, but I wouldn't direct this relationship any more. Maybe I would leave and give Euan the space and time to figure out the mystery of who and what he wanted. Then, if what he wanted was me, he could come and get me. Suddenly I was flooded with excited anticipation. There would be no dithering, no drama and no warning; he would just arrive on my doorstep on a date we both agreed to. The spark of the idea faded in intensity as I began to fall asleep. I had come to him, travelled halfway around the world to show my affection and commitment. It was time for him to take the same risk.

Chapter 38

"Earth! Invisible! What is your urgent command, if not transformation?" – Rainer Maria Rilke, DUINO ELEGIES: *Poetry section, right of fireplace in the gallery.*

And then, in the morning, spring arrived. The warm winds and the spirit of things growing must have pushed out the last of the damp and cold once and for all, because on waking, the sun shone in and noises of birds, people and buzzing crept in through the cracks in the window. The bed was still surprisingly warm, and so was the air outside the covers. Euan had already disappeared downstairs and I got up and happily ran to the window. The scene outside took my breath away.

Wigtown's small green was in bloom. The branches of cherry trees danced in the wind, their delicate pink petals flying free, past window boxes and hanging baskets filled with colourful flowers, and finally landing at the feet of smiling people. Yes, actual people. Smiling. Wigtown filled with cyclists, children and neighbours I hadn't seen in months. As I peered out, it felt as if the town itself had bloomed and had come alive again for spring.

I found Euan sitting in his usual place, behind the long wooden counter in The Bookshop, using the computer at the desk. He looked tired, though I could tell he had noticed that spring had arrived as well. Instead of jeans, he was sporting shorts, and in no time his shoes would be off too. Euan soon would be in his element, as he always said spring was his time of year. He was looking forward to the longer, warm days when free time meant a cold beer, the portable radio and long evenings spent in the garden. His fantasies never included other people, rather him being "left alone" to do what he wanted. Sometimes, I felt lonely on his behalf.

"Anything interesting?" As I approached the counter, I smiled with the satisfaction of knowing someone so well. Over Euan's shoulder I could see he was looking at a gardening website.

Euan wrapped his arm around my waist and pulled me close to him. "I'm thinking of building a polytunnel."

"That will be nice," I said, my thoughts as active as a beehive. Despite the beautiful weather, the night before weighed heavily on my mind. From the dark circles under Euan's eyes, I knew that neither of us had got any sleep. I hated the feeling that we were drifting aimlessly in this uncomfortable space. Things between us wouldn't get better unless we did something and perhaps that did have to involve me leaving. I knew I would have to discuss it, and I was dreading the conversation. Even thinking about it drained me of resolve. I loved it here, I loved Euan. I felt so unsure of myself that any words of protest on his part would easily unnerve me.

"I have a surprise to show you, actually," Euan said, suddenly brightening. "I was waiting for some good weather."

Euan led me out the back of the shop and into the garden. Multi-coloured flowers were blooming every-where, vines and ferns stretched out into the sunshine and butterflies floated on the breeze, accompanied by the soundtrack of buzzing bees. "This is so beautiful," I said, entranced by the change from the bleak winter.

Euan paused, smelling the blossoming clematis that climbed up a trellis, separating the front part of the garden from the back. "It smells like chocolate – here." Euan held out a flower and I leaned in, dizzy from the strong, sweet scent. It smelled just like a Dairy Milk bar.

"That's a great surprise. Thank you, darling," I said and kissed him on the cheek. I felt the strong urge to hug him, in hopes of dispelling the pre-emptive pangs of homesickness I'd have when I returned to America.

"That's not the surprise, Jessy." Euan laughed, and turned me around to face his garden shed. On the door were new iron letters that read: "The Fox's Den".

I opened the door. Euan had cleared out his workshop to make room for a small desk, a chair and a picture, which hung on the wall. It reminded me of Jay O'Callahan's writing cabin in his back garden that he affectionately referred to as "the Chateau". Philip Pullman wrote all of *His Dark Materials* in a small shack like this, and now, like my writing heroes before me, I had my own Thoreau's cabin. The desk was perfectly positioned by the window, from which I could see the glittering garden. On the window sill sat a pot, which instead of holding a plant, was filled with pens and pencils.

"I thought you might want your own space, you know, to plan your films in when the weather is nice," Euan said, shuffling his feet.

"Oh, it's wonderful!" I sat at the desk and tried to ignore a massive spider, crawling up the far wall. I felt both touched and more conflicted than ever. Leaving had felt so right the previous evening, but now, in the bright light of a glorious Galloway spring day, in my own writing hut, it felt horrible, treacherous even.

I stood up. "So you do love having me here."

"Sometimes," Euan said, teasing, and yet that, unfortunately, was the confusing truth.

My mouth moved before I had time to think. "Am I the one for you?"

"Of course. Really, Jessica." Euan embraced me, almost as if he could hug away my concern.

"What?"

"You do know how to spring things on a person."

"You did tell Heather..." The pang of the memory still burned and I winced. The sensation reminded me of when I discovered Grant's journal, the mortification of accidentally stumbling on his true feelings – or lack thereof.

"I know I did. It's just confusing." Euan sighed, and looked concerned as my eyebrows raised. "Sometimes I feel you are, but sometimes I don't."

"Like when?"

"Like right now. I hate talking about these things."

I moved away and slouched back into the desk chair, defeated.

"I don't know, it's just not very British." Euan tried to smile but he wasn't joking. "Can't you just ignore it, bottle it up inside until it goes away?"

I didn't look up.

"Jessy, I want you to be here." Euan walked over to me. "Whenever I think of life without you, I get this feeling; it's horrible and hard to describe."

I wasn't listening. If I had, I would have noticed how much he cared for me, but all my mind could focus on was his doubt. "Would it be easier if you had time and space to figure out what you wanted?"

I regretted it the moment I said it, but now it was floating out in the air between us, alive and buzzing.

Euan's sincere blue eyes flashed with hurt. I wanted him to say it was a stupid idea, swat the suggestion away and repeat that he didn't want me to leave. Instead, he tilted his head thoughtfully and then shrugged. "Maybe. I hadn't thought about that before."

My heart broke but I tried to smile. What was wrong with me? Why couldn't I take what he was saying, that he wanted me, that he made space in his life for me, at face value? Why wasn't it good enough? "Well, we should think about it," I said, and walked out of "The Fox's Den".

Earlier that morning Euan had insisted we go out for the day, "to take our minds off things", as he put it. Then it had seemed like a bad idea, as if it would be impossible to think of anything else but trying to steer our relationship away from crashing into the rocky shore. Now, however, stepping out into the sunshine, it seemed inspired. It was impossible to resist the sheer pleasure of flying through the warm air on a bicycle.

The car sped along, not through the soft greens and browns I knew well, but through a transformed universe. The barren winter landscape was now full of colour, as if van Gogh himself had redecorated Galloway for spring. Pink and white wild flowers lined the curvy country roads and lambs appeared in the green hills, as soft and white as the clouds in the bright blue sky. Everywhere was bursting with beauty and living things and a sense of joy, as if every atom in the universe was shouting, "I'm alive, I'm alive, I exist, I exist!"

Every atom, of course, but the carbon-based life forms in the Citroen Saxo. As we hopped out of the car, bringing the bicycles down from the roof, we said nothing. Our favourite path through the woods was now carpeted with bluebells. It was like a scene from a film about an enchanted wood, with large dark-brown trunks whose green leafed branches stretched over a sea of purple, glittering in and out of shadow. As we biked along the forest path, weaving between the trees, I flashed back to the happy times on my bicycle in Los Angeles, and to almost every birthday in my childhood when I would ramble through Walden Pond's woods in Concord, Massachusetts. A bicycle, to me, had always been a source of bliss, and the woods here were magic at even the worst of times – together today they provided an antidote to my black mood. I felt myself smiling, which was dangerous, given the clouds of insects also enjoying the new lease of life spring had given the world.

*

We returned to Wigtown to the sound of bagpipes. The ancient, mournful blast of the pipes echoed off the stone houses, and Euan and I felt personally heralded as we parked the car in front of The Bookshop. There was an excited commotion in town and masses of people were heading down the street to the old cattle showground. A large plume of black smoke rose from behind the rooftops, covering the blue sky in ashy darkness.

As I opened the car door, I was hit by the smell of burning.

"What's happening?" I said, swept up by the energy. The wind had picked up and I could feel raindrops on my head and arms.

Euan rounded the car and took me by the hand, obviously excited. "It's Wigtown's civic week and there is a massive bonfire. I completely forgot about it. You'll love it, Fox."

As we approached the cattle showgrounds, we saw cars and people gathered around what was a mountain of junk, wood and rubbish. Through the wind and now pouring rain, I could see it was almost as wide as five cars, and higher than any tree or building in the area.

Euan and I took shelter under a tree as four men tried to keep the bottom of the pyre alight. Children ran around the burning mountain as ash and sparks filled the air. Caution tape broke loose and flew into the air, quickly melting as the flames grew larger. Suddenly, a DJ started playing music and "The Chicken Dance" blared out like some bizarre anthem as we watched pieces of Wigtown burn.

Once the first layer of wood on the pyre disintegrated, TV's, computers and old sofas became visible underneath. Anything and everything, and things that you really shouldn't be burning, had been chucked on the fire to make this impressive mound of rubbish. Euan wrapped his arms around me as black chemical smoke cloaked the sky above, and suddenly we were laughing, soaked and covered in ash. I felt alive, and free, in the mounting chaos. This was a rare window of anarchy in the land of health and safety. As the flames grew higher, I noticed two precariously perched recliners at the top of the pyre, and in each of them effigies of a hay-stuffed man and woman. Flames licked their legs.

"Euan, will leaving, and giving you time to figure out what you want, make things better?" I heard myself say as the wind and rain slashed against our faces.

"I think so," Euan replied quickly. I hugged his arms around me tighter and watched as the two effigies caught fire.

"Will we be okay?" I asked, and turned my soaked face towards his. "Not in an existential 'we'll all be okay' way but will you and I be okay, you know, together?"

"I can't promise that," Euan said, lifting his jacket to shield me from the icy rain, "but I hope so."

Bright orange flames towered over the crowd and threw out sparks dangerously close to the children, who stood by as the burning pyre raged. Cries went up around us and the wind whipped debris through the air. Euan and I turned for home as the voice of Johnny Cash sang out, "Love, is a burning thing..."

Chapter 39

"Every man has to learn the points of the compass again as often as he awakes, whether from sleep or any abstraction. Not till we are lost, in other words, not till we have lost the world, do we begin to find ourselves, and realise where we are and the infinite extent of our relations." – Henry David Thoreau, WALDEN: *Special editions, high shelf, by the feet of the skeleton in the gallery*.

Airports have a smell akin to a doctor's surgery. It's a tangy smell of chemicals, air fresheners and stale, reused oxygen. I was becoming allergic to the scent of airports. This morning the smell was mixed with coffee and buttery baked things, as I sat across the way from Euan, slumped into a chair at Costa Coffee.

My chocolate croissant sat untouched before me, as did my tea, which created little steam swirls in the air between us, adding to the already palpable tension in the atmosphere. I was not hungry. I was not one of the excited travellers, about to embark on an adventure that I had been looking forward to, one that would be filled with new experiences and unfamiliar sights and sounds. I was one of those sad travellers, who make you feel uncomfortable by crying on aeroplanes and drinking too much of the complimentary wine.

I wiped the tears from my eyes and shifted uncomfortably. I hadn't even left yet but I could just imagine what it would be like to wake up in my parents' house, in my childhood bedroom, with Euan far away and without any evidence that my old life existed. The thought was too depressing to bear. I was already resenting Boston, hating the fact that its streets, people and pollution would soon feel more real to me than Galloway's twisting country roads, Wigtown's cast of characters and clean sea air. I was hating Euan's absence although he was still here, sitting across from me.

"Fox, aren't you going to eat your breakfast?" Euan looked at me, his blue eyes searching my face. He was smiling and was hoping for one in return.

How could he be so stoic and calm? The selfish part of me wanted him to be a mess, to feel how the universe would cease to exist in the same glorious way once I was gone. Where I felt a great cosmic angst, Euan seemed only to be quietly concerned. I was in the depths of despair while he exhibited an annoying serenity that unnerved me.

"It will be okay, I promise, Jessy." Euan reached across the table, stroking my arm with his warm hands.

"How do you know that?"

When Euan and I had agreed to have some time apart, we had also agreed not to chat between then and the date when he was supposed to "arrive on my doorstep". The latter had been my addition to the plan and had seemed appropriate at the time I conceived it; if my extensive knowledge of period films had taught me anything, it was that men needed a hero moment, and this, perhaps, would be Euan's. However, outside the comfort zone of The Bookshop, sitting on the precipice of losing him on the cold hard seats of Costa Coffee in the airport, my plan looked like a horrific gamble rather than an inspired stratagem.

All I could think of was how nice his hand felt on my arm, and how I might never feel it again.

Euan shrugged and the corners of his mouth twitched. He was trying to suppress laughter. "I just do. We'll be fine. Honestly."

It wasn't that he was enjoying the fact that I was leaving, but he was less worried about himself and more amused by my dramatic outpouring of emotion. I needed to stop my tears, and wondered where the valve in me was so that I could turn it off.

"You don't have to promise me that," I said. With a bold attempt to pull myself together, I smiled. "I want you to figure out what you really want. Whatever that is."

"Jessy, you'll be late if you don't head to your boarding gate now," Euan said gently.

I felt myself standing up and facing him. He wrapped me in his arms. This was a mistake. If we went through with this, I'd never see him again.

*

The plane seats were cramped and uncomfortable, but I stared ahead of me, uncaring. I couldn't hear the roar from the engines, or the chatty woman next to me. Everything was deafened by my depression and grief. How had all my experiences come to this?

Last time I left Wigtown, the moment had been full of sweetness. I had been thinking of all the magic of the festival, the extraordinary series of events that had led me to Euan and the deep connection I felt both to him and Galloway. I had been sad to leave but I had known, deep down, in some mysteriously confident way, that I would be returning.

Now, I felt no such certainty. I felt no sweet connection to a deeper mystery. I felt chaotic and out of control. More than my destiny, my heart was not in my hands. The hands which held my future were no longer those of my imagination, nor those of Wigtown's watchful spirits, but rather Euan's dithering ones.

*

A jolt of turbulence knocked me sideways. Every bump meant that I was going to die. Every movement the buffeted plane made marked the end of my journey. I was no longer the one who made things happen and so I felt my invisible shield of protection had been lifted. Without a purpose, I felt vulnerable. Randomness reigned. Another bump sent me grabbing the woman next to me, who recoiled. I apologised and sat looking straight ahead. The PA system crackled on and the stewardess, in a curt tone, told everyone to return to their seats. My knuckles turned white as I gripped my armrest. I prepared for the worst.

When I was small, aged about eight or nine, on realising the impermanent nature of the universe, I started playing a little game. Whenever I was scared, I would ask myself: if I died now, would I be happy with where I was going? Not literally – what eight-year-old would be happy when they were going to the doctor's or the dentist's? – but figuratively: was I happy with the direction my life was taking, given what I wanted to achieve? (I was a very ambitious child.) If the answer was yes, then there was nothing to be afraid of.

Only once had the answer been no. It had been while I was living in New York, disappointed by my job and the city, despite my friends' and family's love for it; I felt crushed under the weight of the buildings, lost rather than able to rejoice in the anonymity that the place afforded.

On one particularly hot summer's day, I had sat in the thick heat of the subway car, already soaked in sweat from an intense yoga session. The train had started quickly but soon got stuck in a dark tunnel. The lighting had shut off, as had the engine, and we sat in silence as the announcer told everyone that a mysterious package had been found on board. Whispers that it was a bomb suddenly filled the subway car.

I had asked myself the Question. Was I happy with where I was going; with where my life was headed? The answer had come back a resounding "no". Terror had suddenly gripped my throat. I had been on my way to pick up pet food for my boss's cat, in a production job that had turned out to be as enlightening as unemployment. I realised it was true – I wasn't happy with the direction of my life; I had taken the more prescribed route of assistant work in production, hoping I'd slowly circle – through one crap job after another – closer to my goal of being a director. Why was I waiting for someone to give me permission to do what I wanted to do? I could wait for ever for someone to offer me an opportunity to prove myself. If I had been learning more about filmmaking and my craft, that would be something, but all I was getting better at was how to find less expensive cat food. I alone had the responsibility to learn and grow as a director and I was failing myself. I had not taken the risks I should. I hadn't made the films I wanted to and I was not living in the city that was right for me. I had veered into the wrong universe. I had been the Jessica making the wrong choices and there was another Jessica, who had gone in a different, self-directed path.

The lights of the train suddenly turned on and the motor rumbled. The announcer apologised. The mysterious package had turned out to be an elderly woman's shopping. As the subway started moving again, I felt no sense of relief, just an overwhelming desire to resolve my situation. I told myself I could be the Jessica who was on the more self-affirming path; it was all a matter of choice. So I went home and packed my things. I allowed myself to keep four boxes, mostly full of books, and the rest of my belongings I put out onto the street. I gave notice at my job and, as soon as I could, moved back to Boston and decided to make a film. A month later I had asked myself the question again – "if it all ended tomorrow, would I be happy with where I was going?" – and the answer had been an enthusiastic "yes".

I felt the woman next to me inching away to the other side of her seat. I couldn't blame her. I was shaking, terrified, and jolted with every shudder of the plane. She probably thought I was crazy and the assumption would have been justified – I certainly felt it. A "ding" sounded and the light for the seatbelts went off. Sighing, I relaxed into the chair, trying not to think about the fact that under my feet was a vault of sky and below that an endless expanse of shark-infested water.

I had done this to myself. Perhaps then I had it in me to make this trip home meaningful. I could change things, just like I had done in New York. I could take this time to finish my animation, to be with Cole, my old friends and my family.

My face suddenly flushed red at the thought of my parents. In the chaos of the past couple of days, booking my ticket, packing and leaving, I hadn't called my parents once, or emailed. They had no idea I was coming home. In fact, no one did; only Euan knew that I was currently flying half way across the world again, and was barely two hours from arrival in Boston.

Chapter 40

"Madame Sosostris,
famous clairvoyante,
Had a bad cold,
nevertheless
Is known to be the
wisest woman in
Europe,
With a wicked pack
of cards. Here, said
she,
is your card
the drowned Phoenician
Sailor,
(Those are pearls
that were his eyes.
Look!)"

— T.S. Eliot, THE WASTELAND: *Poetry section,
right of the fireplace, under E.*

The cab slowed at a toll booth and I stared motionless out of the window. Beyond my ghostly reflection, dusk settled in sherbet streaks behind the Boston skyline. My heart, in better condition, would have leapt at the sight of the shadowy, yet familiar tall buildings. Now, it remained heavy, full of remorse. I would have done anything to exchange the Prudential Tower for Cairnsmore and the sheer wall of glass on the Hancock building for Wigtown's blue bay.

As the cab driver rolled down the window, the smell of exhaust smoke filled the car. He threw a handful of change into the toll basket, and the red light turned green. I flipped my phone over and over in my hand nervously. My journey home was underway.

The cab drove through a dark tunnel and I welcomed the feeling of being in a long cocoon. I shut my eyes. Blank screen. No one knew I was here; I could do anything without the burden of expectation upon me. I waited for that tingling sense of freedom and autonomy. But instead I felt leaden, like an anchor slipping into the ocean. As I fast-forwarded the movie of my sudden appearance in my mind, I sank deeper into the cigarette-smelling black seats of the cab.

If I appeared at my parents' door, unannounced, I could imagine the anxiety it would cause. My dramatic entrance would ignite their concern and they would ask why, what had happened. I would be obliged to answer, to quell their sudden worry for my welfare. The last thing I wanted to do was explain myself, or talk at all.

As the cab emerged from the tunnel and I blinked in the cheery early-evening light, I wondered if I was clinically depressed. I hadn't eaten anything in days, and I was happiest sleeping, my mind shut off, allowing me the space to not think about Wigtown, and Euan.

I flipped open the phone and called my father.

"Hello? Jessica?" My father was shocked. My mind raced. He would be wondering why I was calling from my American phone.

"Uh yeah, hi, Dad. Surprise, I'm in Boston."

"You're home? Are you okay?"

My grief was so thick I could hardly speak. "Yeah, I'm home. I thought I'd come, you know, for an early visit." My voice sounded flat and distant. I tried to inject some energy into it. "I thought it would be fun as a surprise."

"It's a wonderful surprise." My father's concern was obvious. "Do you need me to pick you up at the airport?"

I couldn't speak any longer, it required too much energy. "No, I'm on my way, in a cab. I'll see you soon."

"All right. I'm so happy you're home."

The cab easily slipped into the darkness of another tunnel. Home. Boston was not my home. I did not want this to feel anything like home. My home was halfway around the world, with Euan. I wanted to call him. It would be so easy to type in his number, to hear his voice. We had made a deal, though: no speaking until he appeared at my doorstep. There was wisdom in having space, taking some time apart. I looked down at the phone, which sat in my hands like a loaded gun. I wanted to hear him, to feel close to him. The silence of his absent presence was overwhelming.

I quickly tucked the phone into my pocket. We had made a promise. I wouldn't be the one to break it.

*

I woke up just as we turned on to Massachusetts Avenue, a couple of blocks from my childhood home. I had travelled those roads over and over again as a sleepy child in the back seat of my parents' car. Bodies can develop an internal knowing, like a GPS. The twists and turns must have signalled that we were close, and I woke instinctively.

Turning onto our small street, I pointed to a classic yellow colonial house on a hill, with large maple trees in front.

"It's here, right here. Thank you."

My parents were waiting for me on the steps. When they saw me emerge from the taxi, they acted heroically calm as if my arrival was planned, greeting me warmly and helping me with my luggage. Walking up the steps, they asked no questions. Their excited conversation was filled only with "We're so glad to see you!", "What a treat to have you home" and "Are you hungry?"

How could they be so good? I marvelled at their consideration, or perhaps their self-control. If it were me, and I were my child, I would have been brimming over with investigative questions, and not resting easy until I had put the pieces of the mystery together. Perhaps it was obvious to them why I was home. On catching a glimpse of myself in the downstairs hall mirror, it occurred to me that you did not have to be Sherlock Holmes to guess what had motivated my sudden return. I looked a mess and my eyes were bloodshot from crying.

With excuses of being exhausted, I slipped upstairs. In my parents' house I knew every floorboard, every crack and every inch of every wall. The familiarity was nause-ating. At the top of the stairs, I turned to face my old room. It was the room I had grown up in, down the hall from my sister, still with "Jessica's Parking, All Others Will be Towed" taped to the door.

Inside my small bedroom, I faced a jungle of child-hood relics, carefully preserved: bedding, books and keep-sakes right where I had left them. A large Kate Winslet *Holy Smoke* poster was pinned to one wall, across from an etching I had picked up when I had travelled to Paris.

I sat on the bed, listening to the sounds of my parents talking in the kitchen below. My heart began to race. I felt as if the walls were as thin as paper. There was nowhere for me to go now, no anonymity, no privacy. I had entered a time warp, and felt suddenly drastically infantilised, thinking of the contrast to the freedom I had had, living in another country, in an adult house with my boyfriend.

My phone buzzed. I had a message. My heart flew into my throat. It was from Euan, I just knew it. He would have wanted to check in, to see if I had landed okay. That was allowed after all, wasn't it? I quickly pulled the phone from my pocket. My heart dropped back into my chest. It wasn't Euan, but my sister. The message read "Happy you're home".

I opened my bag and took out the iPod nano that Euan had given me. Shoving the earphones into my ears and turning the volume up till the music blocked any noise, I moved the stuffed toys off the bed and climbed under the covers. I wanted to disappear, sink into the bed and never emerge again. My eyes closed to the soundtrack of Wigtown and somewhere between thoughts of Euan and Galloway, I fell asleep.

Chapter 41

"That great mystery of Time, were there no other; the illimitable, silent, never-resting thing called Time, rolling, rushing on, swift, silent, like an all-embracing ocean tide, on which we and all the Universe swim like exhalations, like apparitions which are, and then are not..." – Thomas Carlyle, ON HEROES AND HERO WORSHIP AND THE HEROIC IN HISTORY: *Scottish Room, third bookshelf on the left.*

I woke to find Herman Melville sitting at the foot of my bed. He slipped off his hat and surveyed his surroundings, looking as disgusted as I felt. Tucked under a bushy brow, his eyes were full of question marks as he wondered where the *Under Milk Wood* setting of Wigtown had gone.

"You have to get up," he said in an impatient tone. His breath smelled salty, like the sea.

I rolled over and hid my face. The afternoon light poured in between the cracks in the curtain. "For what?"

"To create." Herman looked pleased with himself. I didn't move.

A week had passed and I had barely surfaced for air. Any time I had felt the desire to get up, to leave the room, I thought about the expanse of ocean between myself and Galloway and my energy would quickly drain. Thinking of anything, actually, drained me of energy because it ultimately brought me back to the truth of my circumstances: I wasn't in Wigtown. The pain of not being able to control the next events in my life, where I was going to be, whom I was going to be with, had short-circuited my brain. All I could do was go to sleep to reboot the system.

Herman stood up, annoyed. "It smells worse than Queequeg in here. Get up and greet your destiny." He was losing patience and poked me with the end of his walking stick. "Anyway, you have to get up to answer your phone."

Slowly I realised there was a humming noise and I craned my neck to see my cell phone buzzing on the floor. I stretched my arm over to reach it. True to his word, Euan had never called. We hadn't spoken since I got home and my heart had now stopped jumping at every phone call, thinking it might be him.

I flipped open the phone.

"Hello?" My voice sounded rough and tired.

"Where are you, are you okay?" A deep male voice with a thick Boston accent greeted me on the other end. "We've been waiting like an hour for you. Did you forget?"

My eyes strained to see the big radio clock, a gift I had received for my bat-mitzvah, sitting covered in dust on the table next to the bed. It was 2:30pm. I was an hour late for my production meeting.

*

My silver Toyota with the NASA sticker on the back pulled into the parking lot of a converted mill building outside Boston. Inside, the car still smelled like California, a mixture of coconut and sunscreen. I hazily remembered enjoying the newness of Los Angeles, and the joy of a new dream job, my own apartment and spreading my wings.

Dragging myself up a large stairwell in the main building, I kept my sunglasses on and sipped on my iced tea. That's one thing Wigtown could not offer, iced tea. I had no idea why the British, who loved their tea, never innovated for summertime. When one of Euan's friends had told me it was sacrilege, I pointed out that there was Winter and Summer Pimms. Why not tea?

I enjoyed the tea's bitterness as it slid, cold and fresh, down my throat. Perhaps today would invigorate my spirit. I was in a thriving artists' loft community, walking by sculptures, pictures and paint-adorned walls. I tried to soak in the creative energy on my way down the hall. I was nervous to direct again. My artistic voice felt rusty, lost and unpractised after months without use.

I could hear voices and banging. As I walked over to the familiar studio door at the end of the hall, Will, a dear friend and an enormous talent, whom I had been lucky enough to rope into animating this film, opened the door.

"You made it." He slapped me affectionately on the arm. "Good to see you, Fox."

*

As the animation finished, Will looked from the computer to me, expectantly.

"It's really brilliant. I love it," I said, almost dropping my iced tea. Will had taken my ideas to the next level, bringing to life each film cell with a sensitive, unique touch that exceeded my expectations. It was beautiful, and I was convinced even my producer would have nothing but compliments when he saw it.

"Do you really like it? I was worried." Will sat back and scanned my face.

"The story is okay," I teased, "but your animation is brilliant. Honestly." Though I meant every word, my energy felt low, non-existent. In the past I would have been elated, as if high. Where my insides would have been bursting with exuberance now I felt only a small tremor of pleasure. Why could I not get motivated? This was my dream, after all, to make films. And here I was doing it – I should feel infinitely lucky. Self-pitying tears sprang to my eyes. I felt empty.

"This project is as much yours now as it is mine," I said and slipped my sunglasses on. "I couldn't be happier." I was happy with the animation, just not with myself.

"Well, good, I'm glad." Will rubbed his hands together. "No one else is doing this kind of animation. We're breaking new ground here." He handed me a script. "Let's get cracking. So how long do we have you here for anyway?"

"I think I'm back here for good," I said, not looking up.

Will paused. He softly placed a hand on my shoulder while we waited for the computer to render a new scene.

*

Days turned into weeks, and I began to have a routine that resembled a young professional zombie's: sleep, sleep, work. Sleep, sleep, reluctantly get out of bed to see friends. Sleep, sleep, avoid parents. Refuse to eat. Sleep.

I was creating, as Melville had put it, but I needed an epidural. Every morning I watched myself arrive at the studios in a cloud of reluctance and tried in the old way to make art again. It was not working. I questioned all my decisions, I felt no passion, no thrill shot through my fingers and my connection to the piece was lost. In fact, my desire to make, to affect anything in the world around me, had disappeared.

As the inner world holds a mirror to the outer one, my family watched as I quite literally started to disappear before them. Food had lost its appeal, and I dropped half my weight, my body reflecting the ghostly passivity of my waning spirit.

Being with friends was even more difficult. Time had past since I had left, and like the protagonist in *Flight of the Navigator*, I had returned from what felt like a blink in Scotland to find that their lives had moved on, and they were busy with jobs and relationships. At dinner parties I sat, the single one surrounded by young couples, with a polite smile plastered on my face, while they talked about movies I hadn't seen, politics I hadn't followed and their achievements, which seemed so much more advanced than my own. My friends suddenly had their own apartments, they had pension schemes, health insurance and glittering futures in med school, business school or their careers, while I was living in my parents' house, penniless, with no future to speak of.

"So what do you do, Jessica?" a good-looking Indian medical student asked me, as we sat in Cole's apartment. I looked at Cole pleadingly.

"Jessica," Cole said, "is a director who was just living in Scotland, but came back to Boston to make a film. She's far more interesting than the rest of us." Cole was such a good friend, making my journey home sound triumphant. The way he saw me was so much more complimentary than the way I saw myself.

"I love Scotland," the young medical student said.

"She'll also be winning an Oscar some time soon," Cole added. His blind faith in me filled my heart.

Cole and his girlfriend had been letting me sleep on their couch, an imposition in their small apartment, to give me a break from my family – or more likely, my family a break from me. Not once had either of them made me feel less than at home.

Later that evening, as I was about to leave, Cole stopped me. "Stay, please. Stay as long as you need." I looked over Cole's shoulder to see his girlfriend setting up the couch for me. I felt like their adopted child. I needed to give them some space. I'd find somewhere else.

His girlfriend came over and smiled warmly, leaning against Cole. They were a beautiful, peaceful couple, perfectly matched: a unit, together. It made me hyper-aware of the airy, cold spaces on either side of me, single and alone.

"Things will get better, I promise. He's an idiot if he doesn't come," Cole's girlfriend said, hugging me.

I nodded, with no hope that in three days my ginger-haired knight was going to appear on my doorstep. With a handful of thankyous, I headed out into the crisp Boston night air.

Wasn't I supposed to be rewarded for taking risks? Don't religions, cringeworthy self-help books and poets everywhere tell you to take the path less taken? Well, I had. Like a fool I had followed my impulses and imaginary visions, and instead of leading me to bliss, like Joseph Campbell had promised, I had emerged lost and broken, only to find all the people I loved and cared about had built their own paths and moved on.

*

I woke the next morning and tried to find my bearings. I was on another couch, in a living room surrounded by plants, dolls and stuffed birds, clocks that weren't working and a pinball machine. I blinked up at a seemingly endless high ceiling. The sound of drilling somewhere in the building alerted my senses. I was at the artists' community, outside Boston, on Will's sofa.

I stumbled over to his computer. On the upper right I saw a blinking 8:30am, and I let my eyes adjust to the screen. Facebook was open; the white-and-blue iconic print stared back at me, tempting me to log on. I hadn't used Facebook since returning from Wigtown, knowing any sign of Euan would make me feel worse. I had wanted to log on every minute of every hour to see if I could find clues as to how he was or if he had been thinking of me. I feared, though, that I would become a human archaeologist, exploring things he had or had not written to a depth that suddenly would give them new meanings and motivations.

In my tired, weak state, I stayed at Will's computer, debating whether to type in my password. Surely it would make no difference now. I convinced myself that I was out of the critical window in which Facebook happenings would have an effect on my emotional state; I was close enough to the finish line to be safe.

I quickly logged myself in and went to Euan's profile. I couldn't help smiling when I saw his picture. He had put up a photo I took of him in front of the shop, laughing and leaning against one of the book spirals. It was an attractive image; he looked happy, tall and fit. My eyes flicked over to his wall and then my chest tightened.

Euan's profile was covered in new comments and most of them were by women. Unlike me, his social life had not ceased because of our separation. In fact, the tone on his Facebook page was positively upbeat, back to his bachelor happy-go-lucky self. The women on his profile page spoke to me, their voices chanted loud and clear: you're the last thing on his mind. I cared less about the mysterious new faces who left teasing, snide remarks and more about the ones I knew. Heather had left a message, to which he had responded, full of inside jokes. On reading it I felt excluded, non-existent. It made me panic. I hated the sense of competition it inspired. I did not want to feel as if I were constantly fighting off suitors. He was supposed to be my knight in shining armour, after all, and here I was, brandishing my own sword.

I was breathing deeply now, my lungs trying to catch up with my heart, which was beating as if lightning had struck it. My eyes scrolled down, now addicted, wanting to find every piece of the puzzle that could lead me to Euan during my absence. At the bottom of the page was a message from Heather. My eyes stopped, as if I had found what I had been looking for, the "x" on the map. All it said was, "You better not be late this time, or you'll be buying the drinks."

The phone rang and rang and rang. I was breaking our promise. With three days to go, I had lost all my will power. I did the calculation quickly. It was three in the afternoon here, so about eight in the evening there. Suddenly, there was a click and Euan picked up.

Soft music murmured in background. I heard someone laughing. Euan's voice was distracted and giddy. "Hello?"

"Hi, it's me." Sudden rage swelled over me. "Where are you?"

"Um, look, can I call you back? I just arrived."

"Where?"

"I'm at a party." There was a pause.

"Oh. Whose party?"

"Heather's." He was drunk; he sounded warm and relaxed.

The laughter in the background got louder. My rage was overpowering and I tried to splutter some coherent words out. "In Dublin?"

"Yes," he said. "You sound angry."

"Well..."

"Look, you wanted me to explore, to figure out my feelings."

"Are you two dating?"

There was only silence on the other end. His silence was indignant rather than apologetic. It unnerved me. After weeks of not speaking, this was not what I had pictured as our first reunion call.

"Of course I'm not dating her. I'm dating a crazy American Fox," Euan said unhappily. "Don't you trust me?"

I paused, realising I didn't. "So are you coming, then?"

Music blasted loud from a back room and Euan sounded distracted. "I'm not sure yet."

"But it's only three days away."

"Look, Jessy, this is not the time to talk about it." His voice remained calm. "I've got to go."

I was incandescent, inarticulate.

He hung up the phone.

I called back, and back and back.

Chapter 42

"It is easy to go down into Hell; night and day, the gates of dark Death stand wide; but to climb back again, to retrace one's steps to the upper air – there's the rub, the task." – Virgil, Aeneid, Book VI Line 126: *Classics section, up the stairs on right, third bookshelf.*

In the movies, this part of the story would have a charming montage sequence. I would jog, get into shape, transform my life and premiere my animation, all to a fabulous soundtrack. I would forget about Euan, whether he was coming or not, and get my own life together. Once everything was perfectly in place, and I felt whole in myself, Euan would come, just as he promised, and reveal some gross misunderstanding that made all of his actions look noble in hindsight.

The truth was a lot less romantic.

Later that evening, at my parents' house, I locked myself in my room. I had run out of couches to surf and landed, beached and weary, back on my childhood bed. I could hear my mom watching TV downstairs, and the clinking of dishes as my father washed up from dinner.

My stomach flipped. I thought I'd be sick, and braced myself, looking around the room for something to throw up in. All I managed to grab was my niece's toy pail with a small red shovel clinking inside. *Shpilkus*, as if buried but not forgotten these past months, suddenly flooded my body, as painful as if I were actually sitting on pins. I didn't know what to do with myself. My mind was stuck on one uncomfortable loop: Euan had been seeing other people. He had forgotten about me and I had made it happen.

That afternoon, during my production meeting with Will, I had been in another world. There was nothing I could do about the impending car crash of my life and my mind had disengaged. Will had introduced me to a new intern who had volunteered to work on the animation, and though I had smiled, all I had wanted to do was sleep. While I had been heartbroken, living in my parents' house, my life had been on a constant pause button and I had patiently waited in emotional purgatory for Euan to make up his mind. Now, it had become clear that Euan, instead of pining after me, had been living it up, happy and single, and I no longer felt as if I was waiting for anything. I was no longer on pause.

It started with me throwing my computer off my bed, which landed with a satisfying crack on the floor. The sound made me feel better, awake and alive. I took a jar of marbles and dumped them over the wooden floorboards, exalting in the roar as they bounced in chaotic directions. I was thirsty for more release, so I began to break things.

My parents stood outside my room, facing "Jessica's Parking" sign immobile with worry, calling gently through the door. I was outside my body, watching myself act like a mini-tornado, throwing precious objects off shelves and chucking toys, the innocent bystanders to this scene, across the room. I could feel my insides ripping in two; it was painful but liberating too. How did I let myself get into such a state? I had been such a strong, together woman. How had my whole life suddenly become a mess, and over a man? As I caught sight of myself in the mirror, sobbing onto my childhood bedroom floor, the words of Robert McKee, the screenplay doctor, came to mind: I hit the negation of the negation. Rock-bottom.

Once the wave of Kali-inspired chaos subsided, I crawled into bed, empty, purged. Though I had destroyed the room, at least I was affecting the world around me again; I was making things happen. Feelings, I told myself, were as unique as snowflakes. I had glimpsed the bleakness of self-imposed annihilation in the break-up from Grant, and I had comforted myself that I would never have to, nor be able to have that exact same experience twice. I had got that type of sorrow out of the way and, though this was painful, it was different. I no longer felt like disappearing, nor dying from heartache. I felt raw, shaken and hurt, but also alive – as if I had been in a trance and suddenly woken up. Antonio Porchia, an Italian poet, once said that you mourn the loss of a thing until you lose it altogether. Perhaps that's why, with one great outburst, I no longer felt in despair.

It was then that I noticed the sweet, concerned voices of my parents leaking into the room. Shame rose as high as my cheeks, turning them red.

"Are you all right honey?" My mom tapped on the door.

My father's voice was louder, more anxious. "Jessica, are you okay? Open the door."

"I'm fine. I'm fine."

"Are you sure?" my father asked, not moving an inch.

"Yes, I'm absolutely peachy. Now please leave me alone."

As my parents' footsteps obediently disappeared down the hall, I could only imagine what they were thinking. I was acting like a fourteen-year-old – worse, in fact, than I had at that age – but the truth was, a tiny part of me had begun to feel fabulous again.

Chapter 43

"A woman who thinks that only women can be worthy is like a bird with a broken wing." – Sarah Grand, THE HEAVENLY TWINS: *Fiction section, front room in paperbacks.*

Mending is a satisfying activity. On the days that followed, I cleaned my room, piecing together the wreckage so that, by the time I was done, little remained of the prior emotional entropy. This time I had not only looked into but fallen into the depths of my emotional abyss and come out, if not with my hair ruffled and tempest tossed, stronger for the descent. I had hit the bottom and was now inching my way back out, fearless.

Two days before Euan was supposed to arrive on my doorstep, instead of wallowing in despair, I felt elated. I spent time with my parents, assuring them of my well-being. I even travelled out to see my sister and her family, something I had been too depressed to do before. I tried to go to coffee shops like I used to do in Los Angeles, giving myself time to dream and write. Slowly, I felt energy pouring back in, and like a sponge, I thirstily soaked up the chance to feel fuller, more myself again.

On the evening before Euan was supposed to arrive, I called. It was time to end this ridiculous experiment.

"So any chance you have your ticket?" I said.

"No."

There was silence on the phone. So that was that. The long wait and the muddy indecision were over. I would be staying in Boston. My heart heaved, hurting, and I watched it closely. Where it once would have broken, it remained intact, stretched but untorn.

I exhaled deeply and could feel my breath streaming out of my lips. I surprised myself by how quickly I adjusted to the idea of not seeing Euan again. I was calm. "You're not coming, then. That's okay."

Euan sighed. "I still don't know."

"How can you not know? You have to be at the airport in less than 24 hours."

"I know, I know. I just… don't know." His dithering had reached surreal proportions. I hung up the phone.

*

Some psychologists would say that sleep is like a mini-death. Delving into the unconscious blackness, each night we fall asleep and not only do our minds reboot but our cells die and are reborn. On waking, like the sun at dawn, we are resurrected. We do this phoenix cycle every day, every 24 hours, and each time is a ritual, fuelling the potential for transformation. Or, as Anne of Green Gables' teacher Mrs. Stacy said, "Tomorrow is always fresh, with no mistakes in it."

In the morning light, I stretched on my bed, feeling rested, refreshed and light. I was warm under my childhood blankets, as Kate Winslet looked down at me from the poster on the wall. She was phenomenally brilliant. Only a couple of years younger than she, I'd look at that poster as if it were a carrot before a horse, Kate's expression asking me, "All right, director, what amazing thing are you going to make?"

Even as my mind became more alert and conscious of the previous day's events, I found the sense of levity continued. This was a new beginning, and as I slid out of bed, I was oddly energetic. Even if I was sad and heart-broken, being in control of my own destiny was far more liberating. I was surprised by my sense of relief. There was a bold world of possibilities out there.

My phone rang. I stumbled over to the corner of the room where it lay in a pile of clothes. I looked at the number and my heart sank. It was Euan.

"Hi," I said, my morning voice scratchy and quiet.

He laughed. "Did I wake you up?"

"No, I was just on my way to becoming vertical."

"Well, Fox" – Euan laughed again, this time nervously – "What I wanted to know was, does it still count if I'm a day late?"

"No, it doesn't," I said and hung up the phone.

Chapter 44

"All over the sky a sacred voice is calling your name." –
John G. Neihardt, BLACK ELK SPEAKS: *Biography section,*
across from the fireplace.

Standing outside my parents' house, I stretched my limbs.
I had just finished a run and stood, sweat streaming
down my brow, with my back to the sun. Spring was in full
swell around me, and I looked at the green trees and manicured lawns, wondering what Wigtown would be like now.
I imagined the mountains to be green and lush, and flowers
blooming in the hanging baskets outside The Bookshop.
There would be more people in the streets, the town would
be buzzing like the bees which flew from flower to flower
in the square. I wondered if any of them asked about me,
or noticed I had gone.

Perhaps I had been audacious on the phone with Euan
but I had meant what I said. A promise was a promise and
if he wasn't so much of a ditherer, he would have made it
to my doorstep on time. That was the whole point. I let the
stream of feelings wash over me as I soaked in the day's
warmth like a cat on a hot rock, lazily arching my back as
I relaxed.

A bright-yellow cab pulled onto the street and my heart
fluttered. This wasn't happening. Euan had tricked me,
the monkey, and he had actually kept his word. My heart

thudded in my ears but I watched in disappointment as the cab passed by and disappeared down the road.

My head shook and fell into my heads. I was hopeless. Why, after all that I had been through, did I still think it would be Euan, arriving at my doorstep? The singer Feist, whose album *The Reminder* had been like an anthem album for me in Los Angeles, has a song about a woman walking through the park and thinking she has seen her lover: "It's not him coming across the seas to surprise you/Not him who would know where in London to find you…"

I felt the truth of that sink in. Like Feist's lyrics, I wasn't sure Euan even knew where in Lexington my parents lived. The final lines of the song chimed in my ears and I felt sad, defeated: "…what makes you think your boy could become/ The man who would make you sure he was the one."

The energy from the day's run was wearing off and I could no longer feel the endorphins pumping through my veins. Love intertwined with optimism is a powerful union, almost religious in its tenacity, and difficult to separate. We don't let go easily of hope, but the time had come for me to do so. What was done was done, and Euan, my knight, was not coming. Now the princess had to get down from her ivory tower and get her life together.

As I headed up the stairs back to the house, I focused on the plans for that afternoon: looking at two apartments in Boston. With each step I tried to get excited, and a little murmur of anticipation fluttered in my heart, but nothing more. It didn't matter.

Suddenly, a blur of yellow caught my eye. I turned around to see the cab reversing back down the road and it stopped suddenly, right where I had been standing. Perhaps the people inside were lost or needed directions,

I thought gloomily, so I climbed back down the stairs. As I came closer, one of the passenger doors opened, and a tall, ginger-haired man dressed in corduroys, a jacket and glasses stepped out and stood looking at me on my parents' driveway.

Chapter 45

"No more secrets, no more mysteries, no more adventure. And this, above all else, becomes the real curse of living happily ever after." – Maria Tatar, BLUEBEARD: *Children's section, bottom shelf under children's literature.*

In the hotel room, Euan and I faced each other.

We were in one of the most expensive hotels in Boston, filled with travelling businessmen in designer suits and equally upmarket furniture; the ambience was a bit over the top for our first reunion but it was all I could find last minute. It didn't matter. He was here. With time zones on his side, Euan had gained five hours flying over the Atlantic and made it on the day he had promised, on time.

I stood there awkwardly. "I can't believe you came."

"I can't believe you said a day late wouldn't count."

"I can't believe how much you dither." I smiled weakly. We kissed and I felt my heart expand. I quickly pulled away, unable to give myself into the feeling. "If we are really going to try this again you are never, ever to dither about me again. Ever."

"Okay, okay, I get it." He flopped on to the immaculate bed, covered in a plethora of silk pillows.

Watching him lie there, I felt guilty. I couldn't imagine what time he would have had to get up in order to make it for the early flight. The airport was hours away from

347

Wigtown, along mainly one-track roads through the mountains. It would have been dark, and cold.

Long ago, when Euan and I had started living together, his lack of verbal affection had unnerved me. There had been a tightness to his language that was in direct contrast to his relaxed state of being, his warm, playful manner and his informal, often paint-covered, attire. His had been the art of teasing, not the art of compliments, and on one particular evening, I had had enough: "I would really like more positive verbal reinforcement," I had said, trying to be clear and unemotional.

Euan had burst out laughing.

"What? What did I say?"

"Positive Verbal Reinforcement? Jessy, who says that?" Euan had come over and wrapped me in his arms affectionately. "You know I think you're beautiful. You don't need me to say it."

"Yes, I do." I knew he had been right, but suspected it was laziness, rather than an intimate knowledge of my psyche, that had led him to that conclusion. "Compliments are important, I compliment you all the time."

"I know," he said, sighing. "It's not very British."

Now, in this bizarre businessmen's hotel room, I felt the lack of exuberance like a void in the air between us. Having been apart for nearly two months, I felt out of practice in his company, and my sea legs were getting used to his manner again.

"You're happy to see me, aren't you?" I said and curled up next to him. I knew I was fishing for an implied truth but at that moment I needed to hear some Positive Verbal Reinforcement.

"Of course. I'm more than happy, in fact." He eyed me curiously. "Are you happy to see me?"

"Yes, of course I am," I said, unsure. Euan being there meant that things were less straightforward; and my feelings too were muddled ag ain – where before I had felt calm, now I was a little scared.

*

I stayed awake long after Euan had fallen into a deep, jet-lagged sleep. I wondered if he had noticed my weight loss, or, on seeing me, whether he was regretting everything and was questioning whether the whole ordeal had been worth it. My attention should have been on my own feelings, which were flip-flopping like a politician. If I followed a feeling, it only led to another contrasting feeling, like a massive, well-knotted ball of string.

I heard Euan's deep voice next to me. "Uh oh, I know that Fox look." I turned to find him awake, and looking at me with intense interest. "There's steam coming out of your ears and I can see the gears grinding away." His finger circled my temple.

I batted his hand away.

Euan propped his head up in his hand. "Come on, out with it, Jessy. And don't tell me there is nothing wrong, I know you."

This irritated me. He did know me. It was dawn outside and the room was still dark. "I am happy to see you, Euan," I said. "But, I guess I'm just a bit confused."

"Might we say you're dithering?" Euan sounded almost pleased.

"Well yes, actually."

"Jessy, I don't want you to feel any pressure to come back with me because I'm here." Euan was showing me more wisdom and patience than I had to him, and I felt ashamed. "I would have come to see you either way," he continued. "You are the love of my life, Jessy. You take all the time to decide what you want."

Somewhere, deep inside me, a fortress of feelings relaxed. The constant chatter of my thoughts drained away and for the first time I heard Euan with perfect clarity. I felt free and strong and loved. Suddenly, there was nothing to decide.

*

Euan had given himself five days off from The Bookshop and we toured the city, doing things I never would have done as a resident. Boston is an unexpected treat if you're a tourist. We went on the Boston Duck, a refurbished aquatic vehicle dating from World War II which now housed not troops but tourists, taking them easily from road to water and guiding them through the city's history. After touring the streets, we plunged into the Charles River, boating between Boston and Cambridge.

Euan was thrilled to go to Cheers where a half-drunk Bostonian asked why, if he was Scottish, he didn't speak like Braveheart. I was mortified, having worked so hard to prove that Americans were more culturally savvy than their reputation, but Euan shrugged it off, enjoying his pint of Sam Adams.

We then visited the site of the Boston Tea Party and had a liberty tour, during which Euan kept on referring to the American War of Independence as a "skirmish". He'd studied American history at school, but seemed unfamiliar with our version of events on this side of the Atlantic. He feigned shock when the tour guide told the story of the night tea had been thrown overboard in Boston harbour.

Euan whispered in my ear, "It explains why you lot are crazy."

"Taxation without representation." I retorted, looking at him indignantly.

"It better not have been Lady Grey tea."

"Wait till you come to Lexington – then you can see where the war started."

"Skirmish," he said.

After two days alone in Boston, we returned to Lexington and Euan met my parents. The meeting went better than I had imagined. My father fixed Euan breakfast and offered to set out a vitamin plate for him, the ultimate gesture of welcome into the family. My mother took us to the Isabella Garner Museum, and had long conversations with Euan about American and Scottish colourists. As I walked behind them, allowing some space to grow as they disappeared into another room, I remembered that when Euan left in a couple of days, I would be going with him. I had been so focused on being a good host and tour guide that I had almost forgotten my imminent departure. My parents must have realised this too, but they never once reproached me for having been such a terror while I was home, nor did they make me feel guilty for now choosing to return to Scotland.

At the end of our tour, I found my mom in the gift shop, leafing through a stack of postcards.

"Thank you for letting me work things out and being so, so…"

My mom interrupted me. "Your father and I love you." She smiled sadly and patted my arm. "I'm sorry you weren't happier at home."

"It's not that, Mom, it's just…"

"I know, I know." My mom picked up a postcard, distracting herself. "Euan seems very nice."

Euan headed over towards us, smiling and holding my

jacket. We watched him walk through the crowds and I could feel my mom squeezing my hand. She leant in close, whispering, "I will miss you, though."

Chapter 46

"The returning hero, to complete his adventure, must survive the impact of the world." – Stephen and Robin Larsen, A FIRE IN THE MIND: *Biography section, under C.*

Euan grabbed my heavy suitcase from the trunk and slid it onto the cracked sidewalk of Logan International Airport. The stale smell of fossil fuels filled my nostrils. Once again my life had taken me to an airport – I couldn't seem to escape them. The smells, sounds and glass sliding doors were as familiar to me as an unwanted second home.

Sliding out of the car, my floral-printed dress caught a gust of wind from a passing cab, and swirled up around my waist.

"They'll deport you in that," said Euan as he appeared from behind the car. Luckily he was the only one to see. "A bit chilly in your grandmother's dress?"

I tried to give him my most hairy eyeball stare. "The 1950s look is in, it's fashionable," I said, touching the soft brown flowery fabric. I looked him up and down, noticing his open fly and paint-splattered shorts. "But I forgot you are the epitome of 'en vogue'."

Euan and I smiled at each other.

My parents stood on either side of the car, waiting for their goodbyes. Euan received an affectionate hug from my father while I said a goodbye to my mom and kissed her on the cheek. I could see her face muscles twitch, fighting against tears. Like a coward, I couldn't bear to see her sad so I turned my attention to my father, hugging him quickly.

"The house will feel empty without you," he said, and handed me my suitcase, waving goodbye as we disappeared through the sliding doors.

*

As I walked through the empty, twisting lanes leading up to the immigration desk at Glasgow Airport, my suitcase wheeling obediently behind me, I enjoyed the thought that I wouldn't have to see another airport for a long time.

I was home.

Euan and I had been on different flights, having booked mine last minute. Our plan was to meet at the baggage carousel after immigration check because our flights were to arrive around the same time. I looked behind me, but I couldn't see Euan anywhere.

I shifted my weight onto one foot, leaning against the tall immigration booth. This was taking longer than usual. I could feel my stomach growling and a cold chill crawl up my bare legs. My thin sundress was doing little to keep me warm in the air-conditioned airport.

The immigration officer raised her eyes from my passport. "When was the first time you came to the UK?"

I grew nervous. She could clearly see when I had first come to the UK, and when someone asks you a question that they already know the answer to, it's not a good sign. I tried to peek at what she was looking at, but her hard stare made me look quickly away. Perhaps it was the one eyebrow that was making me most nervous. If both were raised then it would communicate an innocent element of surprise. One eyebrow arched, however, suggested a knowing suspicion. I'd obviously done something wrong.

She repeated the question, this time with no tone of friendliness.

"You mean, like the first time ever I came to the UK? That was with my parents, when I was fifteen." I suddenly felt like Chunk from *The Goonies*, spilling my life story at the first sign of being in trouble.

That was a typical, annoying trait of mine. The statement "if you are innocent then there's nothing to fear" did not hold true for me. I was one of those people who felt guilty even when I had done nothing wrong. When driving and I heard sirens, my heart would pound faster. If a person shouted in a crowded room, I would look around thinking it was at me. It wasn't that I had a guilty conscience, but rather that I assumed responsibility when there was no justification. I was compulsively anxious. Perhaps it was another legacy of being the grandchild of Holocaust survivors; in my DNA was a default deer-in-the-headlights position, like a virus in the software. Or perhaps it was the result of a warped egocentrism, assuming that the whole world, even conflict, revolved around me.

"Not when you were fifteen," the immigration officer sighed. "Recently."

"Oh, well, about half a year ago."

"For how long?"

"About five months… I think."

"You think?"

I could feel my deer-in-the-headlights DNA unfolding, instructing my body to go rigid, my eyes to grow wide. I was on no sleep, and worse, I now had to go to the bathroom.

"Well, I'm doing my best to remember, but it would help if I could reference something, like my passport."

I reached for my passport, which she promptly slid to the far end of her desk. My heart sank. I shifted uncomfortably and looked behind me, watching the empty lanes now fill with people. I scanned the crowd for a mop of ginger hair but there was no sign of Euan. Perhaps his plane had landed before mine, and he was already waiting.

"You know, it's an offence to lie to an immigration officer."

"I know, which is why I don't want to give you inaccurate information." Frustration sliced through the cracks of my exhaustion, giving me a jolt of energy. "It's impossible for me to come up with the exact dates of my travel for the past year without looking at a diary, an email, something."

If Euan was waiting, he'd be wondering where I was by now. I bit the inside of my lip. Perhaps, I thought, suddenly horrified, Euan would see that my plane had landed and when I didn't emerge with the crowd, think that I'd had a change of heart. I could picture him watching confused as the last person emerged at baggage check, wondering why I was not there and then sigh, realising I had decided not to come after all. Rejected, he would leave the airport alone. The image was too awful to endure.

"When was the first time you came to the UK?"

"In September some time." I resisted the urge to pee on the floor. I crossed my legs, squeezing my thighs together as the urge passed but my bladder started to feel tender, swollen.

"So that means" –the immigration officer looked triumphant – "you admit to being here for seven months."

"No, not really," I said slowly. "I only came a couple of weeks for my first trip, then longer the second time."

"Is this your luggage?"

I nodded.

"Is there any more?"

I nodded.

"Come with me."

I froze, unsure of what was happening. She looked over her shoulder beckoning me on. Without knowing what else to do, I reluctantly followed and was led around a corner into some unmarked offices.

Chapter 47

"This aggression won't stand, man." – The Coen Brothers, THE BIG LEBOWSKI: *Film section, across from Children's section, bottom shelf.*

My first exercise in screenwriting had been, when I was fifteen, to write an interrogation scene.

"Two characters, one room," Steven Bogart, my drama teacher in high school, had said. "That's it. Be as specific as you want." He hadn't known what to expect from me. I could see it in his expression and the way he first had handed me my assignment. "Don't just rely on dialogue," he had added. "Tell us about the characters through what we see."

When I had returned the following day with my five-page script, his expression had changed. "This is good," he had said, his eyes flicking curiously from the pages back to me. "I didn't think you were so…"

"Weird?" I had offered.

He smiled. "Imaginative."

The immigration officer took me inside the small room with four bright walls covered in posters: "It is a personal right to have representation" and "If you are seeking asylum, there are organisations to call that could help you". The lights clinked and buzzed overhead, emitting a harsh florescent glow, leaving nowhere unexposed.

In my screenplay, I had made everything dark in the room, which was supposed to add to the growing tension, but now I could see that had been a mistake. Here, in this bright room, I felt more tense, like a turtle without a shell, vulnerable.

"Can I get you a glass of water?" The immigration officer stood before me smiling. She had switched from bad cop to good cop, filling both roles perhaps as a result of the growing public sector cuts.

I took a deep breath, still unsure of what was happening. "No water, thank you, but it's been a long flight. Can I please use the bathroom?"

"No, I'm afraid not yet." She sat down at a long table, which stretched across the small room, and motioned for me to do the same. "Please sit," she indicated, and I reluctantly obeyed.

Two other officers appeared at the door, one with my luggage.

"Can someone at least let Euan know that I'm in here?"

The immigration officer ignored me and started reeling off several of the same questions as before. When did I first come to the country? How long have I been here? How long was my longest stay? I didn't want to give false information by just guessing, but she started pushing me for answers. My brain fizzled with the stress of having to recall exact dates from more than half a year ago.

"Look, I'm not being purposefully evasive, I just don't remember exact dates without my passport or my journals." I slumped back into my chair and a well of tearful frustration overwhelmed me. Don't cry, Jessica, for God's sake don't cry. "I've never overstayed a visa. I know you're only allowed six months with every stamp."

"You're only allowed to stay six months within a year."

"I thought it was six months at a time."

"No."

"Well," I could hardly hear myself speak. My heart was thudding loudly in my ears. "I didn't know that, and no other officer seemed to either. They seemed fine to stamp my passport and allow me into the country."

The immigration officer stayed glued to her forms, silent and unresponsive.

"Please." I could feel myself panicking. "I haven't done anything wrong. My whole life is here."

"What is the purpose of your visit to Britain?" she said softly, without looking up from her writing. The good cop had returned.

"I told you. My boyfriend lives here. That's all. I still work in the States and my family is there."

Her pen scraped against the paper and she started checking off a list of questions. She asked me what projects I had to go back for, what I was working on now and what my website was called. An image suddenly sprang to mind as her voice droned in the background. I was dressed as Charlie Chaplin in *Modern Times*, caught in the cogs of some great machine. Now that my name was on a form, it didn't matter how innocent or guilty I was because I was caught in a process that once started, could not be stopped.

"Did you ever work in film in the UK?" She asked and flipped over the piece of paper. There were more questions waiting to be answered.

"No, of course not, I don't have a working visa."

"But would you like to?" she persisted, staring at me hard.

This was an odd question. My heart, which had slowed, began to race again. It wasn't illegal to have hopes and ambitions, for God's sake. Was she trying to trap me? I hadn't done anything wrong, so why lie?

"Yes, of course. I hope to one day be in a position where I could work, for example, for the BBC." I watched as her pen flashed across the page and wished I had the ability to read bad handwriting upside down. "For now, however, visas are hard to come by..."

My hand restlessly tapped on the table. In my screenplay, I had had my main character do the same. Sweat had started to appear on his upper brow, and I wondered if I looked just as nervous to the immigration officer who sat scribbling in her notepad across from me.

The pen suddenly stopped. "Well, it's good that you've been honest with us. It's very good." She looked at me. "If you're honest, you have nothing to fear." She smiled and stood.

So that was that. My heart lifted. Perhaps they'd be letting me go now.

"Would you like the Koran or the Bible?"

"What?"

"While you wait." She repeated, "Would you like the Koran or the Bible?"

Behind her left shoulder I could see a government-issued poster on the wall, with bold letters that read: "It is your right to ask for books of your faith". I was tempted to ask for anything by Richard Dawkins.

I shook my head. "Neither. But will you please let Euan know I'm in here. He will be worried." Through the open door I could see two officers sipping tea, lounging in chairs outside. It's not as if you lot are doing much anyway, I wanted to add.

"Don't worry," the immigration officer smirked with an "I-know-more-than-you-think-I-do" expression. "We've been talking with him."

My heart suddenly sank. She closed the door. My bladder was beyond the point of exploding. I couldn't feel it any more; it was as if it had emptied by magic, or soaked back into the body. Perhaps it was the dangerous amounts of adrenaline that were now pumping through my veins that made me impervious to any sort of feeling besides panic.

Two officers came in and asked me to follow them into another small room. They took my fingerprints and mugshots of me against a high wall. This was actually happening. They were going to arrest me. Or worse, send me home.

I was ushered back into the interrogation room, past my luggage, which was now waiting by the door. The immigration officer was already there, waiting for me.

"So why didn't you mention, when I asked you about work, that you volunteered at the book festival?" She had the tone of someone who had caught an elusive mouse and I looked to see what she was waving in her hand. It was my journal.

"You read my journal?" I turned red. Not from embarrassment, but anger, thinking about all the personal hopes, dreams and aspirations I had written in there with a confidence that they would not be for public eyes. The sacredness of those words was suddenly soiled.

"I'm the one who asks the questions here." She slammed the journal down on the table. "Did you know it was illegal to volunteer without a volunteer visa?"

I felt like laughing. Her bad cop was not terrifying any more but absurd. This whole thing was absurd. "I was not officially a volunteer, I just helped a friend."

"That still counts."

"So if I wanted to help an old lady cross the street, or set a dinner table for a friend, then that's illegal without a volunteer visa?"

The immigration officer was silent for a moment. "How can we know if you went back to The Bookshop that you wouldn't help your boyfriend with his business in any capacity?"

"Well, now that I know volunteering in my position is illegal, I won't. Look, Euan hires people from our community to work in The Bookshop. As I said, I have work in the States. I'm not taking anyone's job, nor do I plan to, if that's what you're worried about. "

"That's not what I'm 'worried about'." Her face looked as if she'd just eaten a lemon. "I'm concerned that you've been here too long without a proper visa."

"Well, we have months to go before qualifying for a partner visa. Would it be possible to allow me to stay until that time?"

"No. I'm afraid we will have to send you back."

"What? Why? Please, wait, I even have my return ticket for two months from now, printed off here. See?" I pushed the piece of paper across the table but the immigration officer didn't look interested. "I don't see why you need to send me back."

"I'm sorry, you seem like a nice person but this is procedure. We've already done the paperwork for it."

She slid my passport onto the table and stamped it with a black, evil-looking stamp. "We couldn't find a flight out today, so although this is highly unusual, I'm going to let you return to Wigtown for three days to get your things. Usually, we'd put people like you into a holding cell."

She looked at me expectantly as if I was supposed to show gratitude. I remained silent and stared at the floor.

"You're lucky you and your boyfriend's answers were the same. Things could have been much worse for you." Her tone was struggling to be sympathetic. "We'll be holding onto your passport, of course. If you don't appear at the airport an hour before your flight, there will be a warrant sent out for your arrest. An armed escort will lead you from check-in to the boarding gate."

She handed me a piece of paper with my return flight times.

"You are free to go, Ms. Fox" The immigration officer opened the door. The last cog, as smooth as a twist of a Rubix cube, had turned.

Chapter 48

"...a tree began to grow, which got taller and taller till
it reached the sky. It was a useful tree under which boys
would drive their cattle in the heat of the day. One day
two boys climbed up into the tree, calling to their companions that they were going to the world above. They never
returned. The tree has since been called the story tree." –
TRADITIONAL AFRICAN FOLKTALE.

Euan and I sat, hand in hand, in the office of our local
representative. No one seemed to be able to help us,
not family, not friends, not politicians. Three days were
passing quickly and I was getting tired of offices.

I had emerged from the immigration room at the airport
to find Euan waiting at Arrivals. When he saw me he stood
up and wrapped his arms around me. Shaking, I told him
what had happened. Rage flashed across his usually serene,
laid-back expression. They had interviewed him too but
he hadn't expected it to be this serious.

"They're not going to deport you," he kept repeating.
Following Euan's emotions were like watching a tennis
match, bouncing between anger and his desire to comfort
me. "Those shits are not going to deport you. You'll be
fine, Jessy, I promise."

"I don't think that's something that you can promise at
this point," I said sullenly. "You did say I'd get deported

in this dress." My attempt to lighten the mood wasn't working.

"Fuck, we've been here an age." Euan checked his watch. "I can't believe they kept you in there for three hours."

"Three hours?" I had lost all sense of time.

"I'm going to make them pay for our parking."

"No, please." I squeezed his hand. I couldn't take any more conflict. "I just want to go home."

Wigtown had never looked so welcoming than when Euan's van pulled up in front of The Bookshop. I stepped out of the van to breathe in the familiar, cold, sweet air and looked at the central square with a deep sense of longing, knowing I would have to leave it soon. The romantic in me had tried to liken my situation to that of a heroine in a modern-day fairy tale – instead of the red van turning back into a pumpkin at midnight, in three days I would be deported from the ball.

When I walked up the beautiful staircase and into the kitchen, I was surprised to find it full of flowers. Soon people started turning up with cakes and condolences. As always, news travelled fast in Wigtown. When I was interned at the airport, Euan had called The Bookshop to let Hannah know we were going to be late. Hannah in turn had gone to the post office and told them the news, and they in turn had told everyone else.

Over the three days, all my Wigtown friends, and even some people I hadn't met, came over with flowers, cakes and sympathy. The kettle was constantly on and the kitchen continuously filled. I couldn't think of another time where I had felt so supported, but no matter how much the town wanted to help, the reality was that no one could erase the black stamp from my passport and no one could slow down time, let alone stop it altogether.

It was my last day and we had driven all the way out to Dumfries to meet with yet another representative, only to be told that there was nothing he could do. As we walked out of his office, I fought back tears, feeling utterly defeated.

"Aren't we supposed to have a special relationship with Britain?" I said through gritted teeth. I was so angry. I was angry that I hadn't done anything wrong. I was angry that I had held a nonsense belief that being an American made travelling easier. I was angry that Euan couldn't protect me. I was angry that this wasn't logical – all I wanted to do was stay in Wigtown, build a life there and give something back to the place that I loved so much. Why was that not okay?

"Don't worry, Jessy, we'll get you back." Euan led me down the cobblestone alleys towards the van. I looked up to see tears streaming down his cheeks. I suddenly stopped walking. Seeing me in such distress and unable to do anything was killing him and his usual stolid self was overwhelmed.

"Please don't worry." I had been selfish, drowning in my own misery and unaware how it was affecting him. I didn't want to make him suffer. I felt myself squeezing his hand while wiping away my own tears. "You're right," I said, struggling to smile. "I will be back."

*

The following day I walked through the sliding glass doors of Glasgow Airport dressed like a movie star. It had been Deirdre's idea. "If they're going to give you an armed escort," she had said, her eyes twinkling in their usual playful way, "make the most of it, glamour girl."

I did. Dressed in black boots, tight jeans and a long white shirt loaded down with jewellery, I hid my eyes behind bug-sized black sunglasses. Euan held my hand and I could feel eyes on me as I headed to the airport check-in desk. I just smiled and remained calm for Euan's sake. I would try to make this as easy and pleasant for him as possible.

"Name and passport, please." The young man on the desk hardly looked at me as he held out his hand.

I shifted uncomfortably. "I think the immigration offices are holding it," I said and watched as he glanced at me with a curious expression. He quickly disappeared and I turned to Euan, who wrapped me in a hug.

There was a great cloud of confusion behind the ticket desk. The young man was able to find my passport, but not my reservation. Some immigration officers came out and added to the commotion. They had a warrant for my arrest, a notice to leave the country, my passport... but no return flight. The immigration officer who had initially interrogated me had failed to book one.

The desk man smiled. "You'll need to go and buy a ticket with the airline that you arrived on."

I dropped my bags. "No, thanks."

"I'm sorry about the confusion." Another immigration officer appeared next to me. "But it's required that you have a ticket to leave this country today."

"If you wanted me to buy my own ticket, then you could have told me three days ago when I would have been able to find something I could afford." I crossed my arms. Out of the corner of my eye I could see Euan shift nervously. "I'm not going to pay to be deported. I'd rather you arrest me. I've had enough."

The immigration officer looked flabbergasted. I sat on top of my suitcase to make my point. "I'm not paying. I don't have the money, anyway, since I can't work in this country."

"But we need to get you out of the country today, or we'll have to issue the warrant for your arrest." The immigration officer looked from me to Euan and back again at me. It was as if I were short-circuiting his brain.

"Fine then. At least if you arrest me, I could stay."

I glanced at Euan, expecting to see an expression of torment on his face. He was smiling.

The manager of the airport appeared, explaining that the airline I had arrived on was required by law to also take me out of the country in a case of refusal of entry. However, they were required only to get me out of the country, not back to my home. The airline would only pay to take me half the way, to Iceland.

I didn't budge. "That's okay," I said indignantly. "I'll have to live at Reykjavik Airport. It's nice there. I have a camera on my computer. I'll blog about what it's like living at Terminal 3 because I literally don't have the money to get myself home." An immigration officer walked up to me, scowling. "Look, if you wanted me to return to Boston, I had already bought a ticket for two months' time. But that wasn't good enough for you. If you want me to go now, you have to pay for it."

Finally it was agreed that I would be able to go all the way back to Boston. There would be no armed escort, just an apologetic-looking young immigration officer who took my bags.

"I'm sorry this is happening," she whispered to me. "I would have let you in. It just depends on who you get behind that immigration desk." I wasn't sure if that made me feel better or worse. She started to lead me down a long hall, but stopped, looking at Euan. "He'll have to say goodbye here, I'm afraid."

I turned to Euan, unsure of what to say. I felt as if I were dreaming – that I would wake up to see I was still in the air, flying over the Atlantic, into Glasgow. "I'll see you again, very soon."

"I know, Fox. I'll try to come back out in a week or two." He kissed me and I walked away, wheeling my luggage behind me. I didn't want to look back. Like Orpheus, I imagined that if I did, I would never see him again. As I turned the corner, despite my superstition, I glanced behind me and I was glad I did. Euan was standing there, tall, mouthing "I love you".

Chapter 49

"Probability, noun; the extent to which something is likely to happen or be the case..." OXFORD ENGLISH DICTIONARY: *Across from staircase, top shelf, next to the green side door.*

Picture this. A group of strangers, plucked from the routine of their daily existence, are dropped in a large, Tardis-like room, windowless and filled with plastic seats that are perfectly set in long rows. Everyone wears the same bewildered expression, unsure of what to do or where to go until the lights dim and a TV slides into the room, resting on a trolley with squeaky wheels. Everyone sits, and all attention turns to the glowing screen. The scene could easily have been mistaken for an episode of *Doctor Who*. In truth, I had just arrived for jury duty, in a court near Boston.

The film that flickered on the small screen offered instruction in courtroom etiquette and the actor, playing the male courtroom officer, was for some reason wearing heavy lipstick, a wig and blusher – he was either a prime example of an incompetent make-up job or a thinly disguised transvestite. I was relieved to notice that I was not the only one who found the video funny. A young college student to my right was chuckling silently into her jacket.

The smile on my face felt strained and I realised the muscles hadn't been used in a while. I had been home a month when the notice for jury duty came. The month had been filled with constant trips to a visa "expeditor", who had promised to get anyone a UK visa in three days guaranteed. I'd quickly discovered, however, that visa expediting was a questionable business and the guarantee was not for obtaining it in three days, but for the service of submitting the papers on your behalf in that time. Two failed visas later the company was still "expediting" my applications.

My first application, for a simple visitor's six-month visa, had failed, despite the Glasgow immigration officer's assurance that it wouldn't. I was disappointed, but not surprised. They claimed I had been in the country too often to be considered a visitor.

My second application, for an extended-stay visitor's visa, also failed because of the evil-looking black stamp that the immigration officer had placed in my passport. Apparently it was worse than the mark of Cain, like the black sheep of passport stamps. No one would let me into their country now without a hassle, even countries outside the UK. This stamp, I found out, would last as long as my passport – another seven years. I could drop it, damage it, lose it, but the stamp would still be there; it bled beyond the passport, into the ink of their computer system. They had my fingerprints, my picture. I had a file. I was on their radar.

When I got the second rejection I had sat in the office of the visa expeditors, my head buried in my hands. My choices now were more complicated. Every time I applied for a new visa, it cost me a small fortune in fees that I did not get back even if my application was rejected. The nest egg that I had built up so carefully in Los Angeles was disappearing at a worrying rate.

"So what's next?" I had asked, hugging the folder of rejected applications to my chest.

The woman behind the desk sighed. "I'm not sure. You could apply for a partnership visa, but you're months behind the requirement. I'm not sure you'll get it."

"Anything else?" I had become an expert in visa applications because each time you applied, every inch of the submission had to be redone. I knew where to go to get my passport copied, my bank statements certified, my birth certificate duplicated, the cheapest, most secure postage and my biometrics taken. The second time I had gone to get my eyes scanned, I found myself surrounded by refugees from the earthquake in Haiti. They had been homeless and seeking shelter. As I waited for my number to be called, it had put things in humbling perspective.

"There's nothing else that you'll qualify for," the woman's voice trailed off, "unless..."

"Unless?"

"You want to get married."

"I don't think so," I said, focusing on the lint caught in the carpet fibres on the floor.

*

In the jury waiting room someone switched off the video and flicked the fluorescent lights back on. The sea of fellow duty servers blinked and shifted in their seats. An elderly judge in robes appeared from a side door and everyone stood. I quickly followed suit. I had been doing so much sitting down that my legs craved activity.

I had sat in lobbies, in government buildings and in the waiting rooms of the UK embassy. I had become used to waiting. When I had made my first visit to the British embassy in Boston, I had decided there and then to come back day after day until someone agreed to see me. That had turned out not to be necessary. A tall, beautiful blonde woman had greeted me warmly, looking inquisitively as I explained I had no appointment and wasn't there to see anyone in particular.

"I just need to speak to someone, anyone who will listen," I said, trying to sound less desperate than I felt. Desperation was not something that elicited sympathy; rather the opposite. I had observed during my interactions with various organisations that my despair, its sense of urgency and intensity, pushed people away. So now, I tried to sound stoic, confident.

The woman had smiled warmly. "Can you tell me what it's pertaining to?" Her posh British accent soothed my homesickness for Euan and Wigtown.

I quickly related to her the story of how I had met Euan, our relationship and the trouble we now found ourselves in.

"Well now. I'm glad you've come. Please, follow me."

I stood in the hallway, filled with glass furniture and fake plants, dumbstruck. Did she really just invite me to follow her? Or was it the optimistic babblefish in my head translating the usual "I can't help you" response into something more pleasing? I had been pushed to the edge of reason, I thought, and become completely deluded.

"Oh, perhaps would you rather come back another time?" The woman had turned and noticed I hadn't moved. "Do you have something you need to get to?"

"No, no," I said, my feet quickly moving to follow her. "Now is perfect."

She ushered me down a corridor into a nondescript meeting room and indicated a seat across the table from her. She was long-legged, smooth-skinned, and had a mature attitude that suggested she was in her late thirties, perhaps early forties. Her blonde hair was pinned back in a neat, elegant French braid.

"I just want to say I'm so sorry you've had this kind of trouble," she began, leaning forward and clasping her hands together on the table. "I'm not sure how much I can do, but I will try to help."

I felt my shoulders, which must have been pinned up somewhere near my ears, slide down my back, finally relaxing. "I don't know how I can thank you. Even if you decide there is nothing you can do, it means so much to me to find someone who will listen."

"I was actually in your position once. When my husband and I wanted to come to America. He had studied here..." She waved her hand in the air, suggesting that this was long in the past. "I couldn't get in and because his diploma was from America, he couldn't get a job in Britain. We were stuck between countries. It was horrible."

"What did you do?"

"Got married."

I turned red and shook my head. "It's not fair, is it?"

"No," she said, taking a pen from the table. "You said you owned a film company?"

I nodded.

"We could try to get you a small business visa, if you felt like expanding the company to the UK."

"Yes!" I nearly jumped out of my chair. This could be the perfect solution.

Two weeks later, despite great efforts on the part of the woman from the embassy, we ran into a snag. I was a sole trader, and by expanding to the UK, it would not be expanding the company, but moving the company. This was a big difference. I was required to raise £200,000 of seed capital to qualify as a small business. When I argued that the sum was perhaps appropriate for London, but outrageous for anyone starting a business in the Scottish outback, the woman sadly agreed with me. But rules were rules. There was nothing else she could do.

In the end, Euan and I had decided to try and go for the partner visa, an option that allowed people who had been living together for two years to be granted a work visa without getting married. Although we were far shy of the requirement, we now at least had a recommendation from the woman at the UK embassy. It was the last option available to us.

My phone buzzed in my pocket, rousing me from my thoughts. I was waiting for important news, news that was supposed to come that day. My stomach churned nervously.

"And thank you for coming today and serving jury duty, one of the most democratic of American institutions," the judge concluded.

With a billow of black robes, and her short speech done, the judge left as quickly as she had come, through a side door. A courtroom officer, unlike the made up one in the video, stood with a grizzly stare, asking us to look at our numbers. I felt as if I was in a deli, being called to make an order at the front counter. This was the opposite of a lottery. If our number wasn't called, we would get to go home. If it was, I could potentially be stuck in a court case that would last days, weeks or maybe even months.

I desperately wanted to reach for my phone, to listen to my message. My hand fumbled around my pocket until I found it. I glanced down. The number that had called was unlisted. My stomach churned again.

"102, 687, 202, 206, 29, 8, 36…" the officer intoned grimly.

My number was 304. Not all moments could be lucky ones.

"...87, 115, 304..."

I followed my fellow jurors as they funnelled into a long hall, which was equally brightly lit and disorientating. As we turned a corner, I slid the phone out of my pocket and discreetly tried to access my voicemail. Ducking my head down low, I held the phone to my ear, hiding behind the person in front of me.

"You have one new voice message. Press one to hear your message," the automated voice blasted in my ear. Yes, I knew I had one voicemail message, why couldn't it just play it? Why couldn't things be easier? We invented these systems to help us, after all. Press one, get your eyes scanned, go into this room, look at your number, get out of the country, you can go here but not here. Systems complicating systems.

We were instructed to wait before two thick, closed, wooden doors. I quickly moved over to the other side of the hall, away from the prying eyes of the courtroom officer. My finger jabbed at the phone and luckily hit on the right button.

"Hi, Jessica," the voicemail played, "it's Bonnie, from the visa expediting office. Look, we just got your application back and I'm so sorry to say it's been declined."

The phone slipped from my hands onto the carpeted floor. I felt like a gladiator who had watched the last stroke come down on him. I wanted to crumple to the ground, to melt and disappear. I pictured myself, a liquid pool of a person, dripping past the plastic chairs, down the plastered walls of the building and into the ground.

As we filed into the courtroom and lined up in the chairs, we were told that we were going to be hearing a murder case. This meant we might have to serve for weeks, even months. It didn't matter now. What could matter? There was no way I could get back to Euan. Tears were rolling down my cheeks. Sobs welled up in my chest and, before I knew it, were coming from my throat. It was actually happening. I, a repressed New Englander, was crying, hysterically, in public.

The judge looked at me suspiciously as I stood before her, tear-stained and choking on my words.

"Are you available for jury duty?"

"Yes."

"Are you fit and able to judge impartially?"

"No."

"Why not?"

"My visa was rejected." I could hardly spit out the words without letting out snot-filled cries.

The judge asked me to leave her courtroom. The eyes of my fellow jury servers followed me, glaring. One looked me up and down as if to say, "Crying is not going to get you out of your duty honey."

An officer met me on the other side of the door. "What seems to be the problem?" he asked in a surprisingly sympathetic tone.

"I just heard news that my visa was rejected…" I breathed a deep belly breath that my yoga teacher would have been proud of. I needed to ground myself.

The officer patted my arm. "Go home." He took the paper from my hands and stamped it with an official-looking certification. "You've served your time today."

Between sobs I mustered a smile. My world was falling apart but I had officially served my jury duty in a day. Although it may not have been an equal trade, every cloud has a silver lining.

Chapter 50

"There is one elementary truth the ignorance of which kills countless ideas and splendid plans: that the moment one definitely commits oneself, then Providence moves too. All sorts of things occur to help one that would never otherwise have occurred. A whole stream of events issues from the decision, raising in one's favour all manner of unforeseen incidents and meetings and material assistance which no man could have dreamed would come his way." – W. H. Murry, THE SCOTTISH HIMALAYAN EXPEDITION: *Exploration section, to the right of the fireplace, top shelf.*

Name: Jessica Fox
Type: work no funds
Status: 6-month working visa
Expires: January 2011

It had arrived. I found myself touching the visa and flipping it over in my hands to make sure it wasn't an apparition. There was a large sticker with my photo set squarely against a peachy background and an official gold and holographic seal on the top corner. I found myself reading and rereading the clear typewriter-like writing.

On reaching the last line, the thin blue passport suddenly felt heavy as if I were holding a large hourglass: Expires January 2011. Sand was already starting to fill up the bottom jar. Every moment I stood breathing here was a moment I was losing in Wigtown, with Euan.

After I had left jury duty two weeks before, time had gone gooey, like maple syrup. The news that my third visa had been declined had spread as quickly as the Wigtown tide. Euan spent endless sleepless nights emailing, protesting and fighting on my behalf, contacting everyone he knew. Wigtown residents bombarded the Border Agency with words of support and people sent in letters. The town rallied behind me, from Wendy at the picture shop to even the cranky teenager at the post office. Euan read some of the letters aloud and I felt humbled.

I'm not sure what, in the end, loosened the screw that released me from the cog in the immigration machine – whether it was Euan's contacts or the woman at the UK embassy or the support of my friends. But one right call or letter to the right person pushed the right button. A week after my courtroom meltdown, I received notice that my appeal against the refusal of my visa application had been successful. They were granting me a six-month working visa, and I now held it in my hands.

In less than 24 hours I would be once again in Euan's arms, sitting in our home above The Bookshop in the best, biggest, little town in Scotland: Wigtown. It felt too good to be true, a fairy-tale ending to what had been a truly epic, soul-testing adventure. As in any story, though, my granted wish came with massive strings attached. Like the Little Mermaid, who had only a finite time out of the ocean, the UK Border Agency gave me a certain amount of time to spend in Wigtown, after which it looked as if Euan and I would have few options left other than to apply for more visas or get married. At least, if all else failed, I would turn back into a US resident and not sea foam, but the pressure was still there. Every day was now precious.

I pulled my suitcase out from under the bed, trying to distract myself from the questions. There were still options. I could get a job and transition onto another visa, or we could try to get a partner visa instead. As Euan said, in his more lucid moments, this gave us options and most importantly would allow us to be together to make them happen.

I opened the now dust-covered black suitcase and found a bag from the Wigtown Festival still inside. I wondered, as I touched the green, scripted writing, if Euan and I would be different this time. I was not the same adventurer that I had been when I'd first arrived; I was more world-weary, wiser and I had my artistic passion back. I could also now work, I thought excitedly. Things will be different. I'll be more independent. I'll be more satisfied and most of all, I will be making films again. The rhythm that Euan and I were used to would change, and though the thought of this also worried me, I knew it would be the making of us.

Chapter 51

"There is a light that never goes out..." – The Smiths,
"THERE IS A LIGHT THAT NEVER GOES OUT": *Music section,
last bookshelf on the right in the far back.*

The person in front of me pushed back their seat, giving me little room for manoeuvre. Airlines seemed less to reward the first class with luxury seating, than simply to punish the coach class with hardly any seating at all.

I was by the window, watching the world, catching glimpses of the sea between the blanket of clouds. I felt myself rocketing forward. The blue expanse and white peaks quickly metamorphosed into Ireland's rugged green coastline. We were almost there. My heart was racing.

A bell sounded and the ever-present fasten seatbelt sign lit up. "We will be making our final descent into Dublin Airport. Please return to your seats as the fasten seatbelt sign has been engaged."

I tried to conjure up Melville. I needed his sage-like presence and willed him to appear next to me on the plane. This he did, but then quickly got up and stood in the aisle, looking panicked. He was fading in and out of my imagination, like a radio station that was hard to tune into. Surely I can have Euan, Wigtown and my artistic voice too, I thought, though the last was more of a question than a statement. Melville was gone. There was only my own voice now, clear, like a golden bell, which gently rang: why not? why not?

I sat back in my seat, exhaling deeply, and stared avidly out of the window.

Jessica Fox is a writer and film director. She has consulted for Harper Collins and was a resident storyteller and film director at NASA. Jessica's films have been shown at both US and International film festivals. She heads Mythic Image Studios and divides her time between the US and the UK. This is her first book.